Edward Cowley

Jacob and Japheth

Bible Growth and Religion, from Abraham to Daniel

Edward Cowley

Jacob and Japheth
Bible Growth and Religion, from Abraham to Daniel

ISBN/EAN: 9783337099916

Printed in Europe, USA, Canada, Australia, Japan

Cover: Foto ©Lupo / pixelio.de

More available books at **www.hansebooks.com**

JACOB AND JAPHETH:

BIBLE-GROWTH AND RELIGION,

FROM ABRAHAM TO DANIEL.

ILLUSTRATED BY CONTEMPORARY HISTORY.

"WRITTEN FOR OUR LEARNING."

BY
THE AUTHOR OF "GOD IN CREATION," "GOD ENTHRONED IN REDEMPTION," "MRS. WARD WEIGHED AND FOUND WANTING," ETC.

NEW YORK:
THOMAS WHITTAKER,
2 AND 3 BIBLE HOUSE.

Copyright, 1889,
BY THE AUTHOR.

PREFACE.

This book traces the growth of the Old Testament as a preparation for the New Testament. It shows the currents of preparation in various inspired utterances, and that Hebrew theology was not developed from floating myths and legends. Genesis has some matters which are paralleled in Babylonian and Egyptian traditions; they were revised and authenticated by the Divine Spirit speaking to Abraham and others of old time. The true was before the mythical; the legendary arose from thoughts and endeavors to explain facts. Ancient polytheism was derived from ideas about the angels of God and the angels of Eden; animal worship arose from mistaken notions respecting the serpent that tempted mother Eve, and demonology from belief in evil spirits expelled from heaven, with Satan their chief. Genesis and Job spoke of him and of good angels many ages before Daniel.

Hebrew legislation became interwoven with all later Scriptures from Samuel to Jeremiah, just as Homer was interwoven with other Greek writings. The observance of laws ever proves their existence. Israel's ancient judges and priests prove portions of the Pentateuch. A chapter or a book may be forged or false, but not a whole literature; so a wonder here or there may be explained by natural law, but not the series of wonders from the calling of Abraham to the deliverance from Egypt and settlement in Canaan. We find little new theology after Abraham, little new ethic after Moses, and little new in ritual after the dedication of Solomon's temple. But during those centuries prophets gave their expositions of them to successive generations, while the roots and principles of religion remained the same.

The Bible is one long lesson of preparation for the Redeemer. Its aim and endeavor is to educate a people for God. Its voicings are now for one age, now for another, differing in tone and emphasis, sometimes thundering against apostasy and apostate kings, but ever calling in the same direction and urging toward the same goal. We need not weigh and measure the inspiration of one seer as compared with another, for whenever the Spirit speaks by a prophet he utters the word of God, even when the utterance is of local or personal application. Jacob's Bible was a growth of fifteen hundred years, each part being adapted to the age for which it was given, but the purpose was the same in all ages—to educate, to reform, to restore backsliding Israel.

History supplies the authentication of what was believed in the time of Moses and Joshua with as much certainty as in the days of Isaiah. For the prophets of Isaiah's day based their deliverances upon a law then known, a ritual then existing, a history then written, or waiting for a scribe. Thus Sinai prepared for the tragedy at Carmel, Shiloh for the worship of Zion. Circumcision and passover, fast and festival prepared for Him who ransomed the lost, that they might obtain eternal life. The miraculous was illustrated to patriarchs and judges as well as by Samuel and Elijah. It was blended and woven with all Hebrew literature, its songs and its sorrows in Palestine, in Exile, and return from it. Jacob wrote with a pen which was ever guided by a Divine hand, and he wrote for Japheth as well as for Israel. His writings have endured the beatings of many storms—storms of kings and critics; of Antiochus and Julian, Celsus, Porphyry, and modern sceptics. God and His Word can never be destroyed.

We all have an equal interest in these matters. We all are in the same life-boat, needing a Divine Pilot to steer it. If she founder we shall all alike be lost; but if we safely cross the tempestuous ocean, we shall all land on the peaceful shores of the blessed. As during forty years I have studied these matters, seeking to be helpful to others in fresh lines of old thought, it is not presumption to treat of the growth of the Book given as the chart by which to steer our bark while making the eternal voyage. If new objections have arisen, so have new answers to them; new facts have come to light which illustrate Bible foundations and authority. Those who have trod the border-land know that the reasons which established one who doubted the value of certain things may be helpful to others. There are eternal truths which concern us all, and it behooves us, by God's help, to live according to their teaching. Guesses must not usurp the place of Revelation. In such spirit I have tried to say clearly what I have found touching Bible-Growth and Religion, but not to over-color anything. May the Divine Spirit guide us into all the Truth.

THE AUTHOR.

CONTENTS.

CHAPTER I.

Jacob and Japheth: their God.

SUMMARY: PRESENT INTEREST IN ANCIENT BELIEFS—PERVERSIONS—ANCIENT TESTIMONIES DEMONSTRATIVE—HOW CONFRONTED—FALSE PORTRAITURE—AGREEMENT OF GENESIS AND CUNEIFORM INSCRIPTIONS—A BABYLONIAN SPIRIT BREATHES IN THEM, YET TRUE AND NATURAL—INFLUENCE OF HEBREWS, WHY AND WHENCE—DIVINE CHARACTERISTICS—EVER WITNESSING TO MAN—CONSCIENCE THE OUTCOME OF DIVINE INSTRUCTION—GOD THE ACTIVE AGENT—ILLUSTRATIONS—TREND OF HEBREW THEOLOGY AND MORALITY—COURSE OF SEMITIC MIGRATIONS—RENAN CORRECTED—HEBREW TRIBES—HOSTILITY—LANGUAGE—RELIGION MONOTHEISTIC—PERSONIFICATION OF DIVINE ATTRIBUTES—THE DIVINE NAME INCORPORATED INTO PERSONAL NAMES—ABOUT ANGELS, THEIR MINISTRY, AND WORSHIP OF—SEMITES NOW MONOTHEISTS AND NOW POLYTHEISTS—ABRAHAM, SARGON, ELIJAH, AHAB, MAHOMET—IDEAS OF GOD VARIOUSLY EXPRESSED—SEEN IN THE OPERATIONS OF NATURE AND EMPHASIZED IN SONG, PROVERB, AND NOTABLE EVENTS.. 13

CHAPTER II.

The Religion of Abraham, from the Bible and the Inscriptions.

HOW DESCRIBED—DR. SOUTH—REVISED FOR ABRAHAM—CORRUPTED BY OTHERS—NAMES FOR GOD AND PROVIDENCE—DEVELOPMENT OF NATURE-WORSHIP—JOURNEY OF ABRAHAM FROM UR TO HARAN—PASSES THE BIRS-NIMRUD AND TEMPLES OF BABYLONIA—DESCRIPTION OF AND WORSHIP—LEGENDS OF EDEN—THE SERPENT AND SACRED TREE—AUTHORITIES—CAPTURE OF NANÁ AND RESTORATION—ACCADIAN LEGENDS AND IDEAS REVISED BY ABRAHAM—ILLUSTRATIONS OF THE FALL—A DELIVERER EXPECTED BY SEMITES, JAPHETHITES, ETC.—ENDEAVORS AFTER RIGHTEOUSNESS—IDEAS OF IMMOR-

TALITY—PREHISTORIC TREPANNING TO SECURE HAPPINESS AFTER DEATH—BELIEF IN IMMORTALITY IN EGYPT AND BABYLONIA—SABBATH-OBSERVANCE—CHARACTERISTICS OF ABRAHAM—HOW NOURISHED—COVENANT-GRACE, PRAYER, SACRIFICE, DIVINE INFLUENCE—PILLAR TOKENS OF COVENANT—FESTAL RITES AND FASTS AMONG SEMITES—VISIONS AND REVELATIONS—INCORPORATIONS OF DIVINE WITH HUMAN NAMES—FATHER ORHAM AND ABRAHAM, TITLE TO ESTEEM—ANGELIC MINISTRY—MICHAEL AND MERODACH—EVIL SPIRITS AND PRAYER FOR DELIVERANCE FROM—THE NEW TRUTH OF DIVINE COVENANT WITH ABRAHAM.................... 37

CHAPTER III.

The Patriarch in Palestine: Personal Incidents.

BEGINNING OF REVELATION TO ABRAHAM—HIS WORSHIP OF GOD—HIS CONSERVATISM—DIVINE BEHESTS AND BIBLE—A NEW DEPARTURE—COVENANT—ALTAR-BUILDING—LUZ-BETHEL, VISIONS OF JACOB AT AND GOD'S PROMISE TO HIM—LONG VENERATION OF THE PLACE—ITS DESECRATION—SHECHEM, ITS ALTAR AND MEMORIAL STONE—JOSHUA'S FAREWELL—FAMOUS OAK—JUSTIN MARTYR BORN AT SHECHEM—FIRST BIBLE PARABLE SPOKEN THERE—MEN OF, PUNISHED BY SIMEON AND LEVI—ETHICAL STANDARD OF ISRAEL AND PHILISTINES, OF GREEKS AND ROMANS—SAMSON'S RIDDLE—TREATMENT OF SLAVES—JACOB'S ETHIC IN GENESIS COMPARED WITH CLASSICS—CONSCIENCE THEN AS SURE A GUIDE AS UNDER ROMAN EMPERORS—JACOB'S CULTURE AND IDEAS OF GOD—SOCRATES—OTHER ILLUSTRATIONS—ABRAHAM AN EXAMPLE OF DOMESTIC AFFECTION—TREATMENT OF HIS SONS—HIS CHARACTER TESTED BY COMMAND TO SACRIFICE ISAAC—HEAVEN'S PROHIBITION.................... 62

CHAPTER IV.

Israel in Egypt; at Sinai; the Law.

TIME OF RESIDENCE IN EGYPT—HYKSOS OR RULING DYNASTY FRIENDLY TO ISRAEL—MODERN DISCOVERIES CONFIRM BIBLE ACCOUNTS—DYNASTIC CHANGES CHANGED ISRAEL'S CONDITION APEPI AND RA-SEKENEN—HEBREWS ENSLAVED—RENAN'S MISREPRESENTATIONS—THEBANS DOMINANT AND OPPRESSIVE AUTHORITIES TOUCHING LENGTH OF SOJOURN—TIME FOR GROWTH IN NUMBERS—CULTURE—DELIVERANCE BY DIVINE POWER—DEFEAT OF EGYPTIAN GODS—JACOB'S FESTIVALS AND WRITTEN REVELATION—NOT BORROWED—THE TEN LAWS—OTHER PREPARATIONS—ISRAEL SAFE AMONG

CONTENTS. ix

PAGE

THE MOUNTAINS OF SINAI—WONDERS PARALLELED IN OTHER HEBREW HISTORY—RENAN'S CRITICISM OF MOSES—OF PRETENDED ORACLES, GIVING OF THE LAW, AND MIRACULOUS STORIES—ANTIQUITY OF PSALM 68 AND OF OTHER WRITINGS—THE REGAL PERIOD UNFAVORABLE TO THE FORGING OF A NEW LEGISLATION AND RITUAL—WARS AND COMMOTIONS—RELATION OF PRAYER-BOOK TO MISSALS SIMILAR TO THAT OF TEMPLE AND TABERNACLE RITUAL WITH AUTHENTICATED SCRIPTURES IN ISRAEL.................................. 82

CHAPTER V.

At Home in Palestine: Miraculous Events.

COMMENCEMENT AND UNFOLDING OF JACOB'S HISTORY—HIS DEATH IN EGYPT, BURIAL IN CANAAN, AND FAVORABLE IMPRESSION UPON THE PEOPLE—CHANGED TO HOSTILITY IN LAPSE OF CENTURIES—RENAN CORRECTED—HEBREW PROWESS—MORAL FORCE UNITED WITH DIVINE FORCE FOR ISRAEL—HOW EVIDENCED—JORDAN'S WATERS CUT OFF BY JAHVEH—MEMORIAL THEREOF SET UP BY JOSHUA—THE COVENANT RENEWED—AN ANCIENT SOUVENIR—OBJECTIONS CONSIDERED—DR. GEIKIE, CAPTAIN CONDER—DRUID-LIKE CIRCLES IN MOAB—CROMLECH AT GILGAL—SIMILAR INSCRIPTIONS IN EGYPT AND HAMATH—ORIGIN OF CANAANITES—IDOLATROUS AND DEBASED—CULTURED, BUT WITHOUT PATRIOTISM—THEIR GODS CONQUERED—BIBLE ACCOUNTS CREDIBLE, RECORDED BY PROPHETIC WRITERS AND CORROBORATED BY CONTEMPORARY HISTORY—RENAN CORRECTED—GREAT SLAUGHTER OF EPHRAIMITES—ISRAEL'S VICTORIES BY DIVINE POWER—GOD ATTENDS AT THE BIRTH OF NATIONS—JOSHUA RENEWS THE COVENANT—HIS RETIREMENT—THE TABERNACLE A CENTRE OF INFLUENCE—INTELLECTUAL CLEVERNESS OF JEWS—EPISODE OF MICAH—CHASTISEMENT OF BENJAMIN—SEIZURE OF WIVES AT SHILOH—DAN'S IDOLATRY—SUMMARY OF JACOB'S BIBLE EVIDENCE AT THIS ERA....................... 104

CHAPTER VI.

How Japheth Scrutinizes Jacob's Books.

THE ANABASIS AND NUMBERS COMPARED—EVENTS AND RECORD CONTEMPORANEOUS—DR. KALISCH'S VIEW OF BALAAM—SCHRADER AND ASSYRIAN ACCOUNTS—THE MOABITE STONE—BALAK AND MESHA—THE HISTORY AND PROPHECY OF BIBLE AUTHENTICATED—EVIDENCES OF WRITING AMONG ANCIENT HEBREWS—SAYCE vs. RENAN—JACOB WROTE HIS ANNALS—OLD TESTAMENT WORDS IN THE INSCRIPTIONS EXPLAINED—

Renan's Account of Sun Standing Still, and Dr. Egar's—Heaven Gods of Canaan Glorify Jehovah—Lot in Syria—Bible Phrases Original, or not Borrowed from Assyrian Writers; Bible Corrects them—Error of Schrader—How Foreign Words were Adopted by Hebrews—Mr. Lethaby's Letter from Moab—Renan's Objection to Joshua Corrected—Inscriptions Mistake Jehu for Ahab—Growth and Authentication of Scripture—Greek Translation of—Preservation and Multiplication of Copies—Second-Century Collations and Safeguards—Renan's Testimony—Objectors Answered—Acknowledged Prophets Expound Ancient Laws—Anticipatory Legislation Evidenced by History—Reasons for not now Accepting New Chronology—The Lists of Naram-Sin Contemporary Princes whom Sargon I. Subdued.... 131

CHAPTER VII.

The Era of Samuel and David: Jacob's Bible then.

Prophetic and Royal Functions—Catastrophe at Shiloh—Sacrifices of Atonement Cease for Years—Importance of the Ark—Certain Laws in Force at this Period—The Supernatural Manifested from Abraham to David—Samuel not Minimized by Comparison with Elijah—Special and Official Work—Renan Corrected—Samuel at Shiloh and Mizpeh—His Character Suggests a National Chief to the People—Two Centuries of Depression, Disunion, Idolatry—Clericalism and Prophetism—Dynastic Change of Disobedient Saul for Jahvist David—His Character—Consecration of the Temple—Its Theology for Mankind—The Stranger may Worship in Jerusalem—Solomon's Prayer—Liturgic Enrichment—Canonization of a David-like Character in Christendom—Pentateuchal Provisions and Restrictions for Kings—Growth and Contents of Jacob's Bible; About Half the Old Testament then Written—Prophetic Authentication and Writing of New Copies—The Truth Widely Known—Summary of Laws and History in Israel 160

CHAPTER VIII.

The Prophets and their Predictions.

Ewald's Definition of Inspiration—Human Speech Unthinkable Without God—Dr. Kalisch on Balaam and Ruth—His Error—Wellhausen's Error Touching Ahab and

Elijah—Distinction between Prophets of Jehovah and
of Baal—The One Inspired, the Other Augurs and
Soothsayers—Wellhausen Corrected—How Prophetic
Messages were Conveyed—Prophets and Priests Characterized—International Trade and Literary Intercourse—A Constellation of Prophets; Micaiah vs. Ahab;
H. Spencer vs. Micaiah—All Voicings of Seers not
Predictive—Revelations to Jacob—The Twofold Name
of Deity Known by him and by Abraham—Wellhausen
Corrected—"The Swiss Guard of True Religion"—
Non-writing Prophets and a Non-writing Age as Stated
by Wellhausen not Correct—Elijah as Masterful in
Words as in Deeds—The Law not a Late Development
—Ezekiel's Testimony—Ethics and Worship Out of Israel—Prophets of Smooth Things Desired—International and Theocratic Influence in the Sixth Century
—Fulfilment of Prophecy in a Babylonian House of
Exchange—A Second Isaiah and Relation of an Early
Pentateuch to him—False Suppositions—Laws Exist
Before their Incorporation into a Literature—Kuenen
Corrected Touching Hosea and Ezra—Jewish Proselytism of Greeks a Preparation for the Messiah.......... 183

CHAPTER IX.

Jacob's Prophets Serve Japheth's Kings: A Light to Lighten the Gentiles.

Hebrew Language and Prophets Defined by Renan—A Force
Reforming the World—Jonah, his Place, Mission to
Nineveh, and Sermon from its Walls—How Received—
Reigning Monarch Characterized—Repentance of
Later Destruction of Nineveh—Its Ruins—Tomb of
Jonah—"Jahveh not *Unser Gott*"—Isaiah and his
Prophecies for Gentiles—Kuenen on his Era—Predictions Characterized by Dr. Briggs—Lofty Messianic
Reaches—Micah, and how he Saved Jeremiah's Life—
A Bold Truth-teller—Jeremiah and his Predictions vs.
Jerusalem and the Nations—His Career—Ezekiel a
Captive on the Chebar—Location—The Prophet Characterized—His Many Things for Jacob and the Gentiles—Authenticates Daniel—A Captive Honored and
Educated at Babylon—Interprets Dreams of the King
and Saves the College of Chaldeans—Cannot be Relegated to the Second Century B.C. as Describing Antiochus Epiphanes—Predictions of Messianic Kingdom,
a Light to Lighten the Gentiles—Objections vs.
Daniel—Porphyry and Other Critics Answered—Testi-

mony of Josephus, etc.—Former Objections to Isaiah and Sargon Paralleled in Daniel—A Prophet Vindicated by a King.................................... 211

CHAPTER X.

General Review of Matters Considered in this Book.

Story of How the Bible was Given—Its Legislation and Provisions for National Development—Religious Memorials and Prophetic Reminders of them—Laws of the Twelfth Century not to be Relegated to 444 B.C.—Jacob's Bible as Authentic as the Classics—Early Origin of his Religion—Illustrated by Prophets—Authority in the Christian Church Compared with that of Israel—Ancient Observance of Laws and Rites—Disruption of the Kingdom Led to Disruption of the Religion of Israel and to Apostasy from Jahveh—Prophets Exhorted Backsliders to Return—Preservation of Scripture—Stuart's Defence of Daniel—His Prophecy Shown to Alexander the Great—Testimony of Josephus—Justin Quotes Moses, Isaiah, Daniel; he Lived a Century and a Half before Porphyry, and a Higher Authority—Origen—Antiochus Epiphanes Destroyed Scripture Mss.—He is not Compared but Contrasted with Nebuchadnezzar—Fulfilment of Prophecy—Pyrrhonism and the French Assembly—Bible Books not to be Decided by Votes—Fantastic Dogmatism—Homer and Herodotus less Credible than the Old Testament—Writing Prophets Recorded Predictions of those who did not Write—Scripture Authentication—Remarkable Fulfilment of Isaiah in Egypt; of Leviticus and Deuteronomy in the Roman Siege of Jerusalem—Prayer of Esdras—Author's Object in Writing this Book......... 237

I.

JACOB AND JAPHETH: THEIR GOD.

Our interest to-day in the beliefs of mankind forty centuries ago arises from the things believed and from the reasons for believing them. They were preparations for what followed. Those truths and processes of religious thought are important in themselves and grand in their unfoldings. They arrest the attention of scientists, historians, linguists, and critics. But many seek to give their own setting and coloring to them. Some, indeed, reduce God to the Unknowable, who has no revelation for mankind; to a Force in nature that has no concern for men, and they are most emphatic in their voicings about that of which they are ignorant. Everywhere this echo is heard, in books and newspapers, in clubs and halls of assembly. We cannot ignore it, and the issues involved demand that we consider it.

In the chapters on "God Enthroned in Redemption," I treated of the early beliefs about God, the first Sabbath and worship, prayer and sacrifice, the world's legends and expectations of a Redeemer, longings after immortality, the solidaric redemption of man by One promised in Eden, and the founding of a kingdom for the Redeemed; showing by facts and illustrations amounting to a demonstration that revelation, conscience, history, legend—all testify of the same grand truths.

Now we are confronted with attempts to strike off the roots of a God-given Word for man, and of Divine care of him. "He is only one of myriads of existences. Let him run his course to its ultimate issue." Alas! such writers know nothing about that final outcome; about the steps which lead to it, nor what are its tremendous possibilities.

They reduce sacred history to legend and myth, and the Hebrew religion to a natural development of Semitic civilization, according to the gospel of evolution. German and French Japheths encounter Jacob and lay him in the dust of humanity; then slowly make him a "force which sweeps the world of mankind along with it." By such a phantasmagorical representation of history the reader receives impressions which long remain. Thus vast injury is done to the cause of religion and to the souls of men. Jacob is portrayed as an "ignorant slave, yet allowed to make pilgrimages to his local god at Sinai, and becoming dissatisfied in Egypt, was expelled by the Pharaoh who did not want him, and to whom he was useless"! His God is reduced to the rank of a "tribal deity," whose "oracles were of doubtful authority, because of doubtful authenticity, and whose Bible is said not to have been written before the ninth century B.C." So Renan and Wellhausen. We shall endeavor to present some leading facts in the history of Jacob, of his God and his Bible; showing that He was also the God of Japheth, and often sent a prophetic word to him.

Genesis and the cuneiform inscriptions show that the

sons of Noah had much in common of religious instruction, similar ideas of God and how to worship Him. But corruption arose in life, ritual, and theology; distinctions between sons of God and daughters of men, between Sethites and Anakites, which we broadly designate by Jacob and Japheth, the Church and the world; the one accepting Divine revelation and covenant, the other following their own devices and suffering the penalty.

They had descended from the same ancestry, had received similar training in the duties of life, in the knowledge of God and of duty toward Him. From Adam to Abraham there were no Heaven-appointed ecclesiastical differences. But with Abraham arose that distinction which made Israel to differ from the rest of mankind; yet not till the new dispensation was completed under Moses was that difference very marked. First, the Covenant of circumcision differentiated the worshippers of Jahveh from the worshippers of Ilu, Ra, and Bel. The Genesis of Jacob and the inscriptions of Japheth give similar accounts of creation, which are the earliest in human language of the origin of the world and of man upon it; and they have been blended and interwoven into all later histories of primitive man. "The old Babylonian spirit breathes in them still," which is a pretty sure test of their truthfulness, or translators and copyists would long ago have changed them. A false statement of such matters is not true to nature, and, of course, not true in fact and principle. Hence "the old Babylonian spirit still breathes in the" records and legends of creation. Indeed, "the great truth of the unity of the world and of the solidaric unity of all its parts is clearly perceived in them. The nomad pastor would not have invented them, but he perpetuated them," and the Hebrew genius has given them greater simplicity and correctness than the Assyrian scribe. "What was grotesque in Berosus appears true and natural in the Bible. *Israel effected this miracle.*" (Renan's "History of the People of Israel," vol. i., p. 68.) But that Israel could have done such a thing, without the inspiration and guidance of Heaven, is a still greater miracle. She was one of the later nations, with a later history of all that pertained to her; how, then, if she rose from a savage state, could she have given a "true and natural" account of creation and the first men in her Bible? No matter whence came the earliest accounts, the revised and corrected narrative is a "miracle which Israel effected." How? We say by the Divine Spirit speaking to Abraham, to Moses, and by the prophets. In other words, by Divine *guidance*, or by *revelation*. Since it could not have been invented it must have been revealed. Barbarians could not have fabricated Genesis and Exodus. The origin of the world was written in Chaldæan bricks, was early taught, with many other things, to Abraham, who was enabled to transmit a "true and natural" account in Jacob's Bible. The prophets preserved and authenticated the history, the law, and the songs of Israel, while the priests preserved copies of the covenant and the sacred books in and near the Ark of God. But they were a growth, not even all the Pentateuch, as we have it, being as early as Moses, though the later matters generally indicate when they were, or that they were, added.

Semites, indeed, have made their presence felt in our world, but whence came those ideas which differentiated them from other dwellers in Babylonia? for when they left that country, they possessed only what was a *joint inheritance*. It was not native culture and the inventive faculty; for other nations were as cultured and as ingenious as they, and their regal history discloses an equal tendency to polytheistic forms of worship. But the unfolding of their religious character reveals an aptness for Divine instruction and the hearing of Divine voices, together with the faculty of imparting what was communicated to them. They had in large degree the courage of their convictions. From Abraham to Moses they were as surely the subjects of derision as they have ever been, and they were often persecuted. But did ever an Israelite abandon the religion of the God of Abraham merely because he was derided or persecuted? Did not He who created man know this tendency to be rooted in that race, of conservation and perpetuation of what they possessed in religion as well as the material things of life? Differ as we may about the miraculous in their history— about the exploits of Joshua, the frolicking revenges of Samson, the valor of the youthful David, the three young men in the furnace of Nebuchadnezzar, and Daniel in the lion's den—there yet was disclosed in them all a *loyalty to God* which impressed itself upon the nation, and which was as marked when Jerusalem was surrounded with enemies as when David conquered the stronghold of Zion from the Jebusites (2 Sam. 5 : 6-8), or when Hebrew captives wept by the waters of Babylon. From Abraham to John Baptist religious heroism is strikingly illustrated in their kinsmen.

No word-painting is needed to identify the God of Japheth with Him of Jacob. Illustrations will be given that Jahveh of the Hebrews was the Supreme God of the Gentiles ; that He triumphed over the deities of Egypt, over Chemosh of Moab, over the gods of Canaan, over Dagon of Philistia ; and that He was the acknowledged One, supreme in heaven and earth, now by the early kings of Babylonia and Egypt, now by Nebuchadnezzar and Darius. And to Him "the world is to be converted," to Him the Creator, the Father, the Redeemer of mankind. His Fatherhood is distinctly seen in His choice of Abraham for the founding of a new nation ; in His prophetic messages to other nations, warning them of impending judgments ; and in the Son of His love dying upon the cross for the redemption of the world. Ammon and Ishmael, Egyptian and Persian, Roman and Greek may claim Him as Saviour if they will ; for in Him were fulfilled all Japheth's expectations of an Avatar and Mediator by whom the world's ills should be removed.

Even those who relegate Jehovah to the position of a local deity acknowledge those Scriptures which say : God came from Teman, rose up from Seir, and shined forth from Mount Paran (Deut. 33 : 2 ; Hab. 3 : 3.) His efficient presence was manifested at the Ark of the Covenant. He is the Eternal and Personal Energy which acts in all phenomena, orders and causes them. He is supreme in justice, in truth, in love, in power, as supreme in spiritual as in material things; wherefore His creatures need not complain nor despair, but rather believe in Him. Deep soul experiences of faith never lead to apostasy. Neither Judas nor Elsmere cherished that faith in the Christ of God which would enable them to die for Him. The regenerated of God by the Holy Ghost will ever love and serve *their Father*.

In the loss of Eden Adam lost not all his nobility of character, and he looked to the saving seed promised him. There were yet large possibilities for his recovery. Worshipping Sethites, Enoch, and Noah illustrate how they were preachers of righteousness. Abraham and Jacob succeeded them; then followed Moses and the prophets of Israel; Zoroaster, Indian sages, and Greek teachers of Japheth. *God left not Himself without witnesses* of truth, virtue, and loyalty. The dark places of mankind were not wholly dark; there ever shone some rays which betokened a celestial origin. Barbarism has never been universal in our world. It is just as wise to affirm totality of sainthood among men as totality of wickedness. The true man, the true priest, has never died out, nor the Divine Oracles remained silent when they should have been vocal. By some one Heaven's message has been delivered to man. Hence his struggles and aspirations for the higher life and the diviner character; hence his longings and endeavors through the centuries; hence his thoughts and preparations for an expected Deliverer, in Babylonia and India, Judea and Iran, and all those centres of civilization, where "hope eternal sprang in the human breast." For the opposite of this view, see Renan's "History," vol. i., p. 178.

Yet quite characteristically he says: " The human conscience unravelled itself, elevated itself, purified itself, conceived the idea of justice, asserted the principles of right and duty ; *then* came language to define and establish these conquests of mind over matter !" *It lifted itself by itself ?* Just as well try to lift one's self by one's suspenders ! How long could conscience exist before language ? What examples have we in history of any people illustrating the possession of conscience *before* they had a spoken language ? But our wonder at such statements is equalled only by our wonder at this writer of ancient story flying in the face of ancient records and inscriptions, which make God both the Creator and the Teacher of primitive men ; which tell of Sabbath-worship and sacrifice in the earliest times, thus indicating the possession of conscience then ; which tell of belief in immortality and the enjoyment of blessedness with the gods, or of banishment from heaven. Scenes like the Judgment of Amenti, and the region where Queen Allat reigned, indicate a conscience in those who believed them. And they had ideas of the moral difference between virtue and vice. This knowledge was never restricted to Israel. The calling of Abraham was at a time when those ideas of religion were known which our second chapter sets forth. It was not possible for man to civilize and elevate himself before the historic period. Nor have we any instance of a barbarous people civilizing themselves. Our American Indians are pretty hard to civilize, though surrounded with our modern influences. It devolves upon the champions of barbarism developing into a high measure of culture, of conscience, and of language to cite some examples which illustrate their theory. The general progress of man " in diverse centres" is far too indefinite; especially since " primitive humanity" is said to have been " very malevolent; that force was met by force or by imposture; love was accompanied by reverie; the child knew only his mother, women being the common property of the tribe only six or seven thousand years ago!" Compare this with the account of parental love in Genesis; with Abraham's love for Ishmael as well as for Isaac; with Jacob's love for Joseph and Benjamin; with David's love for the child of his sin as well as for Solomon; all which remain unsurpassed after three thousand years. Surely the centre and source of all civilization is the family, where parents *know and train* their children, and need use no " club" to preserve its purity. It is abhorrent to our history and experience that " millions of women stoned to death paved the way to conjugal fidelity; that the male kept guard, and with a club stoned his adulterous female to death; that *thus* emerged the morality which we see under the Aryan and Semitic types" (Renan's " History of the People of Israel," vol. i., pp. 3–7.)

The incidents related in Genesis 12, 20, 26, 34 chapters, whenever written, were true to life, and are not the sort upon which to found such broad statements; rather they contradict Renan's naturalistic theories. Affirmations of later practices of " the natives of the Maldive Islands and of Brittany" do not illustrate the condition of early Semites and Accadians; nor do the irregularities of Olympian deities. We must have examples from ancient Egypt and Babylonia duly authenticated to sustain this charge against woman, and authorities earlier than fifth-century Herodotus. The "club theory" was never true of Adamic man. What *nations* practised it? What women thus became faithful to conjugal bonds? What *moral* ideas did Israel have which had not been divinely imparted to ancient Egyptians and Chaldæans?

Whence arose this difference from the neighboring nations? When the Semites "first appeared in Chaldæa they were less supplied, we are told, with material comforts than the older settlers, but they had inward fire, poesy, passion, and craving for another life. The secret of the future" was strong in them. Be it so; but why this *theological trend in Hebrew Semites?* There were other Semites in early Babylonia, in Assyria, in Phœnicia; but they were not famous for their monotheism. It was not till later that the regions about the Euphrates and Tigris became strongly monotheistic; not till after Cyrus and his iconoclastic successors. The one simple answer is that He who knew what was in those Hebrews selected them to be the conservators of true religion in the world. And amid all their lapses and corruptions they certainly did preserve the knowledge and worship of One Supreme God better than any other ancient people, not excepting those who descended from the same stock. The reign of David brought them into relations with all Palestinians, with Moabites, Syrians, Hamathites, and Edomites; from Joppa to Damascus and the great River, David was respected and obeyed. Pagan treasure, vessels of gold, silver, and brass were dedicated to Jehovah, who thus became known among them. Such knowledge was extended, because David had his *recorder* and *scribes* as well as priests, who kept his accounts, narrated his deeds, and wrote his state papers to other nations, similar to our State secretaries. See details in 2 Sam. 8 : 16–18. But the letter to Joab to compass the death of Uriah was written by the king (ch. 11 : 14, 15). Historians do not fabricate such accounts against kings.

Early Semites cherished self-respect, devotion to God, regard for their tribe, love for their family, purity in women. He generally was more truly a monotheist and less of a polygamist than his Aryan contemporaries. Later Aryans, according to Plato and Aristotle, were both polygamists and polytheists, having gods many and women many. The *tendency* to a simple and reasonable worship of deity, such as some writers claim, is difficult to find among Greeks and Romans, however it appears among early Persians and Iranians ; but even they were often polygamists. History cannot be written in broad generalizations. I do not understand the records of early Babylon and Egypt as showing a *general* practice of polygamy except by some of their kings, though a tendency to polytheism early appears. But by the eighteenth or the seventeenth century b.c. there were efforts in both regions to reassert monotheism ; and who can say how far that endeavor arose from the example and influence of Abraham ? " Semites overflowed the whole plain of Sumer ;" they accepted much of Accadian civilization, and imposed their religion upon that country in exchange. Sargon and Kammurabi consolidated the

Babylonian empire and established monotheism; while in Egypt the struggles of Apepi against Ra-Sekenen had a different result. But Moses at Sinai and Zoroaster in Bactria put forth a manifesto showing that the God of Jacob and of Japheth was One Supreme Being. Such proclamation reappears with Cyrus and his successors in the restoration of Israel. Let those who treat these facts differently remember that truth may be varnished and suppressed, but shall rise again to justify itself. Easier is it to sketch at random than to detail events of far-off ages, and the personal traits and conduct of those who were prominent actors in them.

M. Renan says: "The nomad Semites came from Arabia and Sinai, while on their way to settlement in Southern Babylonia, where Ur was the chief city." But Schrader and others say, "*The Semites were original dwellers on the southern Euphrates;*" that Abraham migrated thence to Syria-Palestine, and *from thence his descendants*, through Ishmael and Keturah's sons, *peopled Arabia*. This latter view is a very different, and probably the true account. The Book of Joshua is authority that God gave Esau Mount Seir to possess it; but Jacob and his children went down into Egypt (24 : 4). When they were travelling toward Canaan, the priest of Midian and father-in-law of Moses met them; he was a descendant of Abraham; so was Amalek, who resisted the passage of Israel through that part of Arabia; showing that two tribes of a common origin journeyed thither, first from near the Persian Gulf to Syria-Palestine, and *thence* southerly to the peninsula of Arabia.

Nor do we find the character of a brigand—so Renan, p. 207—in the opposition of Amalek to Israel. They were cousins, one branch being Jacobites, the other Esauites. The old feeling at loss of the birthright may have incited the Amalekites to avenge themselves on Jacob, now journeying through the wilderness. It was very wrong but very human, and marks the truth of the records. What a different history of those times would have been written if all the descendants of Abraham had early consolidated into one people! See the lists in Genesis 36 and 1 Chronicles 1 : 28–42. Scattered as they became through Southwestern Asia, they yet exerted an influence upon Babylonians and those Japhethites whom they met in their various settlements. But the time was centuries after Abraham left Ur for Canaan, and his Arabian descendants received no civilization from Accad, because Accad was no longer a civilizing power. Any similarity in religious rites and worship between Abrahamites and Babylonians, between Hebrews from Palestine and Hebrews from Egypt, must be traced to him who centuries before had been called out of Ur.

Moreover, the number of those Hebrew tribes whom Israel encountered serves to illustrate the number of Jacobites at the era of the Exodus. Lot in Ammon and Moab, Esau in Amalek, and their cousin Midianites, were their foes while on the way from the Red Sea to the Jordan. Tribe could cope with tribe, and at times with various fortune. All consolidated against Jacob would have extinguished him as surely as Abraham extinguished Chedorlaomer and his allies. Or Israel would have been lost in the multitude of other Abrahamites? But no; consolidation was not to be, or the purpose of the call out of Ur would have been frustrated, and the preparation for the Promised One would have been delayed. National discipline would have been different. Even Midian proved a snare; Milcom and Molech led to apostasy, which neither the priestly tribe of Levi nor remonstrance of Mosaic prophets wholly corrected. Baal-peor was more destructive to Israel than the arms of Amalek at Rephidim. (Cf. Num. 25 : 1-9; Ex. 17 : 8-16; and Num. 31.) All this made an impression upon the national mind, especially Amalek's attempt to be avenged on Israel for the birthright. But Heaven gave victory to Jacob against Esau and against his descendants in the wilderness. One wrong was not to be righted by commission of another, nor by seizing and administering affairs which belonged to God.

M. Renan is careful *not* to emphasize the command to "*write it for remembrance in the book*" (Ex. 17: 14); a clear proof that writing was then known in Israel. While resting under the shady palms of Rephidim, after escaping from the grasp of Pharaoh, Amalek savagely attacked their kinsmen and were defeated. The mission of the tribes was only begun while yet journeying to the promised land and the enjoyment of its good things. As Jacob and Amalek were grandchildren of the same parents, they were in point of numbers able to cope with each other; but that was not the time for such encounter; hence the injunction to record the attack in a book, that it might be ever remembered. The long lists of places, stations, and names of the leaders of each tribe were also written, so Numbers 33 : 2 to 35th chapter. But the Law of the Covenant was graven in stone (Ex. 20 : 2-17 ; Josh. 24 : 25-27). And they set up a memorial stone under the oak by the sanctuary, that it might be long preserved and its influence long endure. The language used was that of Abraham and Lot and of their ten sons. Abraham could talk with the priest-king of Salem, and Moses with the priest-chief of Midian, while the " Moabite Stone" of 875 B.C. proves even then the close affinity of speech between all these Terahites, between the children of Lot and the children of Abraham. Isaac conversed with Canaanites and with Abimelech, the prince of Gerar. Edomites were brethren of the chosen people, not to be abhorred ; while Ishmaelites were not often hostile to their kinsmen of the Jordan. (Cf. Gen. 11 : 31 ; 14 : 16 ; 17 : 20 ; 21 : 12-21 ; 26 ; Deut. 23 : 7.) These Semitic families had inter-tribal dealings with the nations near them, so the inference is clear that Jacob was a benefit to Japheth, and that Elohim-Jahveh cared for the Gentiles as well as His chosen Israel.

Moreover, the tribal relationship, similarity of language, customs, culture, and original identity of religion, rendered communication easy and natural among them. Even the name for God, Jahveh, Elohim, was as readily understood by those peoples as Zeus in Greece. It is mere poetry in Renan to say that, because the Hebrew could not distinguish one *Eloh* from another *Eloh*, he used the plural *Elohim* with a verb in the singular ! A pretty fancy, but at the same time he admits that " Elohim is everywhere ; is universal life and causation ; brings to the birth, slays, and governs all" ("History of the People of Israel," p. 25). Semitic monotheism only needed to express the idea of God by a verb in the singular, because it was so widely understood Who was the subject of that verb, and Who was recognized as the *All* and in all. We also use impersonal words and sentences, as " it rains, it snows, it blows, it freezes," which, by omitting the " it," is like the Hebrew expression, only the Hebrew was more religious in his thought, and would feel that God sent the rain, the wind, and the frost. So, " *God was wisdom*, and imparted it to His children ; was strength, and made men strong ; had counsel and understanding, with which He endowed the wise. He destroyed or broke down, and it could not be restored ; He shut up, and no man could open." I fail to see why any theist, especially any believer in Providence, can object to such expressions, even if of Hebrew origin. Certainly Socrates would so speak. And Pope's Indian " saw God in clouds and heard Him in the wind." Everywhere the Hebrew looked for God and found Him. Dominion and fear were with Him. The moon and stars were impure in His sight, and ceased to shine (Job 12 : 12-14 ; 19 : 26 ; Prov. 8 : 14). To impress God's creative power and ubiquity upon the mind the Divine name, or a part of it, was often incorporated with Hebrew proper names, as in Abihou, Elihou, Abdo, Davdo, which became Abd, Obed, David, etc. (Renan, pp. 26-28). We see it in Elijah, in Elisha, and this form of it in more than fifty names, according to Young's Concordance, while Professor Kuenen estimates " about one hundred and ninety personal names so compounded, or with Jahveh, in the Old Testament" ("Hibbert Lectures," 1882, p. 68, English edition). It was a perpetual reminder of Deity, hence habitual prayer to and invocation of God. In the open fields while tending his flock, or sailing on the rivers in wintry storms, or engaged with an enemy in battle, or when suffering from disease, the Semite prayed to the Supreme Ruler of all things by whatever name he addressed Him. See "God Enthroned in Redemption," pp. 48, 60, 62. Nor did those different names imply a different Deity, but only different thoughts of Him, or different attributes, not in conflict, but expressing the character of the function to which the needs of the suppliant appealed.

And as angels were, from the earliest ages, believed in, some of them were supposed to represent those various functions, and their offices were invoked by man, and they were sometimes adored. Indeed, angelic beings and their worship are so familiar to Bible readers that the statement of the fact is sufficient. It would be easy to trace the worship of *secondary* gods in Babylonia and elsewhere to an earlier knowledge and adoration of angels. There were angels who excelled in strength, who were swift messengers to those in need, and who encamped around God's people for their protection. Now they appeared to utter warnings, as against Sodom; now to announce the birth of a child to Manoah, to Zacharias, and Mary the Virgin; now with a drawn sword to Joshua and to David (Gen. 19; Judges 13; St. Luke 1; Josh. 5 : 13; 1 Chron. 21 : 15–27). The covenant people were ever defended as with a shield, and punished as with the sword of the Lord. Invocation of Him would prevent threatened evils and procure needful blessings for Jacob and for Japheth. This sent them to the study of His law, the eternal law of right living, and to sundry acts of piety. Men believed themselves to be the sons of God, and their conscience and Divine instruction told them of their personal and religious duties. This is seen in the fear and confession of Cain, and in those self-willed sons from whom God withdrew the strivings of His Spirit (Gen. 4 : 9–15 ; 6 : 2, 3, 18, 22 ; 8 : 20, 21 ; 9 : 8–17 ; Job 2 : 1). They are Scriptures which teach at once Divine instruction to man, Divine punishment of him, Divine covenant with him, man's worship and sacrifice in acknowledgment of his duty to God, and the promise of His continuance of temporal blessings to man. These are grand facts of Biblical and monumental history. Semites on the Euphrates and the Jordan were *purer* monotheists than later Semites in Assyria. One striking fact is worth noting—viz., that the Aryan Persians, who succeeded in the government of that country, were for some ages as pure monotheists as the Hebrews in their best days. Aryan Greeks, with their developed Olympus and its celestial denizens, only make the question of *why this was so* more difficult of solution. But the fact is unquestioned, that those ethnic families are found to be now monotheists, now polytheists, alike in Egypt and Babylonia, in Judea and Assyria. It is not to be explained by "Semitic tent-life," for Abraham and Darius were alike monotheists, as were Apepi, Sargon of Agade, and Ezra, the scribe of the law. Even Mahomet did the world some service by his crusades against polytheistic idolatry. From Adam to Seth, to Noah, to Abraham, Sargon and Apepi, Moses and Zoroaster, David and Hezekiah, Ezra and Darius, men and nations worshipped and acknowledged one God, either with the covenant or without the covenant. Renan's *tent-life* does not explain it. Human fancy and caprice do not explain it; but "*an eternal tendency in men*" *to worship*, and in most men to return to their first love, or to the primitive worship of One Supreme Being, does explain it, and explain it according to spiritual laws. This is the alphabet and primer of religion among men. In prophets like Elijah and Isaiah, in kings like Assurbanipal and Cambyses, it became a passion; in philosophers like Anaxagoras, Pythagoras, and Socrates, it was the outcome of calm reason. The portraiture of religion in Genesis and Job finds its reality in those times and as read in the inscriptions. Generations lived in their father; Levi paid tithes in Abraham, and the chief of a tribe was its priest and judge. The standard of right living was at first the inspiration of God, then conscience, then an explicit revelation duly authenticated by Divine covenant with mankind, now with patriarchs, with Moses; renewed under Joshua, under Samuel, and later prophets. During all those ages the history of man was the unfolding of theology and of larger Divine manifestations. M. Naville tells us that Pharaohs, like Rameses II., preferred to mention in their religious inscriptions the names of the Great God, Amon, Tum, or Set, rather than the later local deity of each individual place (the *Academy*, January 21st, 1888, p. 50).

History has its contrasts even in the theology of

Semites. They are now nomads and monotheists, now dwellers in cities and polytheists; at once the most religious and the most irreligious of men, tenaciously holding the faith they profess, whether pure or corrupt; and its effects are seen in their life and conduct. If Persians conquered Semites and protected them in their religion, then more or less monotheistic, Semitic and other Mahomedans conquered all Western Asia, including the holy places of Palestine, and forced their religion upon the vanquished, and they hurled back the hosts which Christians sent to regain those lands to the religion of Christ. Babylonian Semites were the first Puritans who fought for the altars of their fathers and the Oneness of God ("God Enthroned in Redemption," pp. 52, 56-60). Neither naturalism nor culture explains the facts, for the civilization of Sargon and Apepi was as high as that of Arabia at the appearance of Mahomet. In the twentieth century B.C. Abraham, leaving Ur, travelled through Babylonia; in the sixth century B.C. his descendants were carried there captives, and now, in January, 1889, report comes that two Jews of Bagdad have bought up the old capital city, with all its ruined palaces and temples. It illustrates something more than the revenges of history; rather that what was originally true shall be perpetuated. This bridge of time, four thousand years long, despite its broken arches here and there, connects the God of the past with our modern theology, and leads to the One Supreme, who was worshipped as really on the farther side as on the hither side of those millenniums. Conscience and culture do not explain it, but the hand of

God in history and the voice of God in Revelation explain it clearly, saying, "Belief in One God Almighty is *not a growth in man, but a revelation to him.*" It made known the Creator as supervising His work, exercising His providence over the affairs of mankind, directing and preserving all, rewarding the good and punishing the bad, alike in the era of Abraham and Chedorlaomer, as in that of Ahab and Elijah, of Jeremiah and Daniel.

It was "very vague and confused up to the ninth century B.C.," says Renan, "but it was in germ from the first." The size of that germ was pretty large, and its activity great, according to the inscriptions and our Bible, which portray men of the first ages as having definite ideas of God, a day for His worship, ideas of immortality with Him, the power and activity of conscience specially seen in the sons of Jacob when standing before Joseph; all this was as pronounced and emphatic in the days of the patriarchs as when Elijah remonstrated with Ahab and the priests of Baal, or against Israel's halting in the loyal service of Jehovah. The prophet had to deal with an apostate people, whose consciences were seared. A chapel to Baal had been established in Samaria, and the altar of Jehovah at Carmel had been broken down. The people were content to have it so. That never-to-be-forgotten vision at Luz-Bethel, of Abraham and Jacob, and the lesson of the brethren before Joseph (Gen. 17, 28, and 42), demonstrate that ideas of God and the workings of conscience were not vague and confused in those far-off times. Whatever the cause, the facts are indisputable. Those Hebrew shepherds were as truly monotheists as Elijah and the seven thousand who had not bowed the knee to Baal, or as Mahomet and his Arabian iconoclasts. Dwelling in tents or within city walls had nothing to do with it. It was a fact of the soul and its God.

Arabians who had eighty different names for honey, two hundred for a serpent, five hundred for a lion, and a thousand for a sword, before their language was preserved in a written lexicon, might also have many different words for God and ideas of Him, the gift of personification, fertility of imagination and expression of religious thought, without being polytheists. It certainly had little to do with the theology of their remote ancestors, who, though building a temple to the Moon-god of Ur, stood stoutly for Jahveh in Palestine and in Egypt. That they did this in the nineteenth and the seventeenth centuries B.C. is recorded in Genesis; that many of them had become idolaters in the ninth century is recorded in 1 Kings, chapters 18 and 19. It corrects Renan, pp. 38, 39. They are passages which high authorities admit to be ancient and genuine.

Moreover, the Jahveh of Israel did everything which is ascribed to Aryan deities, thus suggesting a common origin. Personification is frequent among both races. "Death comes hastily upon one, and takes hold of him; the earth opens her mouth; the floods clap their hands, the hills skip about, the sea flies away" (Ps. 18:4, 7; 50; 55; 59; 68; 78; 106; 104; 40). That the Hindus applied such activities to their *deva*, who thus affected both animate and inanimate objects, should not prevent Jacob from ascribing them to

Elohim. And it was habitual with him to do so before Aryans had set foot in India; for the Semite was religious by nature. He was less sceptical and less superstitious than the Hindus, and he bore about in his body the seal of his covenant God, when the Hindus doubted the personality of Brahm. That Jahveh had promised to provide for His people quite explains why they saw Divine power everywhere manifested. Others, however, who had no such promise, gave free play to their poetical imagination. Brahm somehow was all and in all, yet an abstraction; inspired their thoughts, increased their joys, charmed the song, pointed the proverb, gave wisdom to philosophers, and skill in prose and in epic. Japheth lived by Brahm, as Jacob lived by Jahveh.

Singularly, however, Renan says "the word Jahveh was never employed in (Hebrew) proverbial literature, *because* it related to an idea *anterior* to Jahvehism" (p. 235). But many Psalms which are anterior to the Exile, and many Proverbs often contain that Divine name. (Cf. Ps. 1 : 2, 6 ; 15 : 1 ; 19 : 7–9 ; 27 ; 37 ; 132 ; Prov. 3 : 5, 7, 9, 11, 12, 19, 26, 32, 33 ; 6 : 16 ; 8 : 13, 22, 35 ; 9 : 10 ; 10 : 3 ; 11 : 1 ; 12 : 2 ; 14 : 2, 26, 27 ; 15 : 3.) These testify to the frequent use of Jahveh in Hebrew proverbial literature. Its songs and sayings were full of Jahveh. The Song of Moses and of Miriam, after the passage of the Red Sea, and of Deborah upon deliverance from Jabin and Sisera, were thenceforth among the most popular songs of Israel. "The sea saw God, and fled ; Jordan was driven back." Very thrilling was the response of Miriam—"Sing ye to Jahveh, for He hath triumphed gloriously; the horse and his rider hath He thrown into the sea"! (Ex. 15; Judges 5). So Balaam, whose written account Kalisch places not later than 1030 B.C., introduces the covenant name, Jahveh, into his prophecy, and repeatedly into his conversations with Balak. The man of Pethor and the men of Hamath knew it well. Kalisch indeed often corrects Renan, who, with all his attainments, has not attained to historico-Biblical criticism. Thus in one volume he objects to "Joshua" for not telling about Samaria, and in another volume accepts the Bible account of its being built in the tenth century B.C., but has not the fairness to cancel his objection. The *Andover Review* smiles at his false derivation of words; Ewald laughed at his "perverted history;" while the *Academy* censures him for calling King David a brigand! ("le brigand d'Adullam," January, 1888, pp. 92, 93): "Renan's poetical history, which treats the Hexateuch as non-historical, cannot stand" before the added light of monumental knowledge, "attesting the accuracy of our Biblical accounts, in the face of all redactors—Jahvistic, Elohistic, priestly, and prophetic editing." The bricks of Pithom prove the bricks of Exodus.

II.

THE RELIGION OF ABRAHAM, FROM THE BIBLE AND THE INSCRIPTIONS.

The religion of Israel is best learned from that of Abraham, which also illustrates that of Japheth. Our authorities are the Bible and monumental inscriptions, which yield fresh light for the elucidation of this subject. They describe man as God-created and God-instructed; not as first a savage who becomes a sage, nor as a nature-worshipper who develops into a worshipper of the God of nature. They say nothing about flintmen and cavemen as progenitors of the Adamic race. But they represent primitive man as a noble and intelligent being who was divinely created and divinely instructed. We find conscience and the religious faculty early developed, with positive ideas of immortality and of deliverance from self-caused evils. Thus we learn that neither the world nor man was a "come-by-chance." It is taught alike in the books of Jacob and the monuments of Japheth. Sin was followed by punishment, and by the promise and hope of redemption. Yet, as Dr. South strongly says, "An Aristotle was but the ruins of an Adam, and Athens but the rudiments of Paradise." Man wandered into devious ways and retained small prospect of return. His best desires could not be fulfilled without Divine help.

Hence God chose Abraham to found a new nation, with a revised or revealed religion. Others of that era knew little and said little about it. But some centuries later Israel emerged into contemporary history, now as slaves in Egypt, and now as tributary to Assyrian kings. Of David and Solomon the inscriptions have little to say, and mistake avenging Jehu for a lineal descendant of Ahab. Still those bricks are no more incorrect than Tacitus, and they contain pretty full accounts of the era of Abraham, of Nimrod who was before him, and of Noah a thousand years earlier.

At the migration of the patriarch from Ur of Chaldea, we find a complex cosmology and theology had taken the place of the religion of Eden. From the different attributes He possessed, from different thoughts of Him, the names for God had increased; and some had transformed the primitive manifestation and ideas about angels into as many deities. Some Divine names were Ilu, El, and Bel, Anu and Ea, Ra and Jah. They were also classified into Triads, and the goddess Nanâ or Istar had become recognized. A god gave name to each day of the week, and to each planet of the solar system. Creation of the heavenly bodies was said to have been by the great God who created man and vivified him by His inbreathed Spirit. A legend tells how the blood which flowed from Bel's head, when severed from the body and mingled with the earth, became the living element in man's creation. Thus man was Divine by nature and by creation. Providence was expressed by deities who presided over birth and death, work and pleasure, disease and pestilence, earth and sky, land and water, heaven and hell. It governed the orbs of light, and they became symbols of deity. Moreover, this religiousness of man found expression in the altars and temples he erected to the Divine Being, in the sacrifices he offered to Him, and in the detailed ritual of His worship. To appease an angry God, to propitiate His favor and the bestowment of earthly good, to thank Him for blessings received and honor Him by worship in a temple or at an altar, this represents the pious practices of the men of the era 2000 B.C. Though primitive purity and simplicity had disappeared, there yet remained, especially among Semites, much which testified of One Supreme God, of His Providence rewarding the good and punishing the wicked, of the hopes of immortality, and of a promised Deliverer from the ills of life.

Myths and legends may conceal the spiritual character of God and of His Providence, but God and Providence are the facts and belief which they conceal, for the counterfeit proves a true original. The popular religion may have become as a wild olive-tree, or, as Schelling happily says, it was "religion growing wild." Paganism could only represent the *world-idea* of spiritual powers imperfectly understood; its elements are called by St. Paul "the beggarly elements of the world." But in Abraham spiritual visions and spiritual realities are clearly unfolded. God dwells again with man and instructs him, lifts him up to a higher plane of life and thought, appoints and ordains him to carry out the grand purposes of Deity, and does not permit him to fail of accomplishing that design, but to become a beacon and a benison to the nations. In Abraham we discover glimpses of Him whose goings forth were from of old, who was the perfection of humanity and its Perfector.

The patriarch believed in a personal God and in His directing Providence. He could not hesitate when he heard the voice which bade him leave a city which had become a worshipper of Sin, the Moon-god and of Istar his daughter. The theology and legends of Sumero-Accadians were familiar to him. From his observation of the starry heavens and his sacrifice at sunset, it is clear that he followed the usages of the people of Ur. And when he left that centre of Moon-worship he went and abode in another centre of Moon-worship. Schrader asks, whether Laban were not originally a name for the Moon-god of Haran, and says the more ancient Assyrian proper names wear a Canaanite rather than an Aramaic form (p. 120). At all events, Abraham and his family long dwelt among the worshippers of Sin, of Istar, and of El, who, like the early Egyptians, made the orbs of heaven symbols and representatives of Deity. And there was an increasing tendency to idolatry and nature-worship, thus debasing that paid to the Supreme Being. Hence the need of a founder of a new nation which should acknowledge and adore Him, and shake off all contamination from its neighbors. But that was only slowly effected, a reformation yet to be achieved.

On his way along the Euphrates, in journeying toward Haran, Abraham beheld the famous temple of Bel at Borsippa. The Birs-Nimrud was then in its pristine glory, with a golden altar to Bel, and with splendid chapels at the base of the structure. Tower and temple he saw, if not for the first, certainly for the last time, passing on northward to Bâbil above Babylon. He did not then know what was later revealed to him, and so he may have worshipped at those temples the God who had spoken to him in Ur. The founder of the Hebrew nation probably visited those temples, one of which was rebuilt by King Nebuchadnezzar, who some fourteen centuries afterward conquered the descendants of Abraham, and carried them to that same country through which he then passed. He was also cognizant of the Tower legends of Babylonia, which Schrader "bases upon the actual existence of some structure erected in former times, whose ruins still exist at Babel and Borsippa." The southern ruin is called Birs-Nimrud, where stood the temple of the "Seven Lights of Heaven and Earth," dedicated to Bel-Nebo, which Nebuchadnezzar restored and dedicated to Bel-Merodach, the chief deity of Babylon at that time. The northern ruin above Babylon is Bâbil, which was a pyramid temple, a "house of towering summit," built in stages like the temple at Borsippa. It was also called the "Palace of Heaven and Earth, the Dwelling of Bel, House of the highest god Merodach." Present information cannot determine which of these ruins marks the site of the famous tower at whose erection "a god confounded their speech," but the trend of opinion inclines to the southern mound. It contains the remains of a large pyramidal structure which was crowned by a temple six hundred feet higher than the plain. Within it was an altar of pure gold; in later times an image of Merodach; but originally the sanctuary was without a statue. Chapels on the first story contained the image of a god sitting on a golden throne, behind a golden altar whereon a thousand pounds of incense were consumed at the annual festival. "The God of a great people was worshipped at great cost." And He was worshipped where our fathers little expected. Schrader suggests that the God of Abraham was known as "Jahveh" to Hamathites, and Stade in his "Israel" that He was so known to the Kenites. *Jahu* seems to have been a synonym for Ilu in Assyrian, and to have worked its way among Hebrews and Arameans. The word indicated a God who was the "Life-dispenser." Dr. Legge says that "King Yew who reigned four thousand two hundred and forty-five years ago, and King Shun four thousand and ninety-five years ago, both worshipped and sacrificed to the Most High God before Abraham was born." These kings illustrate how far true religion had then spread in the Chinese world.

Then, too, the story of Eden and the Sacred Tree, of the Fall of man and the guarding seraphim, had the freshness of youth. Often is the serpent seen figured on the monuments; a tree with hanging clusters of fruit occupies a prominent position in the representations which have been preserved for thousands of years. It is a "fruit-tree" in concrete or generic form, but not the palm; so Schrader (p. 39). And as cherubim were sentinels at the entrance to Paradise, so we find them pictured on the monuments as colossal bulls and lions with human faces, guardians alike of palaces, temples, and city walls. Probably of Babylonian origin, they appear in the account of the Fall, and reappear in the prophecy of Ezekiel, in the cherubim of the Ark of the Covenant, and in the Apocalypse of St. John. Anciently they were the mute sentinels and guardians in front of royal houses and temples, of the king upon his throne, and they symbolized the majesty of Heaven. When placed within a temple, they may have suggested care of the sacred edifice and faithfulness in the ministrations of the priests. Watchful eyes were ever gazing upon them. But whatever was meant by these cherubim, Eden and the Sacred Tree were popular legends in the Ur of Abraham. The word for garden was quite as likely original with Semites as with Accadians; so Schrader (p. 28), who sees no good reason for not regarding the story of the Tree of Life and the Tree of Knowledge as closely connected with the narrative of the Fall on the Assyrio-Babylonian monuments. The differences are a secondary matter, and probably arose with the Hebrews. Existence of such legends among those peoples at that time is a point to be remembered. They did not originate them.

Moreover, the story of the serpent at that time will not budge at our bidding. It is often seen on the monuments, figured in the tree, near the person, at an altar, seen with one head and with seven heads; a tree also is seen with fruit, or with leaves only and branches in sets of sevens, thus early a sacred number. We cannot exscind the tree nor the serpent from those ancient memorials. Thus Eden or Paradise may be regarded as thoroughly historical, locally de-

fined and colored, and blended with the history of the
region about the Euphrates and the Tigris. Schrader
makes it of Babylonian, not Hebrew, origin. Ewald
accepts it as well authenticated. M. Lenormant, the
two Delitzsches, and Fritz Hommel, all emphasize the
historical character of Abraham and of the leading
ideas connected with him. Thus Hommel says his
" exodus from Babylonia, the battle of the Canaanites
with the Elamite league in the valley of Siddim, and
the journey of Abraham to Egypt are historical facts."
Mr. G. Smith suggested that " Amar-phel" of Gen.
14 was to be found among Babylonian titles, and that
" Arioch" is identical with Eriaku or Rim-agu, who
was the son and successor of Kudur-Mabug; showing
that chapter to be in linguistic and historical harmony
with the monuments. From them we learn that Elamite kings exercised at one time hegemony or sovereignty in Babylonia, and that Chedorlaomer of Elam
was the chief of the combination which Abraham routed and extinguished, so that his name no more appeared in the history. He belonged to the Elamite
dynasty of Kudur-Mabug, whose bricks have been discovered, and disclose the power of the Kudurids.
One of those kings, Kudur-Nakhunta, is reported to
have " laid hands on the temple of Accad," carrying
off an image of the goddess Nana, the Istar of that
city, which Assurbanipal, in 651 B.C. or sixteen hundred and thirty-five years afterward, recaptured and
returned to Erech, when he subdued the Elamite
country to his rule. (G. Smith's " Assurbanipal ;"
Schrader's " Cunei. Inscrip.," p. 122; Rawlinson's
" Egypt and Babylon," p. 14.)

That first capture was before Apepi's effort to have only One God worshipped at Thebes, when Ra-Sekenen was sub-king. Efforts to establish monotheism were made in Babylonia, but after long struggles the adherents of Bel-Merodach supplanted the elder Bel. (See Professor Sayce's "Hibbert Lectures" for 1887.)

It is conceded that the Semites of Ur appropriated to their use what suited them in the Accadian cultus and made it their own. Thus Babylonian ideas were scrutinized, perhaps changed in particulars to suit their views before adoption. Abraham may have Hebraized current legends, winnowing the chaff from the wheat, the false from the true, and so reproduced the early facts. True in substance, he preserved the truth in details and significance under the guiding Spirit of God ; true alike for Jacob and for Japheth.

Originality in Hebrew records of the Fall and the Deluge is of less moment than their truthfulness. The monumental writings of Babylonia and Assyria affirm the same grand facts of history which Israel accepted. Careful sifting of the inscriptions from Accad, Borsippa, Nineveh, etc., yields substantial agreement in all important facts. Their Flood account is not later than 800 B.C., so Schrader, though the Hebrews were familiar with it from a *much earlier date*, or when Abraham migrated from Ur. But it is said that the moulding of traditions into literary form was after the settlement in Palestine. Isaiah (54 : 9) and Ezekiel (14 : 14, 20) speak of Noah and the Deluge as long known to Israel, so it must have been a recognized fact of their early history. Its form and that of the creation narrative must have received their last

Hebrew coloring before the eighth-century prophets. Whoever was the original writer, our biblical version bears the impress of antiquity and the guidance of inspiration. Even "the great bow which Anu created" is verified in Hebrew and Assyrian, and was probably an original part of the account when Abraham first heard it; when Accadian legends and poetry were in their bloom, and when critics were not concerned to make them of the date of Assurbanipal, or centuries before him. ("Chaldean Account in Genesis;" F. Lenormant, and the chapter on "Deluge Legends" in "God in Creation.")

Witnesses of the Fall and wickedness of man were to be seen on all sides, in the lives of the people, in their worship, in their historic legends and family records, in their totems and their temples. But it may well be doubted whether the account given by Herodotus of the prostitution of women at religious rites in Babylonia is true in B.C. 2000. Not so early had that people adopted rites which dishonored women. But the explanation of moral debasement may be found in the influence of fallen spirits who dominated the earth, called the dragon, the old serpent, or Typho; among the Japhethites of Iran and India the evil being who led the first man astray, through whose lie the first of our race fell into sin and under the power of evil. Hence were permitted burning heats and freezing cold, disease and death, because the first man listened to the luring words of the serpent. Ejected from heaven he had fallen to earth, and the Divine majesty had departed. ("Khorda-Avesta," 35 : 7, 40 : " Yasma," 9 : 14, 21.)

Deliverance must be the work of another, of a Divine man who will accomplish salvation by the truth He preaches. Some Avatar, son of Zoroaster born in heaven, will effect this by appearing as the Mediator and Redeemer of man. Meantime, let cleansing fire ever burn in sacred offerings; let sacrifice and worship appease the offended majesty of God, save from the evil one, prepare for the Sosiosh and immortal life. Indeed, was not the worship of men derived from that of heaven? Did not the Divine maker of the celestial sacrifice teach it to men? The "Rig Veda" identifies the earthly priest with Agni who sacrificed and prayed as a Mediator. Barth says: "Thrice a day was the offering of libations; a perpetual fire; no idols, no temples; the family hearth was the sanctuary" ("Religion of India"). Thus men were to prepare in life, that when "dying they might go to the gods, the blessed abode where pious men rejoice." The consequence of sin was supposed to be removed by confessing it, and by the mediation of Agni, who was invoked to intercede for man. "O Agni, turn away from us the anger of Varuna!" Such was the early teaching of Japheth. "Conscience or the old man within" quickened the sense of right and duty. In the heart was believed to dwell the Supreme Spirit, the silent observer of all good and evil thoughts; he sat as a god in righteous judgment. Sophocles describes conscience as a god who grows not old. There is much more of a didactic sort in the "Rig Veda" (IV., VII. 93, 7; VIII., X. 40, 11; I. 125, 8; II. 29, 4, 5;) "Laws of Menu" (IV. 175); "God Enthroned in Creation and Redemption" (pp. 68, 76, 30–35). But not so early had the Hindus attained such knowledge ; in the days of Abraham they yet dwelt in their native home. The primitive centre of civilization after the Deluge was Babylonia, whence colonists migrated in all directions, carrying with them similar ideas of religion and the standard of ethics which then prevailed.

"As in this life we pass through childhood, manhood, and old age, so death disrobing us of one body gives us another. The arrows cannot pierce the soul, nor the fire burn it, nor the waters drown it, nor the winds dry it up ; it is imperishable. It is not born ; it does not die ; it is eternal." (Bhishma-parva, V. 1157.) We are enjoined to remember that man is born alone, dies alone, and alone shall receive the recompense of his deeds, good or bad ("Laws of Menu," IV. 240-42). Purity, temperance, truthfulness, self-control, returning good for evil, virtue, knowledge of the sacred books—this was how to attain the perfection of Brahm. Tennyson tersely expresses it as :

"Self-reverence, self-knowledge, self-control."

But the Veda were before the name of Brahm ; and before any Hymns to Varuna, to Indra and to Agni, Egypt had formulated her Book of the Dead, with which Abraham probably became acquainted during his sojourn in the Nileland. He was the equal of his peers in knowledge of human duty, ethics in the broad sense, loyalty to God and to man, and in belief that present conduct would determine man's future happiness. Like Tennyson he would have " more of reverence in us dwell, that mind and soul might well accord." Apart from special inspiration he was an intelligent, well-cultured man, with large religious attainments. From the Saints' Calendar and the Descent of Istar, the Book of the Dead, and the legend of Osiris and Horus, Abraham's ideas of life and death were probably in advance of Hebrews generally in the period between Moses and David. The sacred name of his covenant God suggested to him the Life-giver and the Life-dispenser, the One who ever is, who had breathed the immortal spirit into man and made him a living soul. He certainly had no need to buttress his faith by prehistoric inquiries about trepanning, proving, and illustrating how men of the Neolithic Age expressed their ideas of existence out of the body. To him it would probably appear like a grim joke to see amulets placed in the skulls of dead men in order to secure happiness and exemption from evil in their disembodied state! Writers in "Fossil Men" tell us that some ancients did this, and so disclosed the instinct of immortality which they early cherished. In men who hardly knew how to build a hut better than the lair of a wild beast, there was that which prompted them to provide an eternal habitation for their dead. Quinet is surely right in saying (in "La Creation"), "After such a beginning of evidence of immortal cravings, all that remains is easy of belief." Realm of Allat, Descent of Istar, Life eternal in the land of the silver sky, Book of rules for guidance through Amenti—all might be developed from that small beginning; rather it was the outcome of the inbreathed spirit of God and of original instruction to man; to Abraham in large measure, with knowledge of defeat in Eden to be followed by One who was to be born of a woman in descent from him, and who would drive the evil worker into eternal darkness, and exalt the struggling sons of men unto eternal life. It was then but the morning of God's world, which Satan tried to dominate, and ere the eventide drew on the perfect Light would illume the hearts of men and prepare them for the brighter light of Heaven. Thus the redemption of mankind was revealed to Abraham as the eternal glory of his race. His Son and Lord should sway the sceptre of the world, because He would become the Saviour of the world, and by Divine grace draw all men unto Him. Did not the Spirit of Wisdom enable Plato to say that men are allured to virtue and holiness by Divine influence and by intercourse with good men? The godlike within us seeks its counterpart without. The spiritual loves the spiritual. The lofty soul seeks Divine and lofty souls. So we say with Bishop Martensen ("Christian Dogmatics," p. 307), the "Divine love that knew from eternity the possibility of the Fall, also found from eternity the way of Redemption." It was disclosed to Adam and to Abraham; Japheth had adumbrations of it, dim indeed, but true. (See "God Enthroned in Redemption," Chapters III. and IV.)

Opportunity to prepare for it was the seventh-day Sabbath, universally observed in the first ages. Hence seven became the number for sanctity and for the days of the week. On the seventh day no work was to be done. This was an old Babylonian institution which, as Schrader says, the Hebrews brought with them after their stay in South Babylonia, at Ur Kasdim— i.e., Ur of the Chaldees. The importance of this subject and want of space here may excuse a reference to the author's chapter on "The First Sabbath and Primitive Worship" in "God Enthroned in Redemption." Renan objects to the Semitic observance of the seventh day, because of their *nomad* condition. But where the skies during a long summer were always clear, and where the agriculturist had no difficulty in gathering his harvest or in pasturing his flocks, such objection falls flat. And the inscriptions testify to a week of seven days, to prescribed sacrifices and details of worship for that day. They also name the god who was to be worshipped on the several Sabbaths. Of this evidence Renan says, "Assyria had from the very first her castes of servants and priests and the weekly Sabbath. The seven planets gave their names to the seven days of the week, and the seventh day had special characteristics which marked it as a day of rest," "History of Israel." Again, "the dwelling-place of primitive humanity was Lower Chaldea, with its Paradise and Sacred Tree" (p. 59). Abraham had no relations with the then small Assyria, but he migrated from his native Ur to Haran, carrying with him all he approved of its religion, its art, and its literature. It was many centuries before the supremacy of the northern empire; seven at least before its first Shalmaneser reigned; it was when the Sumero-Accadians were yet strong and their poetry was in full bloom; Sabbath observance was then regnant. The God worshipped on that day disproves Renan's saying, "With our tears we make for ourselves a God." Tears, indeed, may suggest the need of a God, and urge men to seek

Him; but the God of Abraham was not evolved from tears and sorrow. He revealed Himself as his God and the God of all mankind. Jacob and Japheth, Ishmael and Esau knew Him. Not limited to Palestine, Jahu was known at Hamath in the north and by Kenite in the south. All holy men of old felt the influence of His Spirit; Zoroaster in Bactria, Numa in Italy, Socrates in Greece.

Abraham did not lead the life of a recluse in his native city. Legend portrays him as often sitting in public places, speaking words of wisdom and counsel to those who heard him. Some, indeed, affirm that he was persecuted, like the later philosopher of Athens, and obliged to fly for safety. However that may be, we have Scripture authority for saying, he was confederate with Mamre, the Amorite, that he made friends in Egypt, and with Abimelech, King of Gerar. The priest-king of Salem gave him his benediction, and the Canaanite chiefs whom he aided against Chedorlaomer, publicly thanked him for his services (Gen. 14). If his intercession for the sinners of Sodom mark him as the benefactor of man, his bold and strong Jahvehism marks him as the friend of God. Even the covenant-seal of circumcision which he received and administered to his sons was also administered to three or four hundred trained servants. It was available to all who would receive it. By the Arabians who are descended from him, his name is embalmed with precious memories, because of his character and influence. His moral force passed from one centre of civilization to another, blessing the world and preparing the way for Him who took the sting from death and secured immortality for all believers. Jesus could truly say to the Jews, "Your father Abraham rejoiced to see my day; he saw it, and was glad." It has gladdened mankind. We need no other testimony to the religion of Abraham. His faith in God was strong, when faith was weak among men, and they were becoming naturalists and polytheists. For four and twenty years he had lived in Palestine without seal or sacrament, when he received the sign of circumcision. Before that he was sustained by prayer and promise, by sacrifice and by Providence. The old Saints' Calendar may have guided him in the daily worship of God, and he had the assurance that he pleased God. Moreover, he was one of His elect for personal and national benefit. Many of his descendants perished in their wickedness, not because they were not elected to privilege, but because of their rebellion against God, now in the matter of Korah, and now by apostasy; for which they were punished, now by pestilence, now by serpents, now by earthquake. All the twelve disciples of our Lord heard His saving message, yet one of them betrayed Him and went to his own place. Baal or Chemosh called louder than Jahveh to six of Abraham's eight sons. St. Paul illustrates how one may know his duty, but persist in not doing it, till a lightning flash of grace arrests and saves him. Such has been the history of Redemption among men. Some, indeed, expect *grace* to become *violence*, not content that the grace of privilege only precedes grace in activity; the Divine suggests the human side of salvation. So far as we can see in the case of Abraham, there was nothing to prevent other men of Ur and other men in Palestine, as witness the King of Salem, from serving Jehovah, except their own choice, which led them to neglect present opportunities for securing eternal blessings; which allowed them to sacrifice eternal joys for temporal pleasures. Lot was *twice* saved by Abraham, for he had chosen Sodom and the plain country about it. Thus few men of his time exerted a larger influence. "I know Abraham," said the Lord (have covenanted with him) "that he will command his children and his household after him, that the Lord may bring upon Abraham that which He hath spoken of him" (Gen. 18 : 19). This teaches that man must do his part, in order that God may fulfil His promise. Children of the covenant must obey the terms of that covenant, otherwise the blood of the Bull of Mithra would be as efficacious as that of the promised Lamb to take away sin.

The intercessor for Sodom was taught very emphatically to substitute a ram for a sacrifice instead of Isaac. The firstlings of Abel's flock were acceptable to God, while the offering of Cain was not, because not offered with a right spirit, and was not a sacrifice. Noah took of every clean animal and of fowl, and offered burnt-offerings on the altar. Thus the practice became universal and of a sacramental character, for part of the sacrifice was eaten; compacts were thus solemnized, alliances rendered obligatory (Gen. 15 : 7–18 ; 31 : 43–54). The passing of fire between the pieces of a sacrificial victim indicated the Divine acceptance. In Gen. 15 : 17 it probably symbolized the presence of God; the word there rendered lamp also means a flame or tongue of fire; so in the Divine appearance to Moses in the burning bush (Ex. 3 : 2). In both cases there was fire to symbolize, and there was a voice to emphasize the presence of God to Abraham and to Moses; but there was no image or material form. Jacob and Laban made a heap of stones with a central one for a pillar, eating bread upon the heap, as a sacramental seal and witness of renewed friendship. Hence columns placed in the ground and consecrated by pouring oil upon them came into common use, and in later times covered Arabia, especially the region of Mecca; previous to Mahomet they were regarded as sacred. A similar custom of stone use extended northward through Phœnicia (Conder's "Syrian Stone Lore;" Renan's "History of Israel").

Besides the Sabbath, New Year, and royal days, whose observance generally prevailed in the era of Abraham, stated festivals were few. A great feast was made at the weaning of Isaac; Isaac and Abimelech feasted at the digging of a well and to seal a covenant between them (Gen. 26). *Fasting* was practised by ancient Arabs, by Assyrians of the time of Jonah and Nahum, and previously by Hebrews. David fasted for his sick child. Fasting was probably enjoined by Moses; it is mentioned in Judges 20 : 26 as continuing one day; at the death of Saul and Jonathan people fasted seven days (1 Sam. 31 : 13). The custom extended and the time lengthened to forty days at Nineveh. Daniel fasted and prayed at Babylon (Dan. 9). Renan tells of an early Semitic celebration in the spring, characterized by the use of unleavened bread; but he cites no proof earlier than the

Passover, which was a complex festival. Sheepshearing, the vintage harvest, and the new moon were joyful occasions observed by Samuel and David, probably much earlier. Festivals under tents and the feast of tabernacles, with some other rites, were, we are told, common to all Semitics. The feast of tabernacles is said to be a souvenir of primitive life, preserved even by those who had wandered farthest from their ancestral home. It was continued during seven days, and was celebrated alike under Moses and David, Solomon and Ezra, and in the time of our Lord. Its institution is mentioned in Lev. 23 : 33–43 ; Hosea makes its enjoyment a token of Divine favor ; Zechariah speaks of it as to be observed even by nations hostile to Israel (Hosea 12 : 9 ; Zech. 14 : 16-19).

Philo says "the Hebrews had ten festivals (the number of completeness) : (1), a feast of every day with prayer and thanksgiving ; (2), the Sabbath-festival ; (3), that of New Moon ; (4), the Passover ; (5), Feast of First-fruits ; (6), of Unleavened Bread ; (7), the Seventh-day of the Feast of Seven Days ; (8), Feast of Trumpets ; (9), the Day of Solemn Fast ; (10), Feast of Tabernacles" (Bohn's ed., vol. iii., p. 265). Prophets of the eighth century refer to them and to the books of the Pentateuch which treat of them.

Abraham and other patriarchs had visions and revelations, and the latest communications accord with the first ; those to prophets of Jerusalem are of like purpose with those to prophets of Samaria (Gen. 15 : 1 ; 28 : 10–22 ; 37 : 5–10 ; Job 33 : 14–16 ; Isa. 1 : 1 ; Hosea 12 : 9, 10). They disclose similar conceptions of deity and ideas of duty in the shepherd nomad and the shepherd king. Abraham possessed ideas and moral precepts in advance of later times. Fancies yielded to maxims. Life in the tent was as pure and lofty as life in the city, and its memory left an impress on all after ages. The early domestic standard moulded the subsequent character of the nation. It was God-instructed.

Moreover, the Divine name was incorporated with local and proper names, as in Bethel and Bethuel, Ishmael and Raguel, Caleb from Calbel, Isaac from Isaakel, Jacob from Jacobel. The name of the son of promise meant "he whom God smiles" upon, and who was the friend of El. Thus, says Renan, "We may fancy Israel as being a sort of Geneva in the midst of varied populations, surrounded by Moab and Edom, Philistia and Phœnicia ; Puritans begirt with corruptionists in morals and theology" ("History of Israel," p. 92). The covenant name Jahveh was used in Assyria, and the Mesha inscription gives it like the Hebrew as J h v h. That was in 875 B.C. Centuries previously it had been given to Moses (Ex. 3 : 14). Earlier still it was probably known through Abraham to the Egyptian priests as "*Nuk Pu Nuk*," or "I am that I am." Very significant was the inscription on the temple at Sais, which Plutarch rendered, "I am all that was, and is, and will be." In Ra, Jah, Jahu, He was known as the God of Israel and of other nations, already blessed by the chosen man. He founded a people who became stronger than any other in moral force and religious fervor ; who existed when pyramids and temples were being erected whose ruins we study to-day. Old Sargon and Rameses, Shalmaneser and Nebuchadnezzar concern us chiefly because they represent nationalities which mark the course of human development in the ancient world and throw light upon Israel. Father Orham, the reputed founder and king, legislator and saint of Ur, has become interwoven with the early pages of history. He harmonizes with the character of Abraham, benevolent in aspect and seated in an arm-chair, speaking words of counsel and wisdom, if not of urgent warning against corruption in religion. For his chief title to the veneration of his admirers was much more than that he substituted the sacrifice of a ram for that of his son. So explicit and unique are the statements respecting him that it is necessary to regard him as an historical person (Renan, pp. 60–63). Abraham, indeed, was divinely chosen and taught. It was God speaking in his soul that lifted him out of those polytheistic surroundings in Chaldea, and gave him the lofty covenant of a pure faith in Canaan; a covenant which was for him and his descendants. It was not the thought of one who protested against the errors about him, but it was revealed to him by a voice from heaven; a covenant was made and ratified between him and the Divine Speaker, which should never be forgotten.

Moreover, *good angels* were believed to be often engaged in ministry to men. If there were one thousand evil spirits, were there not four thousand good spirits who sang the praises and did the errands of the Most High? Such a belief is evident in the inscriptions and in the Scriptures, from the angels of Eden to the angel who shall sound the last trump. They were of various orders, performing various offices;

angels of sacrifice and prayer, who placed their incense on the celestial altar; angels seen in flaming fire; the Angel of the Covenant, who appeared to Abraham; the angels who delivered Lot from the doom of Sodom; who appeared now to Gideon and Manoah, now to Moses and David, now to Elijah and Daniel, now to Zacharias and the Virgin Mary, now to our Lord and His Apostles, now ministering to little children, guarding the open tomb of Jesus, ready in legions to do His bidding, or to speak words of comfort to broken hearts. The angel or prince of Persia was of a different sort, whom Michael helped another angel to withstand (Dan. 10 : 13-21). The Hebrew word for angel is the same as that for king, malak or melek, acting as an agent, messenger, or counsellor for another; while *sar*, the word for prince, is found incorporated with old names for Deity, as Sar-ili, "King of the gods," to whom Urukh, one of the earliest Babylonian kings, dedicated a temple at Zergul (" God Enthroned in Redemption," pp. 58-60). Thus the angels of heaven became gods upon earth, and under various characters were adored by men.

The angel Michael, which means "like God," is found in the Babylonian Marduk or Merodach, one of its secondary gods, and was regarded as a Saviour by that people, who would raise men to life again and become their judge. A similar idea prevailed among early Zoroastrians and travelled to India. Thus, angelic appearances, Divine voices speaking to man, were commonly believed in, and prepared Abraham to accept God's revelation of Himself without hesitancy. It was not a new thought or experience, but was duly authenticated to the patriarch, and never developed into polytheism with the Hebrews, however they may have added those ideas of Japheth, which grew out of it to their own. Deut. 33 : 2 says the Lord came from the ten thousands of holy ones. Revised Version. (Cf. Job 5 : 1 ; 15 : 15.) The "Faerie Queene," Book II., says :

> " That blessed angels He sends to and fro,
> To serve to wicked man, to serve His wicked foe ! "

And in his "Epithalamium," Spenser thus apostrophizes them :

> " Sing, ye sweet angels, Alleluia sing,
> That all the woods may answer, and your echo ring."

Ages before the angels rolled away the stone from the door of the sepulchre, in ministry to the Lord and to man. It crowned their studies of Redemption.

Belief in evil spirits, who for rebellion were expelled from heaven, was common at this time among Semites, Accadians, and Japhethites, among dwellers at Ur, at Haran, and in Canaan. Witchcraft, too, was then believed in as really as by people of the Middle Ages. And it arose from that early belief in fallen spirits from heaven. Hence, dread of being under their spell, of being possessed, diseased, and injured by them. Hence, prayers for deliverance from evil spirits, and the hope for One to arise who would crush their power. Hence Merodach in Babylon, Horus in Egypt, Krishna in India, was the conqueror of evil and the adumbration of our Redeemer.

The chosen man was familiar with all this ; with ideas of creation and of Providence, prayer and sacrifice,

Sabbath-worship and Divine instruction ; with the existence of good and of evil spirits. The *new truth* revealed to him was that of *Jehovah entering into Covenant with him*, and appointing circumcision as its sacramental seal. It was a covenant and personal relation with God, which lifted him far above others of his race. What chief from Noah to Moses had such a privilege? What old Greek or Roman was so exalted? For it was given to him in a high sense, by this covenant relation, "to repair (as Milton says) the ruin of our first parents by regaining to know God aright."

What if some philosophers by deep searchings found out the necessity of a God, and attributed to Him creation and oversight? What if "Plato and Aristotle rose to the thought of God as a *jealous* God," so Martensen, or of God as a Father, so Origen? What if all primitive nations recognized and worshipped God, Syrians in Hamath, Assyrians in Nineveh, the old Babylonians and Egyptians, Kenites of the era of the Exodus, as the One Supreme, the Creator and Life-giver ; yet it was *not as the covenant Jahveh of Abraham*, Jacob, and Moses, who revealed Himself for the purpose of providing the Saviour of mankind. This exalted Israel above all other nations, gave them a peculiar place in the world, and makes the study of their religion of supreme importance.

III.

THE PATRIARCH IN PALESTINE: PERSONAL INCIDENTS.

In the twentieth century B.C. Abraham settled in Palestine, or rather sojourned there, with hope of remaining. He had brought with him the culture and the religion outlined in Chapter II. He had *no written revelation*, except what he himself had recorded of the Divine utterances. Belief in God the Creator enabled him to believe in God the Revealer, who had spoken to and covenanted with him. His fathers in Southern Babylonia had served other gods (Josh. 24 : 2). A century passed, a thousand miles of country had been travelled, but this could effect no religious change in him, unless enjoined by a Divine voice which told him whom and how he was to worship; which explained why the man who had departed from Ur must accept another ritual in Canaan. He was no Buddha nor Mahomet. He had left the region of one set of polytheists, and was now dwelling among another set equally polytheistic. Some of them, indeed, worshipped El-Eliun, "the Strong God," and some in his more southern home worshipped Sar-ili, "the King of the Gods," which worship Jahveh accepted as to Himself? Urukh had built a temple to Him at

Zerghul; Sargon built another to Sin, the Moon-god, at Ur, and to the Sun-god at Sippara, which were dedicated to the Supreme God, in whom those kings believed; while Melchizedek at Salem was known as the priest of El-Elinn. The One Supreme God of heaven and earth now revealed Himself to Abraham by His sacred and everlasting name, for a saving and world-wide purpose.

Settled in a fertile land, no one of Abraham's practical sense would leave it at the suggestion of a common dream, or the uncertain whisperings of the night wind, to go to an unknown country. No mythical voice or nebulous appearance would root him out and send him off among strangers. He was a man of property and of large practical sense; by birth and temperament a conservative, and his belongings required careful guarding. The voice which spoke to him at Ur spoke again at Haran after the death of his father Terah, in such explicit terms that he left his kindred, passed through Canaan and came to Sichem, or Sychar, unto the plain or oak of Moreh, where he builded an altar unto the LORD, who appeared unto him. Mark the Divine Name here used—Jehovah or Jahveh. Thence he removed to the east of Bethel, builded another altar, and called upon Jahveh (Gen. 12 : 1–8). In these eight verses Jahveh occurs six times. All admit that Abraham was a Semite, a strong monotheist, who had long dwelt among polytheists; yet how account for this building of altars to Jahveh and worship of Him, unless he was assured that he was doing right? This Divine epithet was not the one familiar to his youth; he had not the guidance of a written standard or revelation; if a polytheist, he could not have evolved it from his inner self; the narrative is clearly ancient and credible, so that the rational explanation of Abraham's conduct on his migration, altar-building, and worship of Jahveh, is that he was thus doing the behests of Deity, who had unmistakably manifested His will to him, and that He would be his God forever. Thus began his authenticated Bible.

He had taken this new departure, not as an adventurer or fortune-hunter, but in obedience to what he believed to be the voice of God, and, from the faith of his fathers and according to his own knowledge, was justified in so believing. Mark the words, "Unto thy seed will I give this land"—not an immediate possession for himself, but unto his seed was this charter-right given (ver. 7). Though we are not told precisely how the Divine manifestation occurred, it was by no means an impossible conception to one who had heard of Jahveh talking with Adam, to Cain and Abel, and to Noah, being acquainted with the original Chaldæan legends. The twelve centuries perhaps which had passed since the Deluge made its traditions not very ancient history to one who lived in the full bloom of Accadian poetry. As Noah had built an altar and kings had erected temples to El and Sar-ili, it was quite in order for Abraham to build an altar in obedience to the speaking voice. It is what other chiefs on the Jordan or the Euphrates would have done; what Nimrod and Sargon I. actually did. In fact, the building of an altar to Jahveh became habitual with Abraham in every new place where he made his home; it was habitual with Jacob and later descendants. At every important step of their career they prepared for sacrifice to the covenant God of their fathers, the God of blessing and enlargement, who was at once a Power, a Promise, and a Person, never a "confused nebula" to them.

Indeed, when Israel had no appointed liturgy, their theology was clearly expressed. Before Moses and any Hebrew Scriptures the sacred history of the world was known to them. Whatever may come of Pentateuchal analysis and redactions of its text, the calling of the chosen man and God's covenant with him cannot be exscinded. To Adam was one revelation of Deity, to Seth perhaps another, to Noah a third, while to Abraham was the covenant which prepared for the unfolding of God's plan in the Redemption of the world; it was a Revelation not only to Hebrews but to all mankind. So at every removal of his tent a new altar, now at Bethel, now at Hebron, now at Beersheba, was built, and sacrifice offered thereon, in acknowledgment of duty and a reminder of covenant. The sojourn was never too short for a prayer, nor the place unfit for a sacrifice. In Palestine, the altar and its sacrifice, at the oak of Moreh and the Well of the Oath, certified to the God of that land in distinction from all others, and that He had given it to Abraham. It was in a sense the Divine manifesto to the people of that country that Jahveh possessed it, and that He had bestowed its title-deed upon Abraham and those who worshipped the LORD. This was the idea disclosed at every altar and sacrifice to Jahveh in Canaan. In after times they suggest a similar thought. The many sacred places and altars of Israel are for a purpose, not a fantasy. They dot the whole compass of Hebrew history and cannot be obliterated. There God meets man in covenant.

Luz-Bethel was the place of sacred vision to Jacob, where he saw the celestial staircase or ladder reaching from earth to heaven, with the angels of God ascending and descending on it; angels of whom he had heard his grandfather speak, when narrating the building of an altar there. Here he now enters into covenant and vows a vow with God, that if He will prosper him in his way and restore him to his father's house in peace, then the LORD shall be his God; the stone which he sets up shall be for a sacred pillar, and he will consecrate a tenth of all his gains to Divine service. It was a covenant with God for his preservation and restoration. He was a flying man endeavoring to secure the after-possession of what he had left, that Israel might become a blessing to the nations. Jacob then covenanted for more than he understood. That pillar was a precious memorial, and that place became a famous sanctuary in Palestine. The God of Bethel was Supreme for Jew and Gentile. There Abraham had probably sacrificed a lamb when he called upon Jahveh; but Jacob had only oil which he carried with him for food, and of that he pours upon the pillar as an offering to God. The narrative implies that it was favorably accepted (Gen. 28 : 10–22 ; 35 : 6–15). Here in after years the wanderer returned; he had become a man of substance; renewed his vow to God; received enlargement of God's promise, the change of his name to Israel, and *heirship* of the land given to Abraham and Isaac was *transferred to himself and to his seed*. Esau, Ishmael, and other kinsmen had no share or title in it.

Bethel was held in great veneration by the Hebrews as their oldest sanctuary, given to them by the God of the whole earth ; the place of renewed covenant with Jahveh and of His manifestations to their fathers. It can no more be exscinded from their history than its altar or pillar memorial can be etherialized by modern fancies. Renan suggests that an old Canaanite sanctuary was there, which was a graduated pyramid like an Assyrian temple (p. 210). There, too, Jeroboam set up his calf-worship, which long continued in opposition to Jerusalem, till the Assyrians carried Israel into captivity. But that could not change its original character, nor prove that its Jahveh-worship did not date from the remotest antiquity. There Jacob had his visions of God, and set up his pillar-altar in remembrance of them. There and at Shechem Abraham entered into covenant with Jahveh for his posterity and for the nations that would accept it ; a covenant which Ruth, the Moabitess, accepted when she adopted the God of Israel as her God (Ruth 1 : 16). Were it possible for criticism to redact the entire Pentateuch to " the covenant there made with Abraham and renewed there with Jacob, and again with Moses at Sinai," it would endure as long as the stones of Luz ; for there Jahveh demonstrated His faithfulness. He was at once the God of all Palestine and of mankind, thus seeking to save them.

Yet in Canaan and out of it, man himself must be faithful to his part of the covenant or be rejected by his Creator. The most ancient sanctuary cannot save him; desecrated Bethel became Beth-aven, the house of nothingness, or idols, as the prophet Hosea calls it; while Amos warns the people "not to seek Bethel, nor enter Gilgal, nor pass on to Beersheba; for the one shall be captured, and the other come to nought" (Amos 5 : 5; Hosea 4 : 15; 9 : 15; 10 : 5, 8). It is not even mentioned in the New Testament, and is now a mean village with few inhabitants. Ishmaelite Arabians were more loyal to the God of their illustrious progenitor, for they long continued to offer the firstlings of their flock and of camels to Him who had made them a nation in the land of their choice.

The Shechem of Abraham lay about six miles southeast of the Samaria of Omri, between Mounts Ebal and Gerizim, on the way from Galilee to Jerusalem. It was the place of the patriarch's first stay in Canaan, and where he built the first altar to Jahveh in Palestine. It was the place where Jacob, on his return from Padan-aram, erected an altar on the land which he bought of the Shechemites, and which he called El-Elohe-Israel; not only the God of Abraham as heretofore, but since the vision at Peniel and his change of name to Israel, Jahveh was to be known as his God also and of his sons, God the God of Israel (Gen. 33 : 18-20). It was the place to which Joshua brought delivered Israelites, with the women and children, and the strangers that were among them, to whom was rehearsed all the law as commanded by Moses, and there "upon an altar of whole stones they offered burnt-offerings unto Jahveh, and sacrificed peace-offerings (Josh. 8 : 30-35). And he wrote there upon the stones a copy of the Law of Moses in the presence of Israel and of the *strangers* among them; those strangers were not Israelites, but were now " naturalized" and incorporated with the tribes. For the local God was also the God of nations. Observe that some at least in Israel could then read and write and engrave in stone; a copy of the Law was written or graven in stone; written at that time and published to Israel for preservation. It is a fact of history of a character not easily interpolated, and it was received by all later Hebrews.

It was in the vale of Shechem, where Jacob dug that well which was used by many generations, and which was rendered forever famous by the memorable discourse of our Lord with the Samaritan woman: " True worshippers of the Father must worship Him in spirit and in truth; not in Samaria alone, nor yet at Jerusalem; for such the Father seeketh to be His worshippers" (John 4 : 21–24). As the springtide streams fertilized the vale of Shechem, so the strangers among Israel in the days of Joshua and believing Samaritans in the days of our Lord were alike blessed by the Law of the Covenant and the grace of the Gospel. There, too, all Israel were assembled for sacrifice, and to hear the farewell address of Joshua, who, like Washington, gave them his last advice. He recounted their early history, their deliverance from Egypt, from the perils of the wilderness, and their peaceful settlement in Canaan—but not by their own sword, nor their own bow. Then he told them how they might continue to enjoy their present blessings—viz., by serving Jehovah in sincerity and truth; by loyalty to the Divine covenant. This they renewed and ratified by public acclamation, and by setting up a memorial of it in Shechem. Joshua wrote the words thereof in the book of the Law of God, and set up a great stone there under an oak that was by the sanctuary (Josh. 24 : 1–27). Dean Stanley says : "This oak remained for many centuries the object of national reverence, and the sanctity of the place has continued to this day." We cannot evade the force of such ancient memorials, testifying at once of God and His covenant with Abraham and Israel, and of the public acceptance of it by the people in solemn assembly.

Moreover, the covenant privilege was available to all who would accept and keep it, as witness the strangers then in Israel. It is also illustrated in the case of Justin Martyr, who was born at Shechem, now Nablus, of Greek parents, early in our second century. Israel had failed in duty to God ; the temple and holy places were defiled and possessed by strangers ; among whom were Justin's parents. He was born and educated a pagan ; was in the pursuit of truth converted to Christianity ; but he retained his philosopher's cloak, diligently studied the holy Scriptures, wrote able defences of Christianity, and sealed his testimony to its truth by suffering martyrdom. It was Japheth superseding Jacob in spiritual privileges.

Probably the first Bible parable was spoken at old Shechem—the trees would appoint a king over them ; but they sought in vain among the olives, and the figs, and the vines, for neither would leave its fatness, its sweetness, nor its cheering juice. Then they besought the bramble to reign over them. And the bramble demanded of the trees instant submission and obedience under pain of destruction. Thus Jotham foretold the ruin of those who sought Abimelech to be their king; he at first reigned well, then caused the death of many, till a woman broke his skull (his brainpan, so Coverdale) with a piece of her millstone with which she ground her morning meal (Judges 9 : 7-53).

If Abimelech could reprove both Abraham and Isaac for duplicity through fear of losing their wives, and if Jacob overreached his brother Esau, yet their standard of morality in general was high for those times, of which the unfortunate incident in the matter of Dinah at Shechem is a striking illustration. The conduct of Jacob at that juncture disclosed his prudence and his fair dealing, while the pride and passion of Simeon and Levi incited them to avenge the wrong done to their only sister, a very queen to them. If it suggests little enthusiasm for Shechemites, it shows a high regard for virtue and chastity. The brothers felt that nothing could excuse the treatment by Shechem of a noble lady who was visiting the daughters of the place, and however clear or cloudy his conduct might appear to others, to them it was an awful breach of good neighborhood, which not even a stipulated truce and conformity to their religious ritual should condone. Gen. 34 : 20-25 suggest a treaty.

Their grandfather had earnestly pleaded for sinners, and Moses enacted how certain offences might be atoned, but these brothers decided the case before them, in which their deepest feelings were enlisted. They visited upon the offender the penalty of death, and executed it under aggravated circumstances. It was probable that such offences against chastity would not often occur; with such brothers as fathers and husbands there was ample security for women. But among Hebrews generally the regard for human life was more sacred than among most nations. They are not known to have practised infanticide, when child victims in sacrifice were frequent among their neighbors. The exposal of infants was common in Sparta, and was approved even by Plato in his ideal Republic; it was practised more or less extensively from Rome to China. The Greek Helen and the captive Briseis of Troy, taken from Achilles by Agamemnon, illustrate for Aryans the practice of Philistines with Samson. His wedding guests even sought to win the prize for solving his riddle by *threatening to burn down the house* of his bride and father-in-law, if she did not persuade her husband to tell the riddle! In honor and fairness they had lost by being unable of themselves to explain it; yet so low was their ethical standard that they sought to find the secret by "ploughing with his heifer," and to threaten personal vengeance upon the bride if she did not discover to them the desired answer. Moreover, while Samson was absent in slaying the thirty Philistines for the garments he wanted to pay his forfeit, his bride was given to the chief groomsman! Here is free love and free marriage which led to a double tragedy; the perfidious bride and her father were burned alive by her people for the revenges of Samson, and he avenged himself by a huge slaughter of them. Compare Achilles witnessing the defeat of the Greeks, as sung by Homer, because of the seizure of his Briseis ("Iliad," Book I.),

"Samson," as truly as Achilles, "quitted himself like Samson,
And heroically finished a life heroic."

Now if conscience teaching righteousness is hereditary, or the development of nature, how came the Hebrews, in " an outlandish corner of the world," to excel even the so-called classic nations? Aryan Plato would deprive young children of parental care, and his ideas of women and marriage fall far below the standard of Jacob's sons twelve hundred years before his era. They would hazard the prospect of trade, comity, life itself, in a land wherein they were but sojourners, rather than condone the wrong done to Sister Dinah. Comparing the morality of these brothers in that far-off age with the morality of enlightened Romans under the Empire, we may call that of the brothers very much superior. True, they gave vent to an outburst of righteous indignation and cruel punishment of Hamor, but it was evoked by a dishonor to their sister, which was oppugnant to their every sense of brotherhood and of manhood. The *motives* which prompted that punishment of an unpardonable wrong cannot be condemned. But in the treatment of slaves by Roman masters, what do we see? This—viz.: If a slave poured a little too much water in the wine at dinner, his arm would be broken as a punishment. If he let fall a goblet, he would be thrown into the fish-pond as food for its rapacious lampreys. Indeed, did not senators and emperors glut themselves in the blood of the slain, so that it ran in the streets almost up to the horses' bridles! Who proscribed and killed the famous Cicero? Then, what shall we say of those Roman ladies who much enjoyed the sight of gladiators slaughtering one another; who could not look at the goddess of chastity without a blush for their own impurities! No, the passage of those eighteen centuries developed little improvement in the morals of mankind, and the human conscience was no safer guide to the Emperor Augustus than to Simeon and Levi. Illustrations and proofs of this statement may be found in abundance in Juvenal, in Seneca, in Suetonius, in Tacitus, etc. For misplacement of a brooch on a lady's dress, or ill-arrangement of her hair, the enraged matron would order the offending slave to be lashed, or perhaps crucified! This certainly equalled the treatment of the young Joseph by his half-brothers. His dreams had offended them, and the favoritism of their father aggravated the offence. Hence they plotted against him and sold him into Egypt. "They saw the anguish of his soul when he besought them, yet they would not hear." But when they stood before him as the viceroy of Pharaoh, their conscience smote them for the wrong they had done him, and therefore that evil was come upon them (Gen. 42 : 21-24). We have no record that the cruelties practised by later Romans caused them any compunctions of conscience. So whose ideas of God were the more nebulous, and whose rule of conduct was the more confused? What evidence have we that the Beni-Israel had but mythical notions of Providence? Nay, down to their enslavement in Egypt, God to them was the Powerful One, the Ruler and Overruler, the Avenger and Benefactor of men. He was to be obeyed, trusted, and loved. He was their Teacher and Guide, now of Abraham and Isaac, now of Jacob and Joseph, through the vicissitudes of life and on the bed of death.

The details of the purchase of that burial-field from the sons of Heth, its boundaries, and the weighing of a precise sum of money for it, possibly also the making of a deed of transfer, seem to suggest that Abraham, with others concerned, understood reading and writing. He may easily have learned this at Ur, which was a literary as well as religious centre, or in Egypt, where even boys were then taught to read and write, which was in fact the way for them to rise to honor and position. The probability is that the chosen man had been thus instructed; that he could record the Divine communications made him, and the important transactions touching a large household, which had three hundred to four hundred trained servants fit to bear arms. His great-grandson Judah, under less favorable conditions, wore a signet ring with certain letters graven upon it. And the necessities of a growing tribe called for various skill and handicraft. They had teachers among them as well as shepherds. Early calls to the shop and the factory did not prevent the young Hebrew from gaining a fair education for those days. The long hours of a long summer favored study and converse. Something there surely was about their methods which enabled them to "occupy the foremost place in the history of humanity." They were fathers in religion, in domestic culture, in lofty manhood.

In the departing benediction of Israel we see the clearest conception of Deity—"God, before whom my fathers Abraham and Isaac did walk, the God who fed me all my life long unto this day, the Angel who redeemed me from all evil, bless the lads!" And to Joseph he said, "The God of thy father shall help thee, and the Almighty shall bless thee with blessings of heaven above, blessings of the deep that lieth under, blessings of *food* and of *birth* . . . these shall be abundant upon Joseph who was separated from his brethren (Gen. 48 : 15, 16 ; 49 : 25, 26). Never have the power, the providence, the faithfulness of God been more emphatically expressed as the belief of a dying man. Compare it with the words of Socrates before drinking the fatal cup. He had taught truly, indeed, that the soul of man partakes of the Divine ; that he believed there are gods, in a far higher sense than his accusers believed, and to God he committed his cause. He would follow the intimations of the Divine will ; for it certainly appeared that his soul was immortal, that arrayed in her proper jewels, temperance, justice, courage, nobility, and truth, she would dwell forever in the glorious mansions reserved for the elect. "Crito"—and these were the philosopher's last words—" I owe a cock to Asclepius ; will you remember to pay the debt?" We may call Socrates a prophet and martyr of truth, who did much to correct false notions about the gods of Olympus, and to lead his countrymen to right ideas of the Divine character, yet he fell into the popular superstition by asking for a cock to be sacrificed to the god of health. It marks the difference between the theology of Jacob and

Japheth. Socrates and Plato would save men by knowledge and virtue, truth and nobility, yet allowed them a community of women, so that the father did not know his own child, and children should be brought up in common as wards of the State. Where, then, is the conscious nobility of man? Many, indeed, practised better than they taught, for they also taught that virtue comes by a gift of Heaven to those who possess it. See this in Plato's "Meno."

Such being the moral theology of those times, is it anything better than poetical rhapsody to sing the praises of Greeks as being superior to Hebrews, in all that makes for the nobility of manhood? Nay, is not the reverse of this the fact? Do we not find the loftiest nobility of character, the highest truth and knowledge, the bravest courage, the most reasonable temperance, the most righteous justice, and the sweetest illustrations of domestic life among the Hebrews in all the two thousand years B.C. of any nation under heaven? True, they were not all of such exalted natures, and they attained to only a low measure of artistic and scientific culture. But compare the three Hebrew patriarchs, Moses and the prophets with those who originated or moulded other nations; with Menes and Mahomet, Zoroaster and Lycurgus, Romulus and Numa, Buddha and Confucius; or take the whole collection in "Plutarch's Lives," and say wherein any Hebrew fell short in duty, patriotism, and noblest manhood as compared with persons in a similar position in those nationalities? In legislation and leadership, in reformatory measures, in martial and moral heroism Jacob has ever been the peer of Japheth. Abraham,

Moses, and Samuel were men of robust character, physically and mentally capable, active, and intelligent, with no mythical uncertainty or philosophical absurdity about them, and altogether befitted the dignity of their position. No names of founders read in the brick inscriptions have more reliable evidence of their personality and work. What, indeed, do we really know of Nimrod? Of Chedorlaomer, "the Ravager of the West," we are assured that Abraham cut short his career, so that he drops out of the page of history. Even those who were semi-deified at an early day less impressed their age than the victor of Dan and Hobah (Gen. 14). Nor does primitive history give us a more unique character and personality than his. Witness his intercession for Sodom and Gomorrah. Other men would have furthered their destruction, in order the sooner to possess their lands; but Abraham, who had been promised those lands, prayed for the preservation of the men who occupied them. Instead of portraying their iniquity in dark colors, he set an eternal example of humanity and beneficence. Strong in his faith that God would fulfil His promise to him, he yet reminds Jahveh that the Judge of all the earth will do right, which was an indirect way of pleading for mercy. The friend of God was also the friend of man. Where others were concerned he ever showed generosity, conscience, uprightness, the true nobility of manhood. Witness his dealing with Lot when he chose the rich valley of the Jordan, and then rescued him from the hands of Chedorlaomer, though not having a quarter as many men as the enemy. The brilliant generalship which accomplished the defeat of the allied invaders was followed by refusal to take even a tent thread or a sandal-strap for his pains and risk. Consider his hospitality to stranger-guests; his purchase of the field and cave of Machpelah as a family burying-ground, paying for it a liberal price, though the whole country had been given him by Heaven's deed of transfer; thus setting an example to our William Penn in his dealings with the Indians. Witness his grief at Sarah's treatment of Hagar and Ishmael, and how he atoned for the conduct of the proud mother of Isaac. Read his covenant of fealty and friendship with Abimelech at Beersheba, that ancient "well of the oath," and now called the "well of the lion." Witness his provision for the members of his family before sending them away from the inheritance of Isaac; thus executing and administering during his own lifetime a will which might otherwise have caused much discord after his death. These are illustrations of an upright and roundly developed character, the parental part so natural and touching that both Ishmael and Isaac united in doing honor at his burial in the purchased field of Ephron the Hittite (Gen. 25 : 9). For it was the *character* of the deceased more than the custom of the times which then brought together those half-brothers. And modern Arabs, descendants of the elder son, still cherish and revere the memory of Abraham, while his tomb at Hebron is carefully guarded by the Turk. Not for many centuries, till in 1863 the Prince of Wales visited the Holy Land, was a Christian permitted to enter that sacred enclosure. And now fifteen thousand Mahomedans dwell near it.

This chapter may properly conclude with a remark touching the purpose to be seen in testing the faith and character of the Patriarch in the call to sacrifice Isaac. Every father will admit that it was a terrible trial of faith and character. Hopes long deferred had been just now realized, and these were to be blasted! the father being then one hundred and fifteen to one hundred and twenty years old. He had experienced many providences in the course of his long life, but none like this, none which prepared for it. I venture to say that Abraham of his own volition would not have proposed that ordeal. It was not in his heart to sacrifice his son of promise. Everywhere before this possible tragedy we have found him a life-saving man, a grand intercessor, even a little double in his protecting efforts. It was not in the nature of things that his character should have become suddenly inverted and changed. No matter what sacrificial customs may have prevailed in old Ur of the Chaldees, which he had long left, or in Canaan where he dwelt the internal evidence of the narrative does not admit the thought that Abraham of his own volition proposed to sacrifice his son Isaac. Whatever may have been done in Egypt, we have no historic examples of such sacrifices in Palestine in the nineteenth century B.C. 2 Kings 3 : 27 is authority that Mesha, King of Moab, sacrificed his son and the heir to his throne; but that was a thousand years after the trial of Abraham, when human victims were offered by Carthaginians and legendary Greeks. So this trial of Abraham was a method of indicating *Heaven's prohibition* of offering human victims in sacrifice, and the manifesto was spread abroad. Very significant is it that the Angel of Jehovah called a second time out of heaven, "Abraham, Abraham!" and repeated the injunction to withhold his son Isaac from sacrifice. His seed should possess the gate of his enemies, and be a blessing to all nations (Gen. 22 : 11, 12, 15-18). The provided ram, caught in a thicket by his horns, emphasizes that human beings were not, while certain animals were, acceptable sacrifices to the LORD.

IV.

ISRAEL IN EGYPT; AT SINAI; THE LAW.

Recent discoveries show pretty clearly that the Israelites were in Egypt for several hundred years. Abraham himself was there for a brief period. Joseph went there as a slave, and during a famine which prevailed was gladdened to find his lost brethren and to hear tidings of his father, whom he had not seen for many years. This led to the removal thither of all his kindred, and they may have been among those who sustained Apepi in his efforts to establish monotheism. The defeat of that monarch by the King of Thebes accounts for the Bible phrase "till another king arose who knew not Joseph." He probably was Ra-Sekenen, or his successor, who drove out the Hyksos dynasty and reseated that of Thebes, according to Sayce and Mariette in 1703 B.C.

Whoever those Hyksos were, Hittites, Phœnicians, or Arabians, they appear to have been friendly to Hebrews flying from a widespread famine; supplied their wants, and gave them suitable lands for pasturing their flocks. Herdsmen ranked low in Egyptian caste and estimation. If those Hebrew shepherds were also the friends of the hated Hyksos, they would be regarded with deeper detestation. Add the fact of their being monotheists who would not adopt the

Theban polytheism, and we may see how unfavorable became the position of Israelites in Egypt under the eighteenth dynasty.

There appears no sufficient reason for supposing the Hebrew shepherds migrated to the Delta in different bands and at different intervals; while the governmental state of affairs certainly accords with their going down to Egypt during the Hyksos supremacy, and then being compelled by Theban lords to do servile labor on large private estates and on the public works. The circumstances all fit in with the Bible account of the descent to and humiliation in Egypt. At first the Beni-Israel were quite contented in that land of good pasture for their flocks, "with the bread and onions they ate," and with the position accorded to them. But when their religion came to be understood as oppugnant to that of their masters, and many sharp angles of tribal differences presented as many disagreeable resemblances to the hated Hyksos who were but recently expelled, then Israel felt the weight of the yoke of the oppressor. They were "required to do a large amount of work for a small amount of pay;" to make brick and gather the straw needed for baking them; building storehouses and treasure-cities at little cost to the Egyptians. That was work of no small value to their masters, however much some try to minimize it. Indeed, the ruins of those cities are among the most precious of modern discoveries in the Nileland, and though not yet yielding names of the workmen, they have yielded data of great historical value, enabling us to determine when they were built and the names of reigning Pharaohs. Pictures of relays of laborers may yet be found which will show the faces of the Hebrew slave and of the Egyptian taskmaster lash in hand. Bricks made with straw and without straw have been discovered at Pithom of an early age.

Clearly, escape from that house of bondage and of cruelty was no easy matter for the Israelites. They had lived on good terms with the Hittites of Hebron and with the Hittites near Memphis and Zoan, obtaining favorable position and lands among people of kindred ideas with themselves. Zoan was built seven years after Hebron (Num. 13 : 22), and may have been a chief city of the Hyksos when dominant in Egypt. The presumption is they never "became Egyptianized," or why should they be expelled by the natives? The account says that Apepi, with his Hyksos, was finally worsted in the revolution effected by Ra-Sekenen of Thebes, and the domination of Memphian monotheism thus ceased, after a hard struggle, which Apepi provoked ("Records of the Past," vol. viii., p 3; "God Enthroned in Redemption," pp. 58–60). How long these foreigners dwelt in Egypt is not certain, but they resided there for a considerable period, and after their ejection the condition of the Israelites became oppressive.

Soon thoughts arose among them how to effect their escape from what was now a state of vassalage. The country about Goshen allotted to them supplied the most they knew of Egypt, and the new rulers did not mean they should know much more of it. Brugsch says the men of Upper and Lower Egypt spoke a different dialect. The Zoan connection with Hebron was a ground of hostility. Yet Renan says that some of the Hyksos remained to aid Israel in effecting their escape; who at once increased their numbers and fought their battles. With marked inconsistency, he also says that "the Hebrews had become *useless* to Egypt!" This seems to have been stated in order to contradict the Bible account that they were delivered from that "land of bondage with a mighty hand and an outstretched arm." Surely if they were "useless to Egypt," they would not need Hyksos aid to escape from a people who did not want them? And if they were "allowed to make frequent pilgrimages to Sinai," there was all the less need of such assistance or of Divine interposition. Yet Renan says the "government had no desire to keep by force a band of foreigners whose presence, to say the least, had become useless; who were a small unarmed set, whose escape was hardly missed; that owing to dynastic weakness, fugitives who got beyond the Bitter Lakes were certain of their freedom!" ("History of the People of Israel," pp. 132–40.) This way of writing "how things might have been," if applied to the history of our Southern States, would represent them as disgusted with their slaves and quite willing to be rid of the nuisance. Yet it is precisely how Renan represents that the Beni-Israel were regarded in Egypt. They were useless, and they were allowed to make frequent pilgrimages to Sinai. Routed Hyksos or Hittites were permitted to remain with them to increase their numbers and to fight their battles! Such history will not do for intelligent Americans who remember the late war for our Union.

And one motive for this misrepresentation seems to be to get rid of Moses, or to reduce his work to the least possible value. A people not wanted, and who were privileged " to make frequent visits to Sinai, the ancient abode of their god," would certainly not need a great Deliverer and Legislator to conduct them *via* the Bitter Lakes to freedom and nationality! Nor would they need the aid of God's outstretched arm. But when our rhapsodist gets that " useless" people among the mountains of Sinai, beset by hostile Amalekites, by seducing Midianites, by alarmed Moabites, he rehabilitates " Moses, who must be considered as almost an Egyptian, whose real part was much more, it would appear, that of a chief after the fashion of Abdel-Kader than that of a prophet like Mahomet" (p. 185). However that may be, Moses was no less a chief than a legislator and organizer, whose life-work is woven into the life and history of Israel, whose entire literature identifies him as the man who, by Jahveh's direction, " brought them out of the land of Egypt, out of the house of bondage." It is a characterization which must have been original at the time, and it would not be applied from the era of Solomon to Josiah.

Some reduce the residence of Israel in that house of bondage to about a century; Schrader and others make it at least two centuries; and it may be much longer. The one-century idea is absurdly too short, especially when it is affirmed that the two Hittite capitals, Hebron and Zoan, had large influence upon Israel during their sojourn in the Nileland. It was a century of revolution and migration. Jacob himself left the region of Hebron and dwelt in Goshen among the Hittites there, if there were any remaining. But in the course of a century the Hittites and Hyksos were expelled; a new dynasty reigned over the Delta and all Egypt; a new king arose who knew not Joseph, and had no sympathy with his people or their fortunes. How, during such a revolutionary and transitional period, there could have been any great influence of Hittites upon Israel is not clear; if there were, and it had been known to the Theban Dynasty, the successors of Ra-Sekenen would have cut it short as soon as possible. Still those Hyksos may have rendered the Hebrews more steadfast to the old monotheism during their sojourn, and in other ways have strengthened them in preserving their religious differences. But we can see that a century does not cover the period between Jacob's descent and the Exodus. Professor Maspero says: "Hebron no doubt was acquainted with the Hittite writing of Zoan, adopted it, and possessed writings from a remote date. Hence perhaps Genesis 14. The Ketas were familiar with handwriting about 1300 B.C." ("History," pp. 224, 225). If, then, those Ketas or Hyksos had great influence upon the Hebrews of Hebron and Southern Palestine, and also in Zoan, why should not that influence include writing? It was not regarded as a sacred art, and so kept as an exclusive possession by Hebronites. Rather it is another reason for supposing that the Hebrews of the Exodus understood writing, at least the well-to-do among them; and their sub-officers were Hebrews, Shoterim, writers who kept their own records and reports (Ex. 5 : 14, 15, 19).

Since some formed the opinion that Israel's sojourn in Egypt was about two centuries, facts have come to light which indicate a much longer abode there. Rameses II., of the nineteenth dynasty, was the Pharaoh of the Oppression, the builder of the treasure-cities Pithom and Rameses; and under his successor Menephtah occurred the deliverance by Moses, about 1350 B.C. Add to this date the four hundred years from Jacob's descent to Egypt, and it puts us in the era of Apepi and Ra-Sekenen, making all consistent with the Bible account, with the state of art, culture, and commerce, and bringing the date of the Exodus to the close of the Augustan era of the Egyptian Empire. Thus the four hundred years of bondage (Gen. 15 : 13 ; Ex. 12 : 40 ; Acts 7 : 6) find full confirmation, and Renan's "about a century" is clearly too short.

It also places the wonders of Egypt and of the wilderness by Moses and the exploits of Joshua in Canaan in the full splendor of a civilized age, when Shalmaneser I. was beginning to make Assyria famous, when Phœnicians and Hittites, Babylonians and Egyptians were writing histories which have just now come to light, and when, says a living writer, "it would have been historical madness to associate such extraordinary occurrences with such times, unless there had existed a full knowledge that they were real, and not fabulous events. From the time of Rameses the Great down to the Christian era, the mythological period of the East was closed ; literature and art and historical records were as authentic as in the era of Augustus." This clears away "the mists of a remote antiquity," and brings Moses, Joshua, and the Judges nearer to the brilliant age of David and Solomon. It sets Abraham where he seems historically to belong, dying in B.C. about 1833; naturally Jacob may have gone to Egypt a century later; after an enslavement of four hundred years his children were delivered in about 1350 B.C. Renouf makes the Exodus to have occurred in 1310 B.C.—Mr. R. S. Poole thinks about 1300 B.C. It was an era of civilization, when some Israelites had learned to read and write; had skill to make all the furniture of the tabernacle, and to dye the brilliant colors of its curtains and hangings "violet blue and red purple;" when cities like Kirjath-*sepher* were celebrated for its *books;* and when imposture in national literature and history could be as readily detected as in the age of the Antonines. The researches of modern scholars and explorers shed the light of day upon the night of Egypt. It is remarkable that when the Old Testament was vigorously attacked by historical and scientific rhapsodists, those long buried records should be brought to light which illustrate the very questions they had darkened by over-much criticism. Other "finds" are expected in Palestine, in old Tyre, Byblos, Gibul, Kerjath-sepher, from their literary deposits. But already we have enough discovered to mark the era of the Hyksos, the oppression of Rameses, and the Exodus under his son Menephtah.

It allows of sufficient time for the increase of Jacob's family, so that they could cope in manly force and numbers with hostile Amalekites and other opponents; showing what a loss they must have been to their former masters, and why they would force them to return. Nor were the Beni-Israel the sort of men who in a century would sink to the condition of slaves. In the wilderness they illustrated the spirit of their ancestors in courage and dash against their foes. Even before they reached the holy mount, Joshua with his chosen men routed Amalek and his people (Ex. 17 : 8-13). It recalls how Abraham suddenly extinguished Chedorlaomer and his allies, who had captured Lot and his belongings (Gen. 14). Equipped with the arms of drowned Egyptians, they proved as apt scholars in the art of war as in brick-making and calf-worship. Reliable history represents young slaves in Egypt as sitting side by side with the children of their masters, and learning all that was taught to noble youth. It was the one way to rise to wealth and distinction. See this in Brugsch's " History." We are too apt to compare the condition of Israel in Egypt with that of slaves in modern times. And the schools of "destructive criticism" find it to tally with their purpose of portraying the ignorance of Israel at the Exode, in order to insist upon the inability to write and to legislate for an enlightened and developed nation. They also ignore and try to eliminate the hand of God in the deliverance of Israel. Oehler happily says : " Even in the *heathen accounts* of the departure from Egypt, by Manetho and Diodorus, it comes out undeniably that there was a great religious struggle. The plagues rise step by step until the killing of the first-born." The *obstinate* heart of Pharaoh was to be humbled and his pride subdued by those plagues (Exodus, chs. 7-11). Two of them directly attack the local deities—viz., the sun as the symbol of Osiris, who was then worshipped as a god ; and the river Nile, for causing bountiful harvests, was regarded as a beneficent deity. Both were to feel the superior power of Jahveh, who would be acknowledged in Egypt. The waters of the Nile were changed into a blood-red color, and its fish died therein ; an unparalleled darkness fell on the land for three days, which terribly awed the Egyptians. This was followed by the death of all the first-born, as was threatened by Moses, from the firstborn of Pharaoh to the first-born of the maid servant and of all Egyptian animals, including those regarded as sacred. To mark the visitation as more emphatically that of Jahveh, the Israelites were exempt from these afflictions ; for the Lord would receive honor from Pharaoh. They are specific and terror-striking evidences of Divine power such as no later writer would think of inventing, and which no contemporary writer would dare to affirm if not true. The intelligence of that age of commercial dealings with other nations witnessed the humbling of the deities of Egypt by the God of Israel. It is like the Philistine Dagon falling prostrate and broken to pieces before the Ark in a later age. And the fame thereof went abroad.

Such a record could not have been published during the reign of Solomon, for he had married an Egyptian princess ; nor under that of Rehoboam, for he was punished by Shishak, King of Egypt (1 Chron. 12) ; nor under Jeroboam, for he looked to Pharaoh for recognition in his new kingdom, and ever trembled on his usurped throne (1 Kings 11 : 17 ; 14 : 1–12). Isaiah, ch. 31, tells us of an Egyptian party in Jerusalem which would invoke the help of Pharaoh against Assyria. It assuredly would not provoke Egypt by the publication for the first time of a Book of Exodus, with its groanings of Israel for the cruelties endured in that land of bondage! Every consideration of affairs in Palestine goes to show that the record of the life of Hebrews in Egypt and their deliverance from it must have been originally published before Samuel. During the regal period it was a literary impossibility, and the substance of the Pentateuch is incorporated with the national literature.

Any resemblance between the religious rites of these two peoples must be referred to that early acquaintance. The deep impression made upon Israel by the serpent god and Hathor calves, which Renan claims to crop out whenever they could elude the pressure of the Puritan influence (p. 125), may be otherwise explained—viz., by the healing efficacy once derived from looking at the serpent of brass at the Divine command, and by the royal influence which would hold on to its power by setting up calf shrines at old Dan and Bethel, in order to keep the people from returning to allegiance with the House of David, if they went to the temple worship at Jerusalem (1 Kings 12 : 26–33). The making of a golden calf during the protracted absence of Moses in the holy mount was a symbolism never repeated by loyal Israelites; a symbol of their true God it was originally intended to be. Aaron built an altar before it, and made proclamation that on the morrow was a *feast to the* LORD (Ex. 32 : 5). As it would inevitably lead to apostasy from the worship of Jehovah, who signified His hot displeasure at the abomination, Moses reduced the calf to powder, mixed that with water, and made the people drink it.

Israel may have become prepared in Egypt to accept the appointment and ministry of a priestly class, separate from the people, and without a murmur to acknowledge the tribe of Levi, who, unlike the priests of Egypt, at first had but small provision for their support; no tribal lands in Palestine were assigned them. But such an order is not conceded then to exist by those critics whom Renan follows. However, they claim that the "sacred bark of Egyptian temples suggested to Moses the Ark described in Exodus;" but it could not suggest the details of its making, nor its symbolic cherubim, nor the rich curtains and furniture of the tabernacle. According to Professor Maspero, the temple of the Sphinx was bare of such ornament ("Egyptian Archæology," pp. 63–105; "God Enthroned in Redemption," p. 49). We may therefore grant some genius to Moses and some skill to his myriads of Israelites, whatever our views of Inspiration among them.

There is, however, much which they did not learn in Egypt: they did not learn their theology. This had been revealed to Abraham and Jacob, and repeated to Moses. On Mount Sinai, which was, *par excellence*, the Mount of Jahveh (Ex. 19; Deut. 33 : 2; Ps. 68; 78; Hab. 3 : 3), the grand Olympus of Israel for forty years, the Deity was manifested in Unity as the Jahveh of the Law and of sacrifice. There was proclaimed the Divine manifesto against all polytheism; the long-known Sabbath was re-enacted to be consecrated to God and His worship for all generations.

Circumcision, which was the rite of initiation into His covenant, had been practised since the promise to Abraham. The Passover celebrated a recent event. Autumnal feasts were yet to be established; not for four hundred years had Israel gathered its own harvests on its own lands. Only lesser details of ritual and sacrificial accompaniments remained to be provided. Still, the Hebrew liturgy at the era of the Exodus was very simple. It was little indebted for enrichment to the ritual of Egypt, though, of course, that was known to Israel; and the practice of the patriarchs was better known. With them began a written Revelation from God—a revelation for the establishment of a covenant between man and his Creator, which should prepare for the redemption of the world. That Revelation was now added to; but instead of the forty-two Egyptian commands of obligation, Jahveh, through Moses, gave only *ten laws* for righteous living, later supplemented by certain ritual and ceremonial observances.

Moreover, Egypt had much to say about the dead and return to a second life on earth, and she had a long book of rules how to behave in Amenti. Of all this Moses says so little that some have doubted if he taught anything respecting a future life. Surely the rising again of Osiris cannot have been the origin of Moses being regarded as the prophet who was thus preparing the way for One to whom the people would readily hearken? Indeed, the contrasts between the Mosaic and Egyptian ritual are more striking than the agreements. But even if some ideas and laws were thus borrowed, they were adapted to the people for whose use they were enacted. The borrowing also makes for their antiquity; for the antiquity of the things borrowed, and of him who incorporated them into his system. Singularly inconsistent are they who urge this charge of borrowing; for they also allege a late date for the things so borrowed! Their bootstraps break while trying to lift themselves by them. Hence some objectors admit an early date for the legislation of Moses, though they try to minimize the lawgiver. But there are so many important matters connected with the man and his work, as well as his age, as to make credible all related facts touching his leadership, his legislation, his being the personal agent of Jahveh in doing for Israel all that is claimed in Exodus and some remarkable Psalms. Later additions to a ritual which at first was very simple do not militate against, but rather prove an original; for what was enough for a primitive people might easily be found inadequate for a developed and established nation in the temple of Solomon.

A study of the positive enactments of Moses enables one to understand the additions made by David and his successor. Thus we are prepared for the work of Hezekiah and Josiah, then for that of Ezra. Yet they all disclose a similar idea of the God they worshipped. Throughout the two thousand years of Hebrew history their monotheism is essentially the same, and equally obligatory from first to last. Thus Abraham, "Shall not the Judge of all the earth do right?" does not largely differ from our Lord's saying to the Samaritan woman, "The Father seeketh spiritual worshippers," nor from certain petitions in the Lord's Prayer. So the real question is how far the ritual of one period, as compared with that of another, really tended to promote the worship of God in spirit and in truth? This assuredly may be affirmed of the Ten Laws and tabernacle service of Sinai. It was adapted to the condition of Israel at that time, and it nurtured some of the noblest souls which have ever glorified humanity. Miriam, Deborah and Hannah, Moses, Manoah and Boaz, severally illustrate lofty types of character. In the child Samuel, the young David, the boy-king Josiah, the youthful Jesus, are seen what the system did for domestic life. Its faith, its truth, its purity, its docility—so beautiful, sincere, and strong—are unsurpassed to-day; but was it not equalled by the love which placed the infant Moses in that pitched basket on the Nile, and in that watchful sister's care who, with the wit born of affection, asked Pharaoh's daughter if she might call a Hebrew nurse for the weeping babe? It was thus secured a royal home and education with a mother's tenderness, and due instruction in the faith of that mother's God. This accounts for the learning and the character of Moses, who heard the groans of his people, and was being prepared to deliver them. Ill-advised as was his first attempt, the study of years and the Divine appearance in the bush sent him forth as the spokesman of Israel to Pharaoh, that he must let them go. At length, by the interposition of an Almighty hand, they went forth; were pursued, and their pursuers were destroyed; Israel was safe among the mountains of Sinai.

The wonders which effected this deliverance are objected to as being miraculous; but they are scarcely more so than the events which mark the entire course of Israel. The exploits of Joshua and the Judges are very marvellous, as are certain acts of Samuel and other prophets. The era of Ahab is confessedly historical, having contemporary records in Assyria; but it is only events affecting both countries which are related of Israel in Assyrian inscriptions. Still if the events so related are to be believed because of such confirmation, why should local doings, which do not touch outsiders, be discredited because they too are not narrated by a distant annalist? Nay, if the matters common to Israel and another country are correctly given in Israelitish annals, we may with all the more reason believe those which are local. Thus at Carmel we have the tragedy of Baal's followers and Elijah testing the superior power of Jahveh; at Horeb it was the same Divine power now rending the mountains, breaking to pieces the rocks, shaking the earth, sending forth fire, then heard in a mysterious voice speaking words of encouragement to Elijah, and bidding him to anoint Elisha as his successor, Hazael to be King of Syria, and Jehu King of Israel (1 Kings 18th and 19th). Now as we find these three regal names in contemporary history, we surely ought to accept the record of *all* the prophet did, even though unattested by those whom it did not concern. It is the rule of law. We may also accept similar accounts of wonders by Moses. At Sinai there is hardly more grandeur or majesty or voice than at Carmel and Horeb. At each mountain Jahveh speaks to man.

M. Renan's criticism here is unique, if not witty. Thus he changes the "unto" of Exodus 19 : 3 for *into*, and reads, "Moses went up *into* Elohim," so as to suggest that it was a cloud or mythical something, not a personal God. Is the reader not expected to look at the next clause of the verse, which says, "The LORD *called unto him out of the mountain*"? In the one case as in the other the Hebrew word may be rendered by the same in English. However, Renan does not suggest that we should read "called *into* Moses." Why not? The absurdity would be no greater, nor the irreverence. He interprets Exodus 3 : 18 to mean that the Egyptian Semites made frequent pilgrimages to Sinai, and there offered sacrifices ; for they believed their God resided there ("History of the People of Israel," vol. i., pp. 159-62). This is to mislead those readers who do not see that the narrative means a very different thing. *Not as to a sanctuary* had Moses fled thither, but to be out of Pharaoh's reach ; and when, after many years' abode in that region, he saw the burning bush, he was astonished, but curious to examine it. Then a Divine voice spoke to him. The whole chapter of Exodus 3 corrects Renan, especially verses 5 to 10, making known the God of his fathers, Abraham, Isaac, and Jacob ; also proving the weakness of the assumption that Israelites were wont, while held in bondage, to make pilgrimages to Sinai, and offer sacrifices to a local god ! Jahveh is not thus to be reduced to the character and position of a mere tribal Deity.

Nor does it help Renan to say that it was perhaps at this time (after the giving of the law at Sinai) that "they circulated the pretended oracles of the God of Bethel, who had promised the ancestors of the nation to give them this land. Such a promise from the god of a country was bestowal of it upon whom he wished" (p. 172). However, as he says that "writing was not known in Israel till about the ninth century B.C.," it would be proper to inform us how those "pretended oracles" had been preserved during those dreary centuries for opportune circulation among the people, and that well-known book of Exodus 17 : 14. But his representation of "how things might have happened" contains no evidence that the fathers of the Israel of the Exodus were ever at Bethel, or had ever had that land promised them. Uncertain persons could not be sure of anything, not even of a vision seen when sacrificing at an altar. Of similar character is his comment upon the song in Numbers 21 : 17, 18; it "became the origin of miraculous stories. The spring was discovered by means of a divining rod" (p. 175)! But in Psalm 68 he allows "we possess a religious song which is the most singular composition in Hebrew literature. We seem to hear the distant echo of the triumphal deity travelling across the desert. *The style is a sign of its antiquity.* In it Sinai figures as the place of the highest theophany. The tabernacle of God with men existed from that moment" (p. 177). Now if at Bethel, at Sinai, at Jerusalem, Jahveh did thus manifest Himself to Abraham and Jacob, to Moses and David (1 Chron. 16 ; 2 Sam. 24), why attempt to minimize the oracles which declare it?—which other critics of the Pentateuch admit to be genuine, which Renan himself admits to be of high antiquity, and which perfectly accord with the early religious sentiment and theology of the Hebrews.

It was evidenced by the Law of the Covenant at Sinai, and its supplemental details and exposition. Knowledge of that Law and Ritual often reappears during the era of the Judges; it existed in the time of Samuel, of David, and of Solomon. King Amaziah, B.C. 838-809, acted according to the written law of Moses (2 Kings 14 : 6). Jehu in Samaria, B.C. 884 to 856, took no heed to walk in the law of the Lord God of Israel (2 Kings 10 : 31), while in chapter 11 : 12 and 2 Chronicles 23 : 11 and 18 we find repeated mention of "the testimony" and "law of Moses." This was two hundred and fifty years before the finding of a copy of the law under Josiah, B.C. 640-609 (2 Chron. 34 : 14-19). "Written in the law of Moses" is the reason assigned why a new king did not avenge the death of his father (2 Chron. 25 : 4). Moreover, the Prophet Elijah (B.C. 919-889) sent an epistle in writing to Jehoram of Jerusalem, because he walked not as his father had done (2 Chron. 21 : 12-15). It shows the care of the prophet of the Northern Kingdom for the observance of the Law by the King of the South, and it shows that writing letters was then practised.

We have seen why the Egyptian wife of Solomon, the Egyptian support of Jeroboam, the Egyptian fear in Rehoboam, who lost ten of the Tribes, and the Egyptian party in Jerusalem in the days of Isaiah, would prevent the putting forth such a book as that of Exodus during their time. It was not possible, for reasons just stated, to do so in the ninth century. The eighth century was stirred through and through by reforming prophets, and in 724 B.C. Shalmaneser IV.

discovered King Hoshea to be in hostile communication against him with Egypt. This would prevent the publication of a book which reflected on that country. Shalmaneser marched against Samaria, besieged it for three years, and it fell under Sargon, his successor, B.C. 721, never to be rehabilitated as the capital of the Northern Kingdom, which had been apostate from Jahveh since Jeroboam I. This sweeps away all probability of the origin of the Pentateuch between David and the captivity of Israel. Its history recounts the violations of covenant law. In the remaining kingdom, of which Jerusalem was the head, the chances of a false publication were small indeed. The one prophet to whom such a work is attributed by Renan was the least fitted for it. Jeremiah was too genuine and lofty a character; he had suffered too much, and he knew too well the truth, to attempt to palm off as a work of Moses any writing of his own. While he "lamented Josiah for his goodness and all that he had done according to the Law of the Lord," he would not provoke Egypt by writing a false history. See 2 Chronicles 35 : 20-25, and the last three chapters of 2 Kings. Josiah was slain by Pharaoh-Necho at Megiddo, though he remonstrated against his interference that he had not come against him, but, at the command of the Lord, against Nebuchadnezzar. Babylon indeed triumphed. Even Jeremiah became a forced refugee in Egypt, where he uttered his prophetic voice against her, that she should be given into the hand of her enemies, chapters 40 to 44. That age of commotion and of Exile was clearly unfavorable to high legislative work. The forgery of a book like that of Exodus or Deuteronomy, much more a whole Pentateuch, was out of human possibility in Israel ; so was a new edition of them with large revision of the text. Evidently Daniel, made captive in 605 B.C., had carried with him the Law of Moses and other sacred books, to which he makes emphatic reference in chapters 9 : 2, 11, 13 ; 6 : 5. Indeed, from the Disruption of the Tribes under Jeroboam to the fall of Samaria and of Jerusalem, the local conditions forbade the fabrication of a work like the Pentateuch. War and self-preservation, not literature and legislation, occupied the mind of Hebrews. It was Egypt *vs.* Judah, or Assyria *vs.* Israel and Judah, or Babylon *vs.* each, or all these *vs.* Assyria ; " that the kingdoms of the earth might know that Jehovah was the only LORD GOD." The testimony is unanimous, Moses, Menephtah, Joshua, Samuel, David, Hezekiah, Nebuchadnezzar, Darius—all testifying to the greatness, majesty, and sovereign power of the God of Jacob, who is the Ruler and Wonderworker in heaven and in earth. Read Exodus 15 ; 20 : 2-17 ; Deuteronomy, chapters 5, 6, 7 ; Joshua 23 and 24 ; Judges 5 ; 2 Samuel 22 : 2-51 ; 2 Kings 19 : 15-35 ; Daniel 4th and 6th. The unanimity covers many centuries, and authenticates the testimony. Forgery in such case is impossible.

The *analysis* of the Pentateuch is so thoroughly discussed by Professors Harper and Green that I beg to refer readers who wish to study this question to their pages. My endeavor is to prove the early revelation and covenant of God to Abraham, and the fact of the Law and Covenant at Sinai with Israel, rather than minute analysis of the text. Prophets ever authenticated that text, and even scattered Hebrews in Palestine could as easily know the Law of the Covenant as the early English before printing knew the teachings of the Christian Church. The parallel may include both priests and people in those ages. Perhaps the Book of Common Prayer bears a similar relation to ancient Missals as the worship and ritual of the Temple bore to that of the Tabernacle, while back of each was the duly authenticated text of Holy Scripture.

V.

AT HOME IN PALESTINE: MIRACULOUS EVENTS.

The history of Israel began at the calling of Abraham. The descent to Egypt, departure from it, and receiving the Law at Sinai formed new chapters. The desert wanderings constitute an episode without a parallel in history. Joshua's conquests before the settlement in Canaan accord with the previous record. But we must not fail to notice what a change had come over those peoples. Their fathers had beheld with sympathizing interest the burial of Jacob by his sons, with Joseph at their head, attended by a large company of Egyptians, both in chariots and on horses (Gen. 50 : 7–13). The Canaanites who saw the mourners and their grievous lamentation were deeply impressed. There was not a sign of disrespect, or of opposition. The seventeen years' absence of the patriarch had not obliterated from memory the esteem which the inhabitants had for him, which they still retained. That burial, with such a retinue in attendance, meant that there was the home of the departed and the home of his sons, who would at some future time make it their abode. Machpelah had been bought for a permanent burying-place. There were buried Abraham and Sarah his wife; there were buried Isaac and Rebekah his wife; there Jacob buried Leah; and now his body is laid beside hers (Gen. 49 : 31). It was a sad but peaceful interment, full of hope and promise to the dead who now slept with his fathers.

But when Joshua arrived in the country four hundred years afterward, he found a very different state of feeling in the people, and had a very different reception from them. The Hittites or Hethites rose in force against him; he routed them in battle, hanged their king, and destroyed his people (Josh. 10). It discloses changes since the burial of Jacob, which the absence of his children for "about a century in Egypt" does not explain. The various tribes of Canaan had become more numerous, more warlike, and more wicked. The inhabitants of Hebron were no longer friendly to, but fierce against them. Such Hittites were not the men to stand by them in Egypt, to "increase their numbers, and fight their battles." No wonder Renan regards the Book of Joshua with aversion: it upsets his theory of friendly Hittites helping enslaved Israelites, and of their being only about a century in Egypt. As in the case of his objection, "because Samaria is not mentioned in Joshua," the truth would be jeoparded if such great changes were represented to have occurred among the Hittites of Hebron in one short century. Clearly, three or four centuries are none too long to account for the altered condition of affairs; for the increased numbers and rooted hostility of those old time friendly Hethites.

Home again in Palestine, therefore, is to be among enemies, fierce and well-armed, with walled cities for defence, very unlike the condition in which Abraham found the country, when, with three hundred and eighteen trained servants, he defeated Chedorlaomer and his allies, who for thirteen years had received their tribute, and for non-payment of it, ravaged and devastated their villages and carried the inhabitants captive. Yet within about a century they are enabled to cope with Joshua and stoutly resist the settlement of Israel in their country! Here again the facts of Genesis 14th accord with those of Joshua 10th. And while they say nothing about the length of time which must have intervened between the two accounts, it devolves upon M. Renan to explain how things could have so changed in about a century. He says, " The period is obscure," but not too obscure for $2 + 2$ to equal four; not too obscure to be famous for heroic deeds; to be illumined with the fires of burning cities; to witness the wonders of the same God who had called Abraham from Ur to settlement in Canaan. It surely was no greater marvel to hear that Voice in Chaldea than to see that Hand in Palestine. Failing to see this makes it hard for Renan to believe Joshua to be thoroughly historical. That book, true in its omissions, which the objector deplores, is equally true in those affirmations which he doubts. Had we other and contemporary histories narrating the same events, perhaps he would not as soon believe the legendary age of Greece, " the greatest miracle in history ! For the golden age of the Aryans is only a dream when compared with the patriarchal." Now it is certain that no clearer light shines upon the page of early Aryan history than upon that of Israel at this era. There was stubborn strength in Hebrew mind and muscle then, or those deeds of prowess never could have been wrought. Israel's " exclusive tendencies" do not explain her heroic achievements ; and something more than " fanaticism" was needed to enable her to cross the Jordan after defeating her eastern foes, and go in to occupy the lands and fenced cities of hostile tribes who had been alarmed and aroused at what they heard. Let those who extol the golden age of Aryans not forget the " fanaticism and exclusiveness" of Greece, that called all the rest of mankind barbarians ; that Athens in her glory held two or three hundred thousand human slaves ; that she was venial enough to be bought and sold, now by the gold of Persia and now by the hirelings of Macedonia. Surely the great men of Israel had no larger defects of character than the great men of Greece. If " the hardness and brutal abruptness of Napoleon were part and parcel of his force," the meekness and learning of Moses and the valor and strategy of Joshua were part and parcel of their force. And they succeeded in advancing a movement which swept the world along with it. The effects of those moral forces which they accelerated we, in fact, feel to-day. Whether or not Abraham was the Orham of Ur, he was a character and a power in Palestine, which raised the standard of morals, simplified ideas of religion and of God, gave a legislation and a literature to his country which have blessed the world. Such are the ideas, facts, and characters which constitute the early history of Israel. As a man must live before his biography can be written, so must a nation exist before its history is recorded. In the case of Jacob, his Bible grew up with him. His life, thoughts, and religion form his history; it is what the founder achieved, what the legislator enacted, and the great warrior accomplished. We have enough duly authenticated of the life, work, and influence of each to stamp them as real characters as was Alexander the Great, or Julius Cæsar.

Moreover, a marked peculiarity of Israel is an abiding sense of the Divine presence and power. We see it in the call of Abraham; in the birth of Isaac and a spiritual kingdom, which was confirmed at Peniel and at Bethel; in the Divine voice which spoke at Ur and at Sinai; in each it was just as *super*natural as the wonders of the Exodus and the settlement in Canaan. Joshua is no more miraculous than Moses; and Moses was hardly more wonderful than the manifestations seen by Jacob. From his flight to Padan-aram to his wrestling with the Angel of God, which Ewald transmutes into a ghost or spirit of the night; and from that grand theophany to the famine which sent him to Egypt, where he found his long-lost son, the hand of God may be seen in each event of his life. Theophanies form the striking portraiture of the brightest parts of Israel's history. It is God who fed him and led him through all his one hundred and forty-seven years of life's pilgrimage. Naturally, therefore, may we look for the supernatural in the Home again and settlement in Palestine. It is only the outcome and sequence of what preceded.

Forgetting and ignoring this, Renan " would print his pages with different shades of ink, in order to mark the various degrees of probability, plausibility, and possibility" of their contents (p. 18). Yes, of the contents of his pages, but not of the pages of an authenticated Joshua. For while " the great men of remote antiquity may be depicted without diminishing their proportions; since a giant, even when placed in the background of a picture, is still a giant," quite enough has been said to show that Renan delights in placing our Bible giants too far in the background of his picture, and to conceal their massive proportions. He suggests doubts about Moses, which the narrative disproves, because he assumes the accounts were written some centuries after his death (p. 20). So he paints Joshua, Samuel, and David in colors to express his own ideas of them. This is not history, but *his* story, a rhapsody of conceits and inductions, " in order to know how things might have happened." But the alleged obscurity of Joshua's era may be judged by the fact that it followed the Augustan era of Egypt, whose Pharaoh had just made a treaty of alliance with the Khatti or Hittites of Syria, which is given in the ancient inscriptions, and that Shalmaneser I. had begun those incursions southwest of the Euphrates, which his successors continued till Syria, Phœnicia, and Palestine were subdued and absorbed.

In Israel's forty years' wanderings, which Wellhausen says " were *not involuntary*," the tribes were preparing for their grand attacks on the Canaanites. They crossed the Jordan in a most unexpected manner. A Divine power held it back. It seemed to be miraculous, and was so thought, and so recorded for after ages. It has remained for the naturalism of our day to explain that passage without a miracle. And the action taken at the time under Joshua is, to say the least, unaccountable, if it did not emphasize this belief of God's Hand working for Israel. The first chapter of the Book which narrates his deeds, is better authority than any modern guesses. It represents Jahveh speaking to the new leader and telling him what to do. The people were to prepare three days' victuals, and pass over Jordan to go in to possess the land which the LORD gave them (verse 11). Then spies were sent to view the country about Jericho, which was first to be taken. They came pretty near failing in their errand, but were saved by the strategy of a woman, and so returned with a good report to the camp at Shittim (ch. 2 : 1-24). This is told with the sequence and naturalness which are guarantee of truth. Chapter 3 describes the passage of the River in a quiet, matter-of-fact style, without a word of astonishment; but it gives two names which are rejected by modern critics, who will not allow any Perizzites and Girgashites to be then in Palestine, and do not understand why the great Khatti people should have a fragment of their number west of the Jordan ! Well, suppose some transcriber has made a mistake in those names, or that M. Renan is mistaken in his portraiture of *Hittites in Hebron and in Zoan*, still, the passage of the Jordan by Israel is a *fact* of their history, and their attack upon the inhabitants of Jericho is so well attested that it is universally admitted. But something was done of a *religious* character at which some men cavil ; Joshua set up a memorial of twelve stones taken from the bed of Jordan, according to the number of the tribes, to be a sign to after generations that *Jahveh cut off the waters* and so let Israel pass over in safety. And the people went up from the Jordan on the tenth of the first month, and encamped in Gilgal, in the east border of Jericho (ch. 4 : 19-24). The hand of the LORD was in it. That cromlech testified of it. The covenant was renewed at Gilgal; circumcision was administered, a religious festival was solemnized with the fruits and flour of the land, and the manna ceased thereafter. It is all recorded in chapter 5, and is often spoken of by eighth-century prophets. The vision of a man with a drawn sword, who announced himself "captain of the LORD's host," deeply impressed Joshua, and he paid him reverence; but there is nothing more extraordinary in that vision than in certain appearances to Moses. Surely that cromlech would not offend the god of those Canaanites who had a sacred mound at Gilgal, for it did not intrude irreverently upon the old sanctuary. And the God whom Israel thus honored claimed to be LORD of the whole earth. But, says Renan, "It was *afterward* supposed that in these megalithic monuments had been found a souvenir of the *miraculous passage* of the Jordan" (p. 201). What less could it be? Those Canaanites have left no inscriptions to designate the purpose of their megalithic piles, while here the purpose and end are defined, viz., that the God of all the earth might be glorified (Josh. 4 : 14, 24). Because any part of those events were then recorded in the "Book of Jasher," or in the "Wars of Jahveh," is surely no reason for doubting their truth. That they were subsequently incorporated into the Book of Joshua and repeated in Judges, as Wellhausen states, is, in fact, a confirmation of their supposed accuracy. What reader of Diodorus does not regret that historian's omission of his authorities for the story of Damon and Pythias? It might have removed the seeming uncertainty whether Dionysius the Elder, or Dionysius the Younger, ordered the surety to execution, and whether that illustration of loyal friendship was a contrivance devised by anti-Pythagorians, or a natural occurrence which really astonished the tyrant and others who witnessed it. After going over all the Greek and Latin authors who relate that incident, I feel safe in saying that it requires as much logic and inference to digest and correctly reproduce it for English readers as any incident in Joshua or Judges.

Dr. Geikie, who lately visited "the Holy Land," relates how Gilgal was rediscovered by a German traveller, who heard the Arabs pronounce the words Tell Jiljal and Birket Jiljalia—the former a mound over the ancient town, and the latter its pond (vol. ii., p. 94). It was the place where the Israelites under Joshua erected a circle of twelve stones taken from the bed of Jordan to commemorate its wonderful passage. Dr. Geikie says, "Within a mile of the pond are about a dozen mounds, three or four feet high, which may be the remains of the fortified camp of the Israelites." Captain Conder supposes those stones were set up like a Druidical circle, forming a rude sanctuary like the numerous rings of huge stones still found in Moab and other countries. However that may be, the text says that twelve men who represented the different tribes took each his stone for that purpose. It is mere *inference* that those men had helpers to carry a very large stone ; and certainly twelve such stones as might be taken from the bed of Jordan would make but a small pile for a circle-sanctuary. Perhaps that altar built of whole stones mentioned in chapter 8 : 30–35, is confounded by Captain Conder with this at Gilgal. The last part of verse 4, chapter 3, " for ye have not passed this way heretofore," confirms the whole account. They are words which no late writer could have penned ; the Levitical procession was to be duly spaced and to proceed cautiously by the way, *for they had not passed that way before.* So naturally put, these words prove the record. Preparation was carefully made, yet Divine aid was expected in the passage ; for the Lord of all the earth was to pass over before them (verse 11). The fact of that wonderful crossing over Jordan is as well established as the passage of the Red Sea, and it was attested to all Israel in aftertimes by the dolmen or cromlech of stones taken from the river's bed and set up at Gilgal. It was in accordance with the custom of the times and of the country. So was the altar of whole stones erected by Joshua at Mount Ebal, on which he wrote a copy of the law of Moses in the presence of the children of Israel. Moreover, on an outer wall of the temple at Karnak, in the previous century, the treaty of peace between Egypt and Khita land was written. It is translated in " Records of the Past," vol. iv., pp. 25–32. Rameses II. married a daughter of the Khita king, and thus happily closed the long feud between those peoples. Hamathite hieroglyphics which belong to about this time show Jahveh was known by name at Hamath; so Schrader. Any doubts whether those Khatti are the same race as the Hittites of Canaan cannot change the facts which Joshua created, nor his memorials of them. The change of Hethites into Hittites may at first have been local.

Whether the Canaanites originally came from a Babylonian centre, like the Phœnicians, and the Hebrews, who migrated later, does not concern the fact that Joshua found them hostile, and routed them in different Palestine centres. As in the time of Abraham so now, there appeared to be no difficulty in understanding each other. They may also have been originally worshippers of one God, as was Melchizedec, but they debased and corrupted their worship to such a degree that it became an abhorrence to Jahveh, and their immoralities were detestable. The iniquity of the Amorite was now full. They were not slain without warning, nor proscribed without cause. God who created the world and man left him not uninstructed in his duty and how to live righteously. His worship of Baal, Chemosh, or Molech, if offered in sincerity, purity, and truth, would doubtless have been accepted by Him who was God over all. But the religious practice of those peoples had become an abomination in the sight of Heaven and a degradation in its devotees. Jahveh would no longer tolerate it. Physical and spiritual forces should co-operate in its destruction and extirpation. Prometheus bound, yet uttering defiance against Jupiter, as in classic legend, illustrates the stubborn persistency with which those Canaanites continued in their wickedness. Their rapid increase, their skill, their walled towns; Jabin, with his nine hundred chariots of iron, the giant Anakims of the mountains; these were not to be conquered by the " enthusiastic élan" of Israel, unless the God of Israel went before them. Superior in culture and civilization to the Israelites, Jahveh, God of Israel, caused them to fear Him. Retreating seas, divided rivers, falling walls, yea, the orbs of heaven seemingly halting in their courses; these were scarcely more wonderful or destructive than the thunderbolt and the hailstorm which beat down wicked Canaanites. Admitting Joshua's care in preparations and the enthusiastic élan of his troops, there were yet clear evidences to them and the men of that day that the Almighty God led them, inspired their courage, strengthened their arm, and achieved their victories.

The reasons for such belief, like Wren's monument in St. Paul's, were to be seen all around them; in the deeds they wrought, in the cities they captured, in the terror of the enemy, and in memorable indications of Omnipotence and natural phenomena co-operating with Israel's force. There were human force, natural force, and Divine force all conspiring to one end, or, rather, two ends: victory for the Hebrews and acknowledgment of their God by all the people of that land and of the nations round about.

Now the critics and redactors of holy Scripture require us to believe that Egyptian and Assyrian annalists have correctly recorded the deeds of their kings; Greek historians portray the wonders achieved by the Spartan band, by the heroes of Thermopylæ and the defenders of Athens; so of Roman, German, French, and English, not to say our American, history, we are expected to credit all that is related as history. And when based upon original and contemporary documents, those accounts may generally be accepted as true. Why, then, should we not believe the Hebrew writers in what they say touching the history, the Law, and the predictions of Israel? They are as consistent and consequent, as logical, and no more repetitious than other primitive records. And they are penetrated through and through with a purity and a piety quite unique and national.

In Joshua and Caleb, in Othniel and Barak, in Gideon, Jephthah, and Samson the religiousness and the patriotism are strongly marked. Redactions do not change it; but in the classic accounts of Damon and Pythias, Brutus and Cato, Pyrrhus and Cæsar, it would be as difficult to find the presence and operation of a religious impulse as in Timur and Napoleon. Yet in many Hebrews, even their faults often arose from mistaken views of religion. The accompaniments of the proclamation of the Law at Sinai were much more than "dramatic." Divine voices and forces intensified what was of lasting interest. The ninth century B.C. could not have produced it. Even Elijah was a product of the Law of the Covenant, not the Covenant a product of his age. Samuel and Nathan, Gad and Micaiah, found their inspiration from the Law. It was by it and by Him who gave it that prophets caused kings to tremble on their thrones, and to ask what the King of kings would have them to do? To build an altar, a temple, to offer a thousand bullocks and rams, lambs almost without number and incense in great weight, was small tribute to the Lord of the whole earth. Thus Israel's shrines and holy places were so many upliftings and endeavors after righteousness, from Shechem and Bethel to Sinai and Sion, for at each Jahveh manifested the grandeur of His person as well as the grace and goodness of His character. Carmel and Horeb spoke of God. There the Hebrews found an Olympus; a mount of sacrifice and Divine epiphanies which attested the authority of the messages and of the prophets who uttered them. If Numa claimed to be visited by a goddess who taught him, if Brahmans claimed inspiration for the Veda, if Socrates claimed to hold converse with the Deity, a thousandfold stronger reasons had the teachers of Israel for claiming inspiration and direction from the Almighty. This impelled Abraham to a new departure; it animated Jacob for a hundred years; it revolutionized the career of Moses, sent him from the desert to the throne of Pharaoh, enabled him to perform wonders in Egypt, to deliver his enslaved people, and lead them to the Mount of God. There Jahveh gave him a civil and religious code, the Law of the Covenant, which for breadth and brevity, fulness and conciseness, still remains unparalleled. Given in that age, to that people, under those conditions, it bears on its face the stamp of a Divine Proclamation to mankind. There was nothing in India, Greece, Rome, Egypt, Babylon, which equalled it, certainly nothing to surpass it. Not a clause of that Covenant Law has been repealed; nor does it contain a superfluous sentence for men in the highest state of civilization and culture. Those fifteen verses of Exodus 20 are the Laws of God to man. They have guided the decisions of judges and seers as embodying the principles of human conduct; they have inspired the songs of poets and the thoughts of philosophers; they have curbed the passions of savage men and bridled the anger of kings; for in them God spoke to man from Sinai. The cloud and the thunder have long passed away, but the *Words* then spoken will abide forever. It was impossible that they should be forgotten. Nor has human wisdom yet devised a substitute.

Moreover, the Spirit and power of Him who gave that Law and renewed that Covenant, gave victory to Israel in Canaan, victory over Jericho and over Jabin. There was that in them engaged in those contests which certified to them whence their prowess and their triumphs came. It was confessed at the time; it was ever conceded and so believed. We may well marvel that while modern writers affirm the superiority of Canaanites in arts and arms over Israel, and acknowledge the prodigies of valor which they achieved, they are content to attribute those astounding victories to Israel's "*enthusiastic élan.*" Even those who survived defeat and destruction allowed themselves to be "absorbed" by the invaders in their own country. They had no Alfred with a brave Saxon band among them; no William Tell and Swiss heroes who should annihilate the foreign foe! Art and culture those Canaanites may have had, but *no patriotism;* for God had given away their lands to a people who would better serve Him, and hence patriotism in the old inhabitants died out, and their civilization with it. Yet Wellhausen feebly explains those facts of history by saying, "The extraordinary disintegrated state of the country accounts for the ease with which the Israelites achieved their success!" ("Encyclopaedia Britannica," *ad loc.*) But the history which narrates the victories of Israel also narrates the combinations among the Canaanites: " When all the kings which were on this side Jordan, in the hills, and in the valleys, and in all the coasts of the great sea over against Lebanon, the Hittite and Amorite, the Canaanite and Perizzite, the Hivite and Jebusite, heard thereof [the taking of Jericho and Ai], *they gathered themselves together, with one accord to fight with Joshua*" (ch. 9 : 1, 2). But the Gibeonites, by stratagem, made a league with Israel in order to save their lives, although their city was a greater and better defended city than Ai. " Wherefore the king of Jerusalem sent unto the king of Hebron, and unto the king of Jarmuth, and unto the king of Lachish, and unto the king of Eglon, saying, Come and help me, that we may smite Gibeon ; for it hath made peace with Joshua and with the children of Israel. Therefore these five kings gathered all their hosts together, and encamped before Gibeon ; and made war against it" (Josh. 10 : 1-5). That certainly indicates a *strong combination* for resistance, the very reverse of an " extraordinary disintegrated state of the country." Yet Joshua marched boldly against them, and the LORD discomfited them before Israel, with a great slaughter at Gibeon, and along the way to Beth-horon, Azekah, even unto Makkedah. Also the Lord sent a great hailstorm, cast down great stones from heaven upon them, and they died (verses 7-11). More died with hailstones than with the sword of the children of Israel. The victory was further memorable for Joshua's prayer to the Lord for a lengthening of the day—*i.e.*, for continued opportunity in which to finish his conquests over those combined Canaanites, and to leave them in an utterly "disintegrated state." The account of this marvel seems to have been written at the time, and was later incorporated into our record of Joshua's deeds. Renan's explanation is elsewhere considered. We assuredly ought not to tone down the marvel of nature, much less discard the account, simply because it is marvellous and taken from the Book of Jasher (verse 13). Recent accounts tell us of unexpected and terrific hailstorms occurring in that region. And the unusual phenomena of protracted light or protracted darkness might impress surviving Canaanites with the supremacy of the God of Israel over all the gods they worshipped even more deeply than the terrible destruction wrought by Joshua. Baal, Chemosh, Molech, were only different names for the heaven-gods in that country. And this interference with their authority, making them, in fact, do service to the enemy, was a *defeat of the deities* of Canaan as disastrous, in the people's estimation, as the arms of the invaders. This view tones down no text, and it is in accord with the providence of God over men. They are not proscribed or slain by Him till the end calls for it, till clemency is lost upon obduracy. But whatever explanation we accept of this Divine interposition for man, it would seem that the quotation from "Jasher" was indorsement of that part of the book, which is also referred to in 2 Samuel 1 : 18. The whole is of a piece with the history of Israel in Canaan. The

Creator of man is also his Ruler and his Judge. Prerogative implies duty and responsibility in its exercise. There is nothing contradictory in its manifestation here. The light of the sun was silent, and the moon delayed to shine, till Israel had triumphed over the enemies of Jahveh. The consistency of the record is in marked contrast with the contradictions of Wellhausen, who repeatedly "annihilates Simeon and Levi," yet makes them settlers in Ephraim, though he had destroyed them after having avenged the dishonor of Dinah! For "the Canaanites of the surrounding country combined against them" (p. 400, article "Israel," in "Encyclopædia Britannica"). It illustrates the lowest form of criticism. So does Renan when he says, "The territory of Benjamin was confined almost exclusively to the hill of Gibeah" (p. 293). Yet we know that Benjamin had by lot twenty-six cities or towns, and the country adjacent to them (Josh. 18 : 10–28); Gibeon and Jericho, Mizpeh and Jerusalem being of that number. It was the tribe which gave the first king to Israel. Nor does Renan allow any strong inter-tribal feeling to exist among that people : " A Danite would never slay a Danite, he would always avenge him ; but a Danite would ill-treat a Zebulonite" (p. 299). Then he adds, "There was a bond of fraternity between Israelites. In others every Hebrew would see an enemy." Why, then, tell us that Israel *absorbed* those Canaanites whom she did not destroy? For long they dwelt in the land of Megiddo, Gezer, Kitron, Nahalol, Accho, Zidon, Ahlab, and other places named in Judges 1 : 27–35 ; they became tributaries, not enemies, and there were too often intermarriages among them. To the time of David the Jebusites dwelt with the Benjamites in Jerusalem *unabsorbed* (Judges 1 : 21). On the other hand, a severe punishment was inflicted upon Ephraimites by the men of Gilead ; every man of them who dropped his "h" in Shibboleth was slain ; and there fell of the Ephraimites forty and two thousand (Judges 12 : 6). It was probably the outcome of an old standing feud between them and the Manassehites, which culminated in the terrible slaughter by Jephthah of the proud Ephraimites at the fords of Jordan, because they objected to his going to war against Ammon without their co-operation. They were detected by their *Sib*boleths and put to death (Judges 12 : 1-6). Chapter 20 details the chastisement which the assembled tribes inflicted upon Benjamin for the outrage upon a Levite's concubine ; and there fell on that occasion twenty-five thousand Benjamites who drew the sword, all men of valor (verse 46). No ; the history of those tribes cannot be written in broad generalizations. That tribe which then was almost extirpated gave the first king to Israel ; with Judah it survived the other ten ; gave St. Paul to the Church ; while of Dan, who was the expected Judge of his people, we hear little except deeds of valor and apostasy from the truth ; of his conflicts with the Amorites ; of his frolicking Samson, who was a puzzle to the Philistines and delighted in punishing them ; of idolatry under Jeroboam ; in the Apocalyptic vision of St. John, Dan is omitted from among those sealed in the New Jerusalem (Rev. 7 : 4-8). Thus Israel is unlike every other people. She not only experiences the displeasure of her God on earth, but sinks into oblivion, and the promise of restoration is not universal for her children. Her God rules her in righteousness. He does not punish where punishment is not deserved.

In the days of Abraham the wicked cities of the south felt His heavy hand, while Hebron and Salem, with the chieftain-priest Melchizedek, were in friendly alliance, and so continued till the going down to Egypt. On Israel's return things had much changed, but the southern country, being most corrupt, first felt the power of the avenger. Thus fell Jericho and Ai, Debir and Lachish, Libnah and Makkedah, with the chiefs of thirty cities, notwithstanding their combinations and "enthusiastic élan" against Israel, also the kings east of Jordan (Josh. 12). Such victories in those Israelites inspired other deeds of valor as well as songs of triumph which ascribed the glory to Jahveh, who fought for them. The Pharaohs and Khatti kings, Assyrian and Babylonian monarchs, even Mesha of Moab, in like manner praised their gods for their successes. We credit their stories in the inscriptions; then why not believe Hebrew records of Israel's deeds? There is natural sequence in the narratives of Moses and Joshua, of Caleb and the Judges. Where our science enables us to account for natural phenomena without a miracle, we may do so without violence to the text; but where the text duly authenticated demands the interposition of Almighty power on behalf of the chosen people, in Heaven's name let us acknowledge it! No science of man can measure all the hand of God in history. Did not our Washington often pray to Him, and often experience what he believed to be Divine help? At the disaster of July 9th, 1755, he was the only aid who escaped wounds and death. The stupidity of the British Government then and the blunders of some British generals are a marvel when considered in the light of our day. Reverently may we not say that Providence, like a midwife, attends upon the birth of nations? The Creator rules and overrules in the destiny of mankind, and all the more where His children invoke Him. The miraculous is interwoven with the warp of Jacob's history.

Joshua, immediately after his first great victories, built an altar unto the LORD God of Israel in Mount Ebal, an altar of whole stones, as Moses wrote in the book of the law; and they offered burnt-offerings unto the LORD, and sacrificed peace-offerings. Upon the stones of that altar was written a copy of the law of Moses, in the presence of all Israel; their elders, officers, and judges stood on one side of the Ark, and on the other side the priests and Levites, who bare the Ark of the Covenant; also the strangers among them, the women and the children—all heard the words of the Law read (Josh. 8 : 30–35). They were evidently a brave, devout, and intelligent assembly that there ratified their belief in God, renewed the covenant with Him, and worshipped Him with sacrifices; also the stranger as well as the Hebrew, for the covenant excluded only those who did not accept and observe it. God was the Jahveh of Israel and of all who acknowledged Him.

Israel next assembled at Shiloh, and set up the tabernacle there; the land was subdued and divided among them (Josh. 18–21). Any reader of Joshua must be impressed with the provision made for the priests and Levites. They have no one district of country like the other tribes, forming a community by themselves, but are scattered through all the land in forty-two different towns west and six towns east of Jordan. Thus they were the educational force of Israel; priests and Levites when not on duty at the tabernacle-centre were the teachers and local judges of their towns. They were dispensers of knowledge and of judgment (Lev. 10 : 11 ; Deut. 19 : 17 ; Mal. 2 : 7). The provision made for them under Moses and Joshua, Renan says, rendered them more readily acceptable to the people ; but he ignores the old-time dedication of the first-born to Divine service, who were ransomed by the consecration of the tribe of Levi. That the Levites were favorably regarded in Israel is illustrated in Micah the Ephraimite, who said, "Now know I that Jahveh will do me good, seeing I have a Levite for my priest" (Judges 17 : 13). The episode in that history so fully harmonizes with the local state of the times, that critics generally allow it to be of high antiquity. That the Danites induced that Levite to become the priest of their new tribal centre, Laish, thus making a clean sweep of all Micah's religious establishment, with its ephod and teraphim, emphasizes the truth of the incident and the general esteem for the Levites (chs. 17 and 18). It was the origin of Danite local idolatry, and continued more or less offensively until the captivity of the land (18 : 30). Thus were copied the usages of the Zidonian worship, but not necessarily was that of Jahveh ignored. Danites still went up to Jerusalem. They furnished David with nearly thirty thousand men of war. The altar built by the east Jordanic tribes was shown to be an altar of Witness, not for burnt-offering nor for sacrifice (Josh. 22 : 10, 26). And this explanation was quite satisfactory to Phinehas the priest and the committee of representatives of the people, who inquired into the reasons for that altar. The records do not show that any ecclesiastical schism had then occurred. The apostasy under Jeroboam was much later.

When Joshua had grown old and retired from service, he called all Israel—the elders, judges, and officers—to hear his farewell address. In it he recounted what God had done for them to that day ; that after his death Jehovah would continue to watch over and care for them, failing in none of His promises, if they were faithful to the covenant between them. At Shechem they presented themselves before the LORD, with a great stone of witness set up by the oak of the sanctuary, to certify that they accepted the book of the Law of God, and chose Him as the God of all the people of Israel. So every man departed to his inheritance, as the servant of Jehovah (chs. 23 and 24). The tabernacle at Bethel, at Shechem, at Shiloh, was the representative centre of Israel and its worship. Thither the people of all the tribes flocked at the annual festivals. Such occasions served to keep God in mind and heart. They could easily talk over all their national history, for the memory of three generations would span the time from Joshua to Eli. They were instructed in the law of their God and in the wonders He had wrought on their behalf. No important national event was overlooked. No great variation was made in its recital without instant notice. Our times, with their " three days' wonder," are not the standard whereby to judge of Hebrew affairs in the twelfth and the eleventh century B.C. Rather, they may be compared in this respect to the era of Herodotus in Greece, when poets, historians, and rhapsodists recited the nation's songs, the nation's deeds, and the wrongs she had suffered from Persia, or some nearer foe. The people, without books, well knew their contents, and Homer was carried for centuries in the living memories of Greeks. The siege of Troy divine was a real inspiration to them. Its influence upon Themistocles, Herodotus, and Pericles, are examples of what the public recitation at their great festivals of national events in narrative, poem, or the acted drama did for Greeks in the fifth and sixth century B.C. Similar was the effect of the three great annual meetings of Hebrews.

When the Jews cease to be quick in discerning a chance for a bargain, or to understand debits and credits, social and political finance, or when their Disraelis and Rothschilds wholly fail them, then may we believe that Hebrews from Joshua to Samuel did not know the facts of their history, nor whether Moses had legislated for them, nor whether he gave them *ten* laws or twenty! So long as Shakespeare's Shylock is read will men know that Jews understand bonds and pounds, even as Abraham did when he weighed out his shekels to the Hethites for the field of Machpelah, and as Jacob did in making his second bargain with Laban the Syrian. No, the reason of mankind, especially of educated men, attests to the capacity of Israelites. They have memory, domestic affection, pa-

triotism, common sense, and when opportunity offers
they usually improve it. Now this was all they needed to know the conquests of Joshua, to learn the laws
of God to Moses, the story of the patriarchs, and the
songs of their poets. This formed their national history, and this again was emphasized by the appearance
of angels, by the voice of a speaking God who
wrought wonders for them in the field of Zoan, at the
passage of the Red Sea and the Jordan, by the walls
of Jericho, and at the waters of Megiddo. They all
follow each other in quick succession, from the vision
of Luz and the dreams of Joseph to the vision of Samuel about Eli, from the slaughter of the five kings by
Joshua to the slaying of Goliath by David. From
Moses onward the Ark of the tabernacle was with men,
accessible to all who should ask counsel and guidance
at it. And it was made the duty of the priests to preserve and communicate religious knowledge. At
Shiloh, at Nob, in all the forty-eight districts assigned
them, their light shone out to Israel. Properly may
the Jews brand as libellers of their race any writers
who would have men suppose that from the Exodus to
Solomon the Hebrews did not know whether Moses
legislated for them, what that legislation was, and
what parts preserved to us are true or false, and in
what particulars false.

Micah's idolatry was but an episode in the era of
the Judges, and would seem to have been limited in
extent. It did not flourish under Samuel. Hence the
recurring phrase, " There was then no king in Israel "
(Judges 17 : 6 ; 18 : 1 ; 19 : 1 ; 21 : 25). The
words : " Every man did what was right in his own

eyes," do not apply to the whole book, but to the idolatry of Micah and the seizure of the young women who assembled at the Shiloh festival. That it was not of general application is shown in chapter 20, which narrates how all Israel gathered together even from Dan to Beer-sheba to punish a heinous offence (verses 1–8). The rising of all the people as one man suggests that moral ideas still dominated them. The account also teaches that the tribes were not wholly unorganized and disintegrated. They combined for punishment of tribal wrong, and they assembled for general humiliation, fasting, and sacrifices before God at Shiloh (verse 26). Only six hundred men of Benjamin were known to have escaped destruction. So to prevent the total extinction of the tribe every survivor was permitted to do as he pleased about taking a wife from the maidens who went to Shiloh. At a later time Rome supplies a similar example. But it by no means follows that such capture of wives was the custom from Joshua to Samuel, nor from the rape of the Sabine women to the Law of the Twelve Tables. We therefore restrict such violence to the occasions which justified it in Italy and in Israel. Indeed Judges 20 explains the existence of a law which was enforced against the transgressors of Gibeah. It was in a century after the Exodus. And the punishment inflicted proves both the existence and knowledge of a legal code by Benjamin and all Israel. The tragic incident also illustrates how the tribes might be assembled (19 : 29 to 20 : 13). It is therefore bad logic and poor history to expound Judges 20 by 21 : 25, or by 17 : 6. Remarkable is the idolatry recounted in chapter 18, if it occurred among the grandchildren of Moses. It would seem that verse 30 gives the names of another tribe, and not that of the lawgiver. (See Josh. 21 : 6, 27 ; 1 Chron. 23 : 13–17.) Dan's Jonathan is not among them.

Thus, Hebrew treaties and commerce, weights and measures, law and penalty ; towns like Hebron and Kirjath-sepher famed for its books, the Mesha Inscription and the Siloam Viaduct ; songs like that of Moses, Miriam, and Deborah ; blessings like those of Jacob ; names and stations like those in Numbers ; riddles and frolics like those of Samson ; laws like those of the Covenant placed in the Ark and the Ritual by it, which were often copied and expounded ; the national census, military lists, and tribal allotments ; the obligation of vows in Nazarites and of the annual meetings at Shiloh or wherever the tabernacle was set up ; altars and pillars of witness here and there ; Joseph and his brethren in Canaan and in Egypt—all these certify to the genuineness and credibility of Old Testament history to Israel and the world.

VI.

HOW JAPHETH SCRUTINIZES JACOB'S BOOKS.

Every boy who knows his Anabasis also knows that the writer of it could not have carried in mind the several stations and parasangs made, the places visited, and the eventful details of that enterprise. The author must have taken notes on the spot or after the day's halt, in order to reproduce for his reader a true account of the ill-advised expedition of the younger Cyrus. That was four hundred years B.C. A comparison of the Anabasis with the Book of Numbers, apart from the rest of the Pentateuch, will show that it must have been written near the time of the events recorded. They are so various; so many stations or haltings, so many names of persons, so many places and dates, with the numbers of the several tribes mentioned, could not have been carried in the memory of an Israelite. Even admitting the "Episode of Balaam" was later incorporated, there is too much left, too great a variety of matters to be preserved, without a contemporary record of them. To memorize the "Iliad" would be easy in comparison for a Greek, even with its catalogue of forces; for they were all familiar names, and it formed the chief part of a youth's education. But Numbers was only a portion of what a Hebrew must learn, if he would know the early literature of his country. The reader can try this for himself, and commit to memory the first four chapters of that Book. "According to the commandment of the Lord they were numbered by the hand of Moses, every one according to his burden ; thus they were numbered of him, as the Lord commanded Moses." These four chapters required to be written at the time ; so did chapters 7, 9, 10, 11 ; while no later Hebrew would have forged or invented chapter 12. The 13th is so full of names and timemarks that no one would invent it. The national and personal pride, not to say patriotism of Hebrews, would not have originated chapter 14. The 15th, like the 5th and 6th, comprises legal enactments and duties, and tells how the law of the Sabbath was executed upon one who had broken it. Chapter 16 records the first serious ecclesiastical rebellion which, from the signal punishment which was inflicted, must have made such a deep impression upon Israel as to be long remembered. It assuredly could not have been originated after the calves of Jeroboam and his new-made priests, for it would have *convicted* Jeroboam's successors of wrongdoing in Israel and legally condemned them, which they would not permit (2 Chron. 11 : 14–16 ; 2 Kings 15 : 17–30 ; Lev. 10 : 1–7 ; Num. 16–19). The death of Miriam ; the striking of a rock which yielded an abundant supply of water to murmuring Israel ; the gentle message to Edom for safe passage through that land, and the refusal ; the death of Aaron, appointment of his successor, the mourning, and the announcement to Moses that he was not permitted to enter Canaan, are all historic matters quite in accord with its unfolding in Israel, and put the seal of authenticity upon chapter 20. The account of the plague of serpents, and of the brazen one made for the healing of those bitten (chapter 21), could not be palmed off as historical among that people, unless genuine. The record finds confirmation in the fact that the serpent of brass then made was preserved to the time of Hezekiah, who destroyed it because the people had learned to burn incense before it, which was an abomination. The lifting up of that brazen serpent by Moses for the healing of the wounded was made a type of the sin-healing power of our Lord to all who sincerely look to Him (St. John 3 : 14, 15 ; 2 Kings 18 : 4).

It hardly detracts from the historic credibility of chapters 22-24, if originally written by Balaam, who figures conspicuously in them. Dr. Kalisch, with some others, regards it as a separate document, later incorporated into our received text—about 1030 B.C. Because Balaam predicts the coming time when Assyria will carry the Kenites captive, " this threatening presupposes that *when it was uttered* the Assyrians had already acquired an imposing position in Western Asia ; and that the words had as their background the age of Tiglath-pileser II., or of Sargon II., or of Sanherib. So the inference is drawn that a redaction of the first four books of the Pentateuch was made in the second half of the eighth century B.C." Schrader well says there is no sufficient warrant for this conclusion. We know that Israel came in contact with Assyria at a much earlier period, being tributary to her in the ninth century B.C. Her king, Rimmon-nirâri (812-783), mentions the land of Omri, Sidon, Tyre, Edom, and Philistia as tributary to him. Assurnâsir-habal (885-860) possessed the boundaries of Lebanon, marched to the great sea of the west country, gathered his faithful ones, and sacrificed to the gods. He received tribute of Tyrians, Sidonians, and other nations of the west country; the latter probably included Israel. Wherefore the redaction of a pre-Deuteronomy Pentateuch may have belonged to the last quarter of the ninth century B.C. But why should any relation of Israel with Assyria in the ninth or the thirteenth century B.C. have anything to do with the prediction of Balaam? The real question is, Did Moab oppose Israel while on her way to Palestine? Did her king send for Balaam to curse the intruder? Have we the account of that opposition and the utterance of the seer? The Moabite stone of 875 B.C. is evidence of Moab's hostility to Israel then; for Mesha "dragged the females of Jahveh before Chemosh, and slew seven thousand men and boys, women and maidens!" It discloses a fiercer oppugnancy than Balak exhibited; for his *fear* of Israel was aroused, not his religion. The narrative is in accord with other events. Balak sent for a man to help him against the people he feared and the God he did not adore. Assyria was then distant, and her kings had not yet marched so far to the southwest. There was no motive for adopting the episode of Balaam and Balak, unless it accorded with Israel's historic tradition; but the account being credible and genuine, that it was

Balaam's own gave it the greater value. The objection to it largely arises from its containing a prophecy—"The Kenite shall be wasted; Assur shall carry her captive" (Num. 24 : 21–24). This came to pass in part under Sargon after 721 B.C., under his son Sennacherib, and again under Nebuchadnezzar, who devastated that country. See the "Speaker's Commentary," *ad loc.* The last quarter of the ninth century, when accepted by the redactor, still leaves at least *two centuries before the fulfilment* of the prediction; when there was no seeming probability that Assyria would sweep the whole country to the southwest of the Euphrates. Whatever effect Balaam's deliverances may have had on Balak, the son of Beor was in fact slain before Israel crossed the Jordan. It is pitiful criticism which would explain away what he said, because he was not a recognized prophet of Jahveh, or because the country in question was not then a likely agent to fulfil it. Deeds and dates may be matters of sequence, but a prophecy must belong to a period earlier than its fulfilment. So does this of Balaam's.

We have dwelt on the character of the Book of Numbers to illustrate how very difficult it would be to memorize its verbal contents; much more so would it be to invent them in a late age. Then there is the plague at Shittim (chapter 25), inflicted because of lustful idolatry. Chapter 26 is an impossible conception unless true, and its place in the book proves it is true. Mad indeed must an author be who should try to invent it or chapter 27. Its historical genuineness ought not to be questioned. Writers do not fabricate such literature. The introduction of verses 12–23 in that relation sounds like a thunder-clap in a clear summer day. Passing to 33 : 38 we have the death of Aaron, which, and the subsequent matters related, show how much easier it would be to invent the expedition of Cyrus, or remember all its details of stations and parasangs, than to fabricate the contents of the fourth book of Moses. It must have originated in the age of its events, which must have been written out then, though some chapters may have been transposed or added since 1300 B.C.; according to Kalisch in 1030 B.C. Read Bible references.

That the early Hebrews were familiar with reading and writing appears in Genesis, in Exodus 5 : 18–20; 17 : 14; 34 : 27, 28, and in the national census of Moses and David; in the letter of David to Joab touching the treatment of Uriah, which David wrote to compass his death (2 Sam. 11 : 14, 15); in the writings of prophets and seers—Nathan, Gad, Iddo; in David's Psalm and his charge to Solomon, and in the long lists of famous men. (Cf. 2 Sam. 7; 1 Chron. 16; 21 : 9–30; 23–25 chapters; 2 Chron. 12 : 15). They are details and matters not carried in a stranger's memory. The men of Hezekiah copied out Proverbs of Solomon (25 : 1). It suggests authorship, and that writing was known in the eleventh century B.C. The now famous Siloam inscription could not have been later than Hezekiah, and may have been Solomon's work. Professor Sayce says, " While there are several reasons which assign it to the age of Solomon, there are others which place it in the reign of Hezekiah" (2 Kings 20 : 20; 2 Chron. 32 : 30). "The forms of the letters used in this inscription make it quite clear that the engraver was accustomed to write on parchment or papyrus and not on stone. They are rounded, not angular, like the characters on the Moabite stone. Indeed, the alphabet employed in Judah was that of a people then in the habit of writing and reading *books*. The engraver was probably one of the workmen delighted at the success of the conduit. Skill in engineering was then so advanced as to allow the workmen to commence tunnelling the hill simultaneously at the opposite ends and to meet each other in the middle of the tunnel, which winds in its course and is one thousand seven hundred and eight yards long from mouth to exit. This inscription was in a place never likely to be seen, was carefully executed, proving that writing was common at that time." Only by an accident was it discovered in June, 1880. Scribes, priests, and prophetical schools were as well practised in this art as writers in our day. "This conclusion," says Sayce, "is confirmed by the monuments of Egypt and Assyria. Books were common there from the earliest times ; the profession of scribe was held in high esteem ; public and private monuments were covered with characters presumed to be read by every one. Long before Abraham libraries were well stocked with clay or papyrus books which had numerous readers. New works were frequently added, and copies of old ones made. They were arranged and catalogued as in a modern library ; treated of every department of knowledge, and represented every known class of subjects. If the Israelites had been illiterate, living midway between Assyria and Egypt, and bordering on the highly-civilized cities of

Phœnicia, it would have been nothing short of a miracle. That they were not is put beyond cavil by the Siloam inscription. Consequently no arguments can be drawn against the credibility of the Old Testament Scriptures on the ground that their historical statements are false or mythical, or that they could not have been written at the early date to which they lay claim. There is no reason why Abraham should not have been able to write; most of his contemporaries in Ur could do so; there is still less reason why his descendants, who had been brought into contact with the literature of Egypt, should not have written too. Biblical books composed at the time of the events described have the weight of contemporary evidence. A writer does not give a false account of things well known to his readers, or imagine events which his contemporaries can show never happened. The history of writing in the East makes it probable that the Biblical books were written at the time to which tradition assigns them. It is not likely that the Israelites abstained from composing books when they were acquainted with the art of writing, and when they were surrounded by nations long in the possession of libraries. That the Biblical books belong to the time which tradition supposes is confirmed by the deciphered monuments of Egypt and Assyria, and by the accuracy they display in the matters related by contemporary histories." Renan's positive statement to the contrary, which I have been disproving, excuses the length of this quotation. The proof is cumulative and irresistible. Witness the contents of 2 Chronicles 10, relating the interview between the party of Jeroboam and Rehoboam pending the disruption of the tribes. That was not left to Ezra after the Exile, but was doubtless recorded at the time. Its credibility is beyond cavil, and with all the evidences previously mentioned of writing by Solomon, David, Joab, and those who aided in taking the national census, illustrates how common writing was in the tenth and the eleventh century B.C. That letter of Elijah to Jehoram was written by a prophet who illuminates his era with moral heroism, and who, judging from the place of his birth, had not the highest educational advantages in his boyhood; yet he wrote an epistle to a king. From Moses to Samuel writing was the medium of preserving prophetic deliverances, and they were thus preserved. The early Hebrews were competent to write their history, compose a literature, and read books; witness the well-known book mentioned in Exodus 17 : 14; Josh. 18 : 9; 8 : 30–34.

But the existence of similar phrases in the Old Testament with certain cuneiform inscriptions decides not the priority of the latter, nor that one account was derived from the other, and is therefore more ancient. Schrader compares the words, "Burned the city with fire, or consumed with fire" (Judges 18 : 27), with what is said of Tiglath-pileser I. at nearly the same period in his col. V., 60, 72, where Isatu=ash or esh is found, which by some vowel changes makes the word like one in Hebrew. No such device is needed to show that both Joshua and Tiglath-pileser I., like others before them, made ashes of hostile cities. Exodus 9 : 7 says, "The heart of Pharaoh was hardened or obstinate;" so Sennacherib's col. (Taylor cyl., V.,

7) has the phrase, "Their heart was obstinate, so that they offered resistance" to him; the Khors. 91, 33 reads, "The heart . . . obstinate." Other resemblances between Hebrew and Assyrian are seen in the same word designating certain colors—viz., those of the sanctuary of the tabernacle, violet-blue, red-purple, seal of agate, etc. (Ex. 25 : 4 ; 28 : 19 ; Khors. 142, 182 ; Schrader, "Cuneiform Inscriptions," p. 143). He also says Pharo is found on the monuments; Pethor, the home of Balaam, was on the west bank of the Euphrates, and called Pitru by the Syrians, and Shalmaneser took possession of it for himself. It fulfilled the prediction noted above. Expressions " like the stars of heaven" (Gen. 22 : 17 ; 27 : 4) are used by Assur-nasir-habal, who carried away prisoners and booty, which, "like the stars of heaven, were not to be numbered." He flourished 886–858 b.c., and was the father of the Shalmaneser just named. But it would be folly to say that *therefore* the phrases in Genesis were written after those of this Assyrian king.

The use of the word seven in Leviticus 26 : 21, 24, 28, and in Deuteronomy 28 : 7, 25 is similar to its use in Genesis and in Daniel as the number of completeness. In Deuteronomy 28 : 36, 64, Leviticus 26 : 29, 30, we have emphatic proof that the passage was *not* written by a fifth-century Jew. Hebrews and Persians were then decided monotheists, and would not provide *idolatry as a penalty* for transgression of Jehovah's covenant, which would be adding sin to sin. Nor could the verses refer to the Babylonian captivity, because Abraham had come from Ur of Baby-

Ionia; and a nation is spoken of which their fathers did not know. The reference must therefore be to the Assyrian captivity, and was palpably written before 721 B.C., when Sargon took Samaria. So the verses clearly make against the fifth-century-origin theory, whose advocates must either exscind the reference or admit its early origin. It is amazing how some critics ignore dates. Again, Leviticus 26 : 29, Deuteronomy 28 : 53-58 are demonstrably prophetic, and did not find their complete fulfilment till the last war with the Romans, described with some attendant horrors by Josephus (" De Bell. Jud.," VI., 3, 4). Though strongly forbidden by the law, which did not permit one to touch a dead body without subsequent cleansing, the famine was so great that parents ate the flesh of their children for food. The terrible extremity softened even the hearts of the tyrants who ruled the city, and verified the prophecy.

So the fact that Abraham began his public life in Canaan by defeating a combination of invaders who were as five to his one has no relation to the fact that Joshua began his career in that same land by defeating one combination after another of hostile forces, taking five kings at one time, " whom he crucified," and a popular song celebrated this victory. " In it," says Renan, " were found two lines :

> "' Sun, stand thou still upon Gibeon,
> And thou, moon, in the valley of Ajalon.'

The poet would express the astonishment of nature at the prodigious effort of the Israelites. This rhetorical figure afterward gave rise to some curious mistakes. The two lines were ascribed to Joshua, and in changing the meaning of the word which signifies 'stood still with astonishment' (struck with terror), it was supposed that the sun really stood still at the order of Joshua." In the song of Deborah the stars are said to fight against Sisera. Some would feel relieved if the original narrative warranted Renan's explanation. He acknowledges the personality and leadership of Joshua. While his version of the lengthened day differs from that of many, it removes a difficulty; but it also removes the honor done to Jahveh; for Joshua makes the heaven-gods glorify Him by aiding His Hebrew servants. A sermon on the passage by Rev. Dr. Egar, in the *Churchman* of October 13th, 1888, suggests that the "battle was fought in the night, and the prayer was for the sun not to rise and frustrate the advantage of this night attack. It was not yet dawn; let the sun be silent and not shine; let the moon be obscured and the storm continue until the enemy be destroyed!" Let Jahveh be glorified in Israel's victory. So also sang Deborah.

What Renan says of Lot and the Rotenu, the Egyptian name for the Syrians, accords with Gesenius; they were the people of the country about the Dead Sea. Lot was among the new-comers into that region, and left his name in the Rotenu of Syria. His sons were Moabites and Ammonites, now at war with Israel and now seducing them to the worship of Chemosh. They were more often hostile than friendly to Jacob, and ever ready to aid Japheth against him. To-day they have no place in history.

"He said in his heart" (Gen. 17 : 17)—*i.e.*, he

thought to himself, is found in G. Smith's "Assurbanipal," and also the Accadian legend which gives the creation of the moon as *before* that of the sun, following the usage of the Accadians, who placed the female before the male, and gave the goddess Istar an independent position. Error of the inscriptions is also seen in locating Edom between the land of Omri and Palestav—*i.e.*, between Samaria and Phœnicia, when, in fact, Edom was south of those two countries. Why, then, shall we correct the Bible by Assyrian records? Their forms of greeting: "I salute you—my good wishes to you—peace be to you," neither prove nor disprove that the forms in Genesis are later than the inscriptions, or that those of Assurbanipal, 667-47 B.C., are before our Bible forms. (Cf. Schrader's "Cuneiforms," p. 125 ; II. Rawlinson's "Asurhaddon," and G. Smith's "Assurbanipal.")

Moreover, if details of Israel's history do not appear in the inscriptions till the era of Shalmaneser II., the omission does not militate against the probability that the Bible record was the earlier, nor that its idiomatic phrases—words for violet-blue, red-purple, seal of agate, its prophecies, and the facts of local history—were not original ; for Jacob had artistic and linguistic skill enough at and after the Exode to imitate or originate bright colors and expressive phrases for all his needs, before the Assyrian set foot in Palestine. Even before the house of Omri was known east of the Euphrates, Solomon, David, and Saul had reigned over a unified Israel. So, because the Persian word *pahat*, meaning vicegerent, is used in 1 Kings 10 : 15 ; 20 : 24 ; rendered governors and captains, in the tenth and the ninth century B.C., it by no means follows that it was first written in Hebrew after the time of Cyrus, nor that the passage is an interpolation. For careful examination finds the word used by Sargon II., who established his *paháti* over South Babylonia, and that he was enthroned in his palace amid his *paháti* near two centuries before Cyrus (Khors. 22, 178). Yet some will have us suppose that this word came to the Hebrews through the Persians, when in fact it was used in Israel and in Assyria long before Cyrus conquered Babylon. Evidence is conclusive that the word for viceroy existed in Hebrew as early as we find it in Kings. Schrader rightly says that "interpolation in such cases is absurd" (pp. 175, 176). It was quite historic for Shalmaneser II. to mention the "land or house of Omri;" for Rimmon-nirári and Tiglath-pileser II. mention it, and Sargon II., who extinguished it. But Schrader *errs* in saying that "according to the Biblical account the king who captured Samaria can only have been the same king who laid siege to it"—viz., Shalmaneser IV. (p. 181). For 2 Kings 17 : 6 only says, "The King of Assyria took Samaria," without naming the king. It is not relating the history of Assyria, and so only states what was done to Israel; therefore the inference of Schrader that Shalmaneser took Samaria is his mistake, not the writer's in Kings. Indeed, verses 4, 5, 6 do not mention the king's name, but leave it to the general history of Assyria. Schrader correctly says that the Samírena of Assurbanipal, after 668 B.C., is not the Samaria of Israel and Omri (p. 182). Its national existence terminated more than half a century before.

Assyrian kings punished her for disloyalty to the Lord God of Israel. Japheth chastised Jacob. Egypt and Babylon chastised Judah. These are truths of history. It would not make them false if the record of them were not found in contemporary annals. So of words used in describing any of those events. Dialects differ; words used by a people at one stage of their history are not used at another period. We find this in the English of Chaucer, Shakespeare, the "judicious Hooker," in Johnsonized Latin, and in De Quincey, who tried to Anglicize "parvanimity" as the natural counterpart of magnanimity. Among the myriad of *domestics in Solomon's establishment* were many non-Israelites, some of whose words may have become incorporated into Hebrew with the dawn of the tenth century B.C. This readily explains some supposed verbal anachronisms in our Bible. Some so-called "Americanisms" are clearly traceable to the English of the seventeenth century. Professor Green shows that in the decalogue is found the so-called Elohist writer, the Jahvist, and the Deuteronomist, all in a few verses; so in other passages.

Mr. William Lethaby recently wrote thus: "On the east side of the Dead Sea, at the top of the mountain where Lot fled for refuge after the overthrow of the cities of the plain; where since the Crusaders no Western couple has resided, and which, we are told, we must not think of as a possible abode, I find that Farrar, Geikie, Harmer, Thompson, etc., have not conveyed one half of the force of the argument for the utmost credibility of the Biblical books which residence in the Holy Land conveys to an Occidental.

If you lived in Moab, to suggest that Moses was midway between a dupe, a braggart, and a myth, the sons of the desert would regard you as needing a close-fitting strait waistcoat for your suggestion, so supremely ridiculous would it appear to them. Anything approaching to infidelity is not to be found in a single Arab or native of these lands; nor, if he could read, and had the Bible in his hands, could such a thing be possible, when every page speaks to him, in emphatic language, of his forefathers."

It may cause a smile to note Renan's objection to "the Book of Joshua, which relates the conquests of Joshua, but does not mention that of Samaria" (vol. i., p. 208). *Because Samaria was not then built!* Late in the tenth century "Omri bought the hill Samaria of Shemer for two talents of silver, and built on the hill, and called the name of the city which he built, after the name of Shemer, owner of the hill, Samaria" (1 Kings 16 : 24). This Omri was the father of Ahab, and flourished 929-18 B.C. He and the name of his city are found on the Assyrian tablets, but he could not have been known to any *early writer of the deeds of Joshua, who died several centuries before Omri built Samaria!* The contents and the silence of the Book will survive Renan's objection, although he calls it "the least historical of the Bible" ("History of the People of Israel," p. 212). In his second volume, while accepting the record in Kings, he does not cancel his false criticism.

The Assyrian tablets say that Shalmaneser II. subdued Ahab with the loss of ten thousand men; but Ahab was slain in battle in 892 ; and Shalmaneser in his sixth year defeated Israel and her allies, when fourteen thousand soldiers were put *hors de combat*. He reigned from 858 to 823, or, according to Schrader, 860-25--*i.e.*, he began to reign thirty-two years *after* Ahab's death. He twice came in conflict with Jehu, whom he wrongly calls the "son of Omri"! Surely we shall not change our Bible record to suit these errors of the inscriptions! It is only a *verbal* mistake, but it is a mistake in the bricks. Jehu was the son of Nimshi, who destroyed the house of Omri-Ahab, and seated himself on their throne, according to the word of Elijah (1 Kings 19 : 16 ; 2 Kings, chapters 9 and 10). Yet we may accept the Assyrian account that he paid tribute to Shalmaneser II. or to his predecessor, Rimmon-nirâri II., . . . " bars of silver, bars of gold, a golden bowl, a golden ladle, golden goblets, golden pitchers, bars of lead, a staff for the hand of the king, and shafts of spears," a great many things of no great value, but paid to Shalmaneser's father. The text may be seen in Schrader's " Cuneiform Inscriptions" (p. 199). Another fragment says that Shalmaneser II. " received tribute of the Tyrians, Sidonians, and of Jehu ;" this was about 842 B.C. Thus early was the independence of the Northern Kingdom assailed. Indeed, an inscription of Tiglath-pileser I. about 1100 B.C. and in the time of Samuel's judgeship says : " With the assistance of Assur, Samas, and Ramman, the great gods, the King of Assyria, ruling from the great sea of the west country [Mediterranean] to the sea of the land of Naïri, marched three times." That west country probably included Phœnicia-Palestine and Philistia, to which

Israel was then partly subject. Only indirectly could it be said to be under Assyrian domination. Tiglath does not say that he conquered them, but only as "ruling from the great sea." He does not claim to be receiving tribute from Israel then, which his annals would have claimed had the facts justified. As they read, they illustrate how the inscriptions were wont to embellish rather than omit royal exploits, and are certainly not more reliable than our Biblical accounts. Yet Renan says : " It is only by modern criticism and philology that an insight has been obtained into the truth of these ancient texts. These, trustworthy in their way, with theocratic after-touches and sacerdotal revisions, are often met one upon another in the same paragraph, requiring a practised eye to detect them. The different wordings and the scissors of compilers capriciously used often make impossible the attempt to sort them out" (p. 21). But after this brief examination we can see how very much more of doubt and uncertainty he suggests than his citations or the inscriptions warrant. Reuss, Graf, Kuenen, Noeldeke, Wellhausen, and Stade do not prove his version of how things may have been. In going through his first volume I marked every passage of seeming importance, and have now fairly considered most of them. In "God Enthroned in Redemption" (pp. 61, 62), I anticipated what might be said here of "Moses meeting Elohim in mountain defiles," and the attempt to mystify the Divine Personality (Renan, (p. 28). No; the Ten Commandments will not budge at his bidding. Jahveh then as now reigns over all, and gives laws to all, amid the thunders of

Sinai, or by the voice of conscience speaking in the hearts of men. Equally in the thunder and in the whisper a Personal God speaks, and speaks to be regarded : not often to destroy, but to guide and save.

The learned logomachy about redaction, compilation, and use of the scissors finds its sufficient answer in the fact that each inspired writer and editor did for his time precisely what was then needed for that time ; adding to the historical parts of sacred history to date, explaining the laws, enforcing its precepts, composing its Psalms, combining scattered accounts, and making the whole more complete and adapted to the new conditions of new generations. This culminated and, so far as we know, ended for the Old Testament under Ezra after the Exile, and with the prophets to Malachi. They were enabled to judge under the guidance of the Spirit of Truth what was of God's truth for future use to men. Thus it had been from Abraham to Moses, when revelation was small in volume, and when it was added to under Moses the people knew what was God's truth for them. So it was under Samuel and Nathan, Hosea and Amos, Elijah and Isaiah. Under Judges and Kings the Law of the Lord was, or might be, as well known to the men of Israel as the laws of the Government at Washington, applicable to the several States, are known by Americans. For Israel was a federation of tribes having Jahveh for their Head, who was honored by being obeyed. Hence He was to be worshipped at His sanctuary. Hence loyalty was seen in Sabbath observance and sacrifice at His altars. Hence exhortations to obedience to the Divine covenant ; for national loyalty implied faithfulness to Israel's God, just as regard for the laws and for the flag are implied in faithfulness to our America. The Law of the Covenant was to be kept in the Ark of God, and a copy of the appointed ritual was preserved beside the Ark. (See Deut. 9 : 9 ; 31 : 24-26 ; 2 Kings 22 : 8-11.) The priests would seem to have been the guardians of the books, and were aided by prophets in expounding them. Only by their consent could additions and expositions be made. Each king was required to have a copy of the law which he executed (Deut. 17 : 18-20). Probably another copy was made by each school of prophets. New Psalms were composed from time to time for public use and to be sung in the service of the temple. Thus the sacred books were authenticated, edited, and copies of them multiplied. Each copy was security for others ; the priests and prophets were joint security for all. Thus the Hebrew Scriptures became, *par excellence*, the Bible for future generations. Such authentication is what no other books possess, while it marks the Bible as the Word of God for all His people.

That Word has been preserved to this day with remarkable care and exactness. Two centuries before our era it was translated into Greek at Alexandria, and was the best and fullest example of Alexandrine literature, as the Greek Testament was of the Syrian Greek literature. Thus in the Old Testament and in the New we have the best example of the Greek language in each period, as the Hebrew of the Old Testament was for its day. Jewish colonies in most of the centres of Roman civilization rendered translation of the Hebrew Scriptures necessary. This required authentication of them, and multiplication of copies. From Ezra and Malachi, the last inspired editors, to the commencement of its translation into Greek, the time was too short for spurious books or amended copies to pass as genuine. Each book must be known at its true, recognized value before it passed to the translators at Alexandria. From the tenth century B.C. onward prophets like Elijah and Elisha, Joel and Hosea, Amos, Micah, and Isaiah must have known the sacred books, and they had the courage to repudiate and denounce the false. Never was Israel without a witness or without a testimony or law of God; never before the Roman era were all the people driven from the land of their birth. After Sargon there were tens of thousands of Israelites left in the country of which Samaria had been the chief city; after Nebuchadnezzar there were other thousands of Hebrews left who had gone up to Jerusalem to worship. Among these it would be rash to say that not one copy of the Pentateuch, nor of the prophets who had then written, nor of the Psalms which had been chanted in the temple and committed to memory, then existed in Israel, and that the Hebrew Scriptures at that date could not be found in Palestine. No; we are not restricted to the existence of but one Hebrew copy of the Bible. Private copies, we may believe, were ever accessible, which could verify the official in the possession of prophets and of priests, and as read at the three great festivals. Nor is it too much to assume that many who returned with Ezra could verify his text of Scripture as easily as they could compare or contrast the new temple with the greater magnificence of the old one destroyed. Philometer, who is called the good Ptolemy, and who was killed B.C. 146, consented to build a temple at Bubastis, after the model of the Jerusalem temple, to be dedicated to Jehovah, where should minister Jewish priests and Levites, and in which Philometer, his queen and children, should be honored as θεοὶσυνάοι, or companion gods, as was then the fashion in Egypt (Mahaffy's "Greek Life and Thought," pp. 501, 508; Josephus, Book 13, chapters 3, 4; Isaiah 19 : 19). Hence arose the temple at Leontopolis, which lasted till A.D 70. It shows the deep interest which Alexandrian Jews and Egyptian rulers took in their writings and their ritual. The new learning at that centre produced fresh and improved copies of the text of earlier writers both in sacred and secular literature. Justin Martyr, a Greek convert to Christianity, testifies to Moses, Isaiah, Jeremiah, and Daniel. Origen, in the second century A.D., took great pains to collate and arrange Hebrew and Greek versions of the Bible. These Jerome had to aid him in his Latin version two hundred years later, and since then there has been vast labor expended on the sacred volume. Josephus, Justin, Origen, the whole Christian Church, and our Lord Himself, testify to the Law, the Prophets, and the Psalms of the Old Testament, the three divisions into which it was then classed and divided. They reached back in two short centuries to the era of the Alexandrian version, and that in two more centuries reached back to the last Old Testament prophets. So the apostle might truly say, we have a very sure word of prophecy. Religious sects, Samaria upon Jerusalem, and Jerusalem, with her colonies, upon all, were guardians of the Scriptures. Devout men watched the text of the several books, and that no unauthorized additions were made. The law and the history find illustration in the Prophets and the Psalms. The 119th Psalm is a good exposition of the spiritual meaning of the Law, and may express the writer's opinion of Deuteronomy. The statutes of Jahveh were his study day and night. Thus Jacob certifies to the Divine Word for Japheth. Appointed judges, anointed priests and kings, inspired prophets composed, expounded, and authenticated that Word for Israel and the world. It is not an *ipse dixit* of any one man. Its history demonstrates its character and purpose, resting upon evidence which commands conviction of its truth.

Any occasional or protracted lapse from the law or the ritual was met by the voice of warning prophets, "who burned with anger over the abuses of the world, and whom to-day we should denounce as socialists and anarchists. They were impetuous in the cause of justice ; if they could not reform they would destroy the world. This led to deeds of heroism, and awakened the forces of humanity. The founders of Christianity were successors of the prophets, invoked the end of the world, and so transformed it." This strong testimony of Renan (p. 10) makes against his theory that Jahveh was only a local god. "For the Bible," he says, "is the great book of consolation for *humanity*. The prophecies of the ninth century B.C. have their root in the ancient ideal of patriarchal life—an ideal partly of the imagination, but it was a *reality* in the past of Israel. It lay at the root of a movement which swept the world along with it." Now those prophets were Elijah and Micaiah, Elisha and Joel, all true and earnest men of God, but not the originators of their religion. The *root* of the movement which swept the world along with it dates from the patriarch who left Ur of the Chaldees, sojourned for a time in Haran, and then travelled southward to Shechem, Bethel, and Beersheba, thus taking possession of the land promised him by his covenant God. "A small tribe in an outlandish corner of Syria supplied the void which Greece never felt of the need of a just God and a universal religion." *That*, and not "Greece herself, is the greatest miracle on earth." *That* has given mankind a universal religion and a Bible for the world. O that Renan saw this!

Moreover, if the inspiration of God was given to men for the preparation of the Coming One centuries before He came, why may not Divine inspiration have enabled Hebrew legislators to formulate laws for that nation in anticipation of its actual needs? The two, in fact, are often found together in Holy Scripture; prophets, judges, kings, uniting in edicts and exhortation for observance of the law and for the worship of God. A "thus saith Jahveh" both *enjoined* and *explained His will*. But from the positiveness which some critics now assume, one might suppose that important discoveries had been made in the text of the Old Testament, which at least warranted, if they did not suggest, a new method of interpretation. But examination shows that Professor Green, of Princeton, for example, has possession of all the facts and data possessed by Professors Kuenen and Wellhausen—*i.e.*, the *same text and the same* MSS. I have looked through Kuenen's "Critical Inquiry into the Hexateuch," of 1886, for the purpose of seeing the grounds upon which he bases his claims for a late origin of the Pentateuch as we have it, and why he relegates now one part to the reign of Solomon, now another to Hezekiah, now another to Josiah, now another to some post-exilic date, while allowing this or that part to the era of the Exodus. But I fail to find any stronger reason for such redistribution of the several portions than that, *a priori, they are legislation in anticipation of the national history!* In a word, it is an "I think" against "thus it is written." Such and such things were *not* enacted till after the settlement in Canaan, *because* it was not needed, not called for! That is the method of procedure. As ropes, for example, were before hanging and trees before fruit, so *offenses* were before the enactment of penalties, and before the laws which enforced them; the law of the Sabbath before penalty for its violation; settlement in Canaan before cities of refuge. These critics, however, admit that Hebrew prophets exhorted the people to obey a law which existed before the reformation under Josiah, and before the reformation of Hezekiah; that Amos, Hosea, Micah, Isaiah, and perhaps Joel, delivered such utterances about the law which prove it must have been well known in the ninth century B.C.; and that Elijah complained, "Lord, they have broken down Thy altars, slain Thy prophets, and I only am left in Israel!" But the Divine answer told him that *seven thousand* were still faithful to the law of the covenant in that apostate land. Isaiah also complained that Judah had *transgressed the laws, changed the ordinance, broken the everlasting covenant;* hence a curse upon the land (24 : 5 ; compare 34 : 16). That was in the last quarter of the eighth century B.C. The antiquity of these prophecies is unquestioned. No recent "findings" qualify them ; though some ask what law was meant ? Professor Briggs, of the Union Theological Seminary, who is not likely to die of conservatism, holds to this old legal teaching of the prophets named above (" Messianic Prophecy," pp. 109-219). The exhortations to obey legal requirements imply their existence. Though often blended with predictions of the Coming One, they cannot be relegated to a later date than when spoken. All fair principles of interpretation suggest that the commentary and the urging to obedience were later than the laws so enforced. Laws existed before exposition and penalty. Transgression was only passing beyond what was permitted. The eye of the great legislator foresaw by prophetic vision the needs of his people. Hence much of his code was anticipatory of actual needs, and clearly referable to later requirements. To assume that nothing *anticipatory* in legislation is to be received as genuine and historic is to sweep away a large part of those *national* codes which are supposed to have originated in the early ages of mankind. Indeed, those nations which have made the largest mark in the world's history are all guilty of *anticipatory* legislation—Egypt by her Menes and " Book of the Dead ;" Eran by her Zoroaster ; India by her " Vedic Hymns ;" China by her

Confucius; Sparta by her Lycurgus; Athens by her Solon; Rome by her Numa; Babylonia by her "Liturgy and Saints' Calendar;" Darius in reorganizing his empire; Charlemagne in legislation for the Franks; William and his Normans legislating for England; Napoleon in his "code" for France. Not till these can be explained away can critics explain away the anticipatory legislation of the Hebrews from Moses to David. When you have *blotted out the Samaritan Pentateuch*, and have discovered genuine MSS. *and an authenticated text, which contain no anticipatory enactments for Israel, then, but not till then*, can you decide upon all the dates of Hebrew legislation. We have no fears for the results of any discoveries, whatever they may be—Sinaitic, Alexandrian, Jerusalem, or Vatican. The Law of the Covenant, much of the ritual for worship and sacrifice, laws respecting vows, Nazarites, eating flesh with the blood, prohibiting witchcraft, and limiting the royal prerogative of Israel's king, were *before* the establishment of the Hebrew monarchy.

Moreover, we need stronger evidence than that of Nabonidos, that "Naram-Sin, the son of Sargon, founded the temple of the sun-god at Sippara, B.C. 3750 years." And as this is the now accepted date by many current writers—Professor Sayce, the new Chambers' Encyclopædia, etc.—we are surprised to see how little noticed this chronological revolution has been, which radically changes so much of previously received Babylonian data, library collections, culture, and governmental development. As it adds about two thousand years to the supposed chronology heretofore followed, it is worth considering whether we are critically historical in accepting those additional two thousand years without some further proof. I base my reason for rejecting these added millenniums, at present, upon the facts of history, Babylonian and Egyptian. We all know that in Egyptian history the era and dates of several dynasties were *contemporaneous*. This, I suggest, was so with the tables of those Babylonian kings mentioned by Nabonidos, found in that Cyprian temple.

Consider: Sargon I. was the great *unifier* of Babylonia, and consolidated the adjacent princedoms into one nation—viz., his own Agadé and Ur, with Babylon, Nipur, Sippara, and Zerghul; but it was not till the reign of Kammurabi, the third in succession after Sargon I., that Babylon was made the capital of the empire. And so Sargon's *son* actually incorporated into one series the names of all the kings or princes of those districts which the father had absorbed and consolidated into the new empire over which Naram-Sin reigned. It is assuredly *probable* that such a reckoning was made for the twofold purpose of glorifying his ancestry and of conciliating his subject peoples, who were restive under his government, when they remembered their former and larger liberties. Example of this procedure he had in Egypt, while thus lauding the antiquity of his royal ancestors. Indeed, I have seen this principle acted upon in certain incorporated institutions of New York, and I feel confident that it explains the tables of the long list of kings claimed by Naram Sin as his predecessors. It is literally true that *he was the successor of each king or prince of each of the united districts of his empire.* And he needed to be strengthened on his throne ; hence the claim of a long line of ancestors was a short and pretty sure way of doing it. Hence his royal and thus lengthened pedigree. A thousand years later Sargon II. of Assyria likewise claimed descent from certain kings whom he called by name— viz., Bel-bani and Adasi, which claim his courtiers readily admitted. But both these Sargons were probably *usurpers*, certainly the latter. And "the three hundred and fifty kings" said to have preceded Sargon I. doubtless included all those who had reigned over the several districts which his arms subjugated. They are easily embraced in our former chronology, *four fifths* being contemporary princes. Wherefore there is no present cause for changing "the bloom of Accadian poetry" to a period before 2300 B.C. We thank translators for telling us what the inscriptions say, but we claim the right to explain those sayings according to the custom of the times and the methods of procedure then and now practised.

VII.

THE ERA OF SAMUEL AND DAVID: JACOB'S BIBLE THEN.

We have to deal with these celebrated Hebrews in their official relations with the theocracy. Personally they stand high upon the roll of fame. To call Samuel the Aristides of his country is to put an incident for a character, a part for the whole. Samuel, indeed, was an example of justice; he was also the Reformer and organizer of a scattered and disunited people whom he moulded into a nation. Its centre was now at Ramah, now at Mizpeh, now at Gilgal, and then transferred by David to Jerusalem. In their civic position they represent to us Washington as the first President of America, while in their religious position they represent the body of American clergy in bringing the people to the God of their fathers, who had given them a free country and a Divine religion.

From Joshua to Eli the centre of worship and of tribal meetings was Shiloh. There only during that period atoning sacrifices could be offered for the people. The catastrophe which led to the capture of the Ark also involved the death of Eli and his sons. There was no high priest left in Israel. Samuel was but a Levite in pedigree, though a highly-honored prophet of Jehovah. At his home in Ramah, he built an altar, and offered sacrifices there and at other centres of assembly; but they were sacrifices which acknowledged Jehovah's victory over the Philistines; which recognized Him as the Bestower of tribal blessings, or renewed the kingdom before Him, with Saul as its earthly sovereign, while the Lord alone was their King; sacrifices of thanksgiving, of invocation, and of worship might properly be offered by Samuel or by Elijah, but not sacrifices of propitiation and atonement for sin; these were prescribed to be offered by the priest alone before the door of the tent or tabernacle. And from the capture of the Ark to its reinstatement in the tabernacle by David, who brought it from the house of Abinadab to Jerusalem, there is no record of prescribed sacrifices of atonement for the nation's sin (2 Sam. 6). The call for Ahijah to bring the Ark of God to Saul (1 Sam. 14 : 18), was for a different purpose. Chapter 22 relates how Saul himself had put Ahimelech and the priests of Nob to death; the young Abiathar alone escaped to David for protection. Thus no sacrifices of atonement were made at the door of the tent of the Ark during all that time. The burnt-offering of a lamb in 1 Samuel 7 : 9 was for invocation of the God of Israel against Philistines, which any prophet or national chief might properly offer, as had been the custom from Abraham to David at the threshing-floor of Araunah (2 Sam. 24 : 18-25). Hence, while sacrifices for purposes of atonement for sin were localized at the place of the Ark, other sacrifices were not thus restricted in Israel. The best explanation of the meaning of a law is the practice under it soon after its enactment. Thus we interpret the seemingly restrictive passages in Deuteronomy 12, which were doubtless known to Samuel and David. (Comp. Lev. 6 : 6 ; 5 : 14–19 ; 19 : 21 ; 17 : 9 ; 16 : 33, 34.) So of 1 Samuel 14, which mentions Saul's calling for the Ark of God ; it certifies to the fact of its being with Israel at that time, while the related verses tell of his rash objurgation, made obligatory by the law then known and understood, against eating flesh with the blood in it (verses 24–35 ; Lev. 17 : 13, 14 ; 19 : 26 ; Deut. 12 : 16 ; 23 : 21–23 ; Num. 30 : 2) ; passages of high antiquity. So the later incident of Saul's life, when he inquired of the Witch of Endor, certifies to the law and its penalty (Lev. 20 : 6 Ex. 22 : 18 ; Deut. 18 : 10, 11). Saul had himself cut off those that had familiar spirits in obedience to that same law, and had disguised himself so as not to be known by the woman whose aid he sought (1 Sam. 28 : 3, 8–10). I repeat, the practice under a law proves its existence, and illustrates its meaning. Shiloh even when desolate, Samuel at Ramah, Saul lamenting that God no longer answered him, neither by dreams, nor by Urim, nor by prophets, suggest what comfort the Hebrew had in inquiring of his Covenant God at His Sanctuary.

Our study of the Hebrew Scriptures of that time shows that they tended to produce one grand result— viz., to mould and educate a people to conserve the true knowledge and worship of God among men, and to bring the nations to Him for Redemption through His Son. The same Spirit breathes in all Divine agents to this end, the same Hand guides in all Divine providences. The supernatural permeates all the series of preparations for the Saviour of the world. During many ages it seemed that the chosen people were those alone for whom Jehovah manifested Himself; made a way for them through the Red Sea, through the wilderness, across the Jordan; threw down the walls of Jericho, destroyed wicked Canaanites, crushed Moab and Jabin, humbled the Philistines. His epiphanies were for Abraham and Jacob, Moses and Joshua, Othniel and Gideon, Deborah and Barak, for father Manoah, Nazarite Samson, and the rash Jephthah. Then He appeared to Samuel as the vindicator of His Law against the sons of Eli, whose merited death caused his own, through shock at their fate and the capture of the Ark. Never again did the glory of Israel return to Shiloh. The sun of that place went down with Eli's house. With Samuel was ushered in a new and national era, a school of prophets for the Hebrew people, and a king for their state. He should lead their armies to victory over enemies far and near, over Amalek and Midian, Moab and Philistia.

I can see no reason for minimizing Samuel while lauding Elijah, as is now the fashion with some critics. He was a judge and organizer, prophet and priest, while Elijah was a voice of warning from the wilderness, an ascetic in life, a reformer who struck at the root of evils. Both had a Divine mission to fulfil, and they fulfilled it. They were two centuries apart in time, which largely accounts for the different character of their work. Elijah wrote one notable letter, Samuel compiled some national annals; Elijah anointed two avenging kings, Samuel anointed the first and the second king of Israel, who unified the tribes, consolidated the government, and established the kingdom, of which he wrote the account and laid it by the Ark of the LORD (1 Sam. 10 : 25). Even Renan admits the practice of writing in Israel at this period, and that progress was made in the art under David (vol. i., pp. 309-311). He seems to forget that it was the eleventh century B.C., and only two centuries after the Exodus ; an era of wars and adjustments not favorable to the literary art. That it then flourished in the school of the prophets and elsewhere disproves the theory of Israel's previous illiteracy.

Under Samuel were formed guilds for the education of young men in the law of God and for service in the State. They became advisers of the king, teachers of moral and political economy among a people who were fast becoming a nation. They pointed out the real bond which held the tribes together. Heretofore it was much like that which united our colonies after their Independence, not strong, nor defined, but felt ; now it was to be understood and acknowledged, a *union* of which God Himself was the centre and head. The new prophets expounded this idea with greater emphasis than priestly teachers. They were preachers of righteousness in prince and peasant ; Divine agents for uttering the Divine voice to men ; literally "men of God" in a higher sense than Levites ; they were cohens or priestly functionaries armed with supernal powers, seers of what others could not see, and readers of the inward thoughts of those who consulted them. Samuel in his dealings with Saul, Nathan with David, Elisha with

Hazael, the minister of Ben-hadad King of Syria, illustrate this power of prophetic thought-reading. Dwelling at Damascus or in Israel, the prophet read the mind of the royal messenger, divined the conduct of his servant Gehazi, just as Ahijah had discovered the wife of Jeroboam in spite of her disguises, when she consulted him about the recovery of the young prince (1 Kings 14 ; 2 Kings 5 and 8 ; 1 Sam. 9 and 10). Such powers are as wonderful as miracle, and must have been of vast influence with the people. Distant from the Ark of God, at Damascus, at Shiloh, at Carmel, at Gilgal, without an ephod or a breastplate, wherever one found a prophet of Israel there he might learn the will of God toward him and hear the Voice of a speaking oracle. The attested facts admit of no other explanation. At the door of the Tabernacle and at the house of the Seer Jacob might receive the word of Jehovah for himself and for Japheth. This alone suggests the influence of Samuel and Nathan with Saul and David, as well as the terror which Elijah caused in Ahab, who dared not hurt him, when he could hardly tolerate his presence, leaving to his Zidonian wife to be avenged without scruple.

In face of the record Renan says that "Samuel was always Saul's dreaded prophet," yet he "had been his good genius ; deprived of him he could no longer live" (p. 346), but he did live many years after the rejection for disobedience about Amalek. It shows the importance of adherence to historic truth. While a writer gives his own coloring to a narrative, that narrative should seek to harmonize the several characters which it portrays. Thus the ruling ideas of that age correspond with the description of the writer respecting the downfall of Saul. There is no contradiction between the account and the times depicted. The king is represented as a strong, rough man, cruel, yet of generous impulses; at times as mean-acting as any king need be; brave, too, patriotic, and passionately desirous that Jonathan shall succeed him; religious withal, he died nobly on the field of battle, and his son with him. Never was tenderer elegy penned than David composed upon Saul and Jonathan in the eleventh century B.C. It amply refutes the charge of illiteracy. In one day fell the pride of Benjamin and the first regal dynasty of Israel. We never tire of reading 2 Sam. 1 : 17-27, a passage which Renan carefully conceals in the background of his story; rather a novel way of writing about heroes.

Though priest and judge, Eli permitted his sons in a course of corrupt practices and of imposition equal to anything in the priests of Egypt and India, which caused the ruin of his house (1 Sam. 2 : 12-17; 4 : 3-21). The Philistines became the avengers of Heaven; they seized the Ark of God, which had been profanely carried from the tent at Shiloh into battle; but they became terrified at the mischief it wrought when placed in Dagon's temple, and after seven months' captivity they sent it back to Israel. Cared for by Abinadab it blessed his house for many years. This was at Kirjath-jearim. Shiloh's annual festivals ceased, and Israel lamented for Jehovah's worship. It was during this time of spiritual widowhood that Samuel commenced his work of reformation. He assembled the people at Mizpeh, the place of his famous victory over the Philistines, at old Bethel, and at Gilgal, urging them to loyal service of the God of their fathers, to put away the Baalim from among them, and to renew the covenant with Jehovah, allowing no compromises with the false religion about them. Like a true prophet-priest he offered a burnt-offering to the Lord, who heard him, and accepted the renewed service. The men of Israel fought the Philistines with fresh courage, and routed them as fugitives flying before them. This victory they commemorated by Samuel setting up a stone near Mizpeh, which he called Eben-ezer, the Stone of Help, where Jehovah then helped His people (1 Sam. 7). The place was in the canton Benjamin, some four thousand feet above the sea, and became a rendezvous for the tribal meetings for some years. The hill of Zion is said to have been visible from the heights of Mizpeh; but no American would call it "the Washington" of the tribes; rather it was their Philadelphia, lasting only for a time. Of special importance under the last judge of Israel, it was the local witness of the developed idea of tribal federation, and where the diet assembled which chose Saul to be their king (1 Sam. 10 : 17-25). The strong character which Samuel exhibited as Reformer and Judge, Prophet and Priest must have suggested the advantages of national unity under a true leader, whom all would recognize and follow. His many virtues pointed to tribal federation under a national chief. The people thus paid a high compliment to the man who, most of all then living, had nourished, if not indeed evoked, the feeling which was expressed by asking him to appoint a king over them. True, Jehovah was supremely their King, but they wanted a sub-king, a Ra-Sekenen or Naram-Sin, who visibly should lead their armies and manage all federal and extra-tribal affairs. Only Gideon since Joshua had approached to such an ideal, and he had erred in following after Baalim. Now, a school of prophets had arisen which could conserve religious purity, while a recognized sovereign would conserve political interests. Moreover, Samuel's annual circuits to Bethel, Gilgal, Mizpeh, and his abode at Ramah, where was his house, a sort of court, and where he built an altar unto the LORD, all illustrated, perhaps unconsciously to the prophet, those centralizing ideas then maturing in the public mind. Scarcely more than Eli's were Samuel's sons fitted to succeed him, whose personal and official success emphasized the revived longing for a national chief. It was part of his life's work to render the people more religious and more observant of those rites which all acknowledged, though all did not practice, each man having learned to do what was right in his own eyes (Judges 21 : 25).

The religion of Israel, after two centuries of corrupting influences from their neighbors, was revived and enthused with a new spirit by Samuel. Clearly there was no evolution of a new theology, but a restoration to a new life of the old covenant religion, and a wider, perhaps, deeper appreciation that Jehovah was its Head. Very similar was it with our colonies after their independence. Religion had declined among them. Some shepherds had left their flocks to the wolves, while they went with the army ; others had returned to their native land. Schools had become neglected, literature did not flourish, the art of writing languished. Israel's hostile neighbors, like Philistines and Zidonians, were poor teachers of letters; rather they kept them as ignorant and untaught as possible. The power which could prevent the forging of an agricultural implement would not favor the cultivation of the liberal arts. Not even a smith to forge a spear, a sword, an axe, a coulter, or a mattock, was allowed in Israel while dominated by the Philistines (1 Sam. 13 : 19-22). It was a heavier oppression than that of hostile Indians and French Canadians upon our colonies. East of the Jordan, Ammon and Moab kept them subject; in the south, Edom, Midianites, and Amalekites. The record narrates the religious and military disorganization, and the new-born hope under Samuel; what he did to consolidate the tribes and to restore the powerful influence of religion. Jehovah was their King; judges, prophets, even anointed sovereigns were only His vicegerents, administering, teaching, judging for Him. This was true in theory at Mizpeh and Jerusalem; Tirzah and Samaria became apostate. It bears repeating, that the distinctive mission of Samuel was Reformer and Organizer of the Israelites into religious and political unity. He sought to restore the old ways, to exscind the polytheism copied from Canaanites, and to make Israel strong against all who were enemies of Jehovah. It was disintegration which had invited domination by neighboring cantons west and south of the chosen people. From Joshua to Samuel there had been no national chief over Israel. The leaders who had risen were but local captains of bordering tribes, who often disputed for supremacy. Shiloh, indeed, had been a religious centre rather than a national capital of political unity. Its two centuries of attraction ceased after Ichabod was named upon a grandson of Eli (1 Sam. 4 : 21). National enthusiasm did not radiate from it. Even the young priest Ahiah, who survived the fall of his family, was but a weakling at the behest of Saul (14 : 18, 19), who would bring again the Ark of God to battle! But the prophet revived patriotism and a common interest and purpose in the tribes. He would have them Jehovists by walking righteously before Him, as well as by sacramental seal of His covenant. Such revival was the outcome of the prophet's work, and in furtherance of his nation's needs. It set an example to Elijah and Micaiah, to Elisha and Jonah.

Nor does it minimize the importance of his grand mission to add that Samuel was a defender, if not the founder, of clericalism in Israel; for then the clerical party was the Lord's party, who were profoundly concerned, jointly with the prophets, to elevate the people in the religious life as well as in civil privileges and aspirations. Saul had slain the priests of Nob, who were only just recovering the loss of Shiloh, and however much he might need their aid, he was too reckless to regard their lives. Renan says they were "too powerful to be dominated by the king," yet he slew them at their innocent offending! In David they found a more congenial chieftain, which, with the mandate of Jahveh, effected a change in the dynasty even before the death of Saul. Jonathan had the good sense to recognize and yield to the Divine choice. It discloses the deep and far-reaching influence of what is called prophetism in the era of Samuel. Before his death his teaching had penetrated the minds and hearts of high and low in Israel, so that it dominated the government, changed a regal dynasty, won over the priests, and set an example of State control which Elijah could follow but in part; for while he could change Ahab for Jehu, who avenged the wickedness of Jezebel, he failed in winning over the priests of Samaria to his side. But the prophets of Ramah and the priests of Jehovah were united in efforts for the national and Divine honor, and they were quite as successful as the prophet of fire and the guild of Elisha. They also had the courage of their convictions and of their order; they as publicly proclaimed the son of Jesse as their successors proclaimed the son of Nimshi. But they patiently waited for the chances of war to remove Saul, and to put David, the chosen one, in his stead. In this also Elijah followed that first example. Jehovah is not precipitate in His dealings with mankind (1 Sam. 15; 16; 19: 18-22; 1 Kings 19; 15-21; 2 Kings 8: 7-15; 9: 1-37; Renan, vol. i., pp. 325-35).

Saul's great offence was disobedience to the Word of God, which established a very bad precedent. If prophets could be disregarded and priests slain at will, what would become of religion in Israel? How could preparation be made for the Advent of the Redeemer? At the root lay the danger. The redemption of man was jeoparded in the disobedience of Saul and rejection of the Divine voice. Here Japheth had an interest in Israel's loyalty to the God of Jacob. No altar erected by an erring king would compensate for the moral terpitude and after consequences of his sin. It was inexpiable. Very characteristic is Renan's remark, that "man is thus shown to be punished for the good he does, and to be compensated for the evil. History is quite the contrary of virtue rewarded" (*ib.*, p. 331). It is, however, apparent by the facts that Saul was personally a no better man than David, who was often obliged to fly from his deadly weapon while at dinner, though as often as Saul's life was in David's hand, he scorned to take it, choosing rather to seek a home among Philistines, or in the cave of Adullam, or among the wild slopes of Carmel. It is pitiful criticism to ridicule the "pretty story of David in a cave; taking the lance and pitcher of water from Saul, while improving the opportunity of a good laugh at the sleepy Abner," who should have guarded his king. (Renan, vol. i , pp. 341-46). It certainly speaks well for the son of Jesse, and suggests that his conduct had nothing of the "brigand" in it. Compare his character as portrayed in 1 Sam. 24 to 29 ; cutting off the border of Saul's robe at Engedi ; taking his spear and cruse of water in the wilderness of Ziph ; restraining his anger against churlish Nabal ; seeking refuge with Achish at Gath and at Ziklag, then marching after invading Amalekites rather than lift his hand against his king. What gentleness and justice, what patriotism and faith are there illustrated ! Not doubting its historical correctness, we must accept the whole account. Even if legendary, we have no right to pick and choose this or that item or incident which may best support our *theory* about a famous king of Israel. Salient facts in the life of David are correctly narrated in Samuel ; there is no extenuation or condonement for wrong doing, nor aught recorded of malicious purpose. The choice of the LORD's prophet has his human weakness and sins, which are frankly told, as well as his valor and nobility of character, his gentleness and devotion, his strategy and successes. He captures old Jebus and makes it a city of the great King, but sins upon the housetop and in ordering a census of Israel. Then David the Jehovist became David the penitent, and prepared to erect a magnificent temple to his God. Thus the founder of Jerusalem as the capital of Israel became the founder of a perpetual habitation for the mighty One of Jacob, of which glorious things are spoken. "The outlaw of Adullam, the fugitive of Engedi, became the author of Psalms, and an ancestor of the Redeemer of the world. JESUS as incarnated was a lineal descendant of David and of Ruth the Moabitess ; one the slayer, the other the Saviour of men." "A bandit has supplied the finest books in the ancient liturgy. A Roman convict has redeemed mankind." Be it so. We accept those Psalms as the precious outpourings of pious souls ; we accept that salvation as the one way whereby man is restored to the Divine favor, and made the child of God by purchase as well as by creation. We also accept the theology of the time of Solomon's temple as the authorized expression of Jehovah's character as then understood by Hebrews.

That grand *consecration service* demonstrates a fact which cannot be eliminated from history, nor omitted by redactors of the narrative, nor pulverized by critical chemists. The worship of Jehovah at that time in that temple is evidence of the character of God as understood by His worshippers then. It was Jehovah, as the God of Abraham and Jacob, who was thus worshipped. The account of it given in 1 Kings 8 crushes by the weighty facts recorded all the fine-spun theories of "fifth-century" rhapsodists. There was no recent development in the ideas of Jacob touching the being and attributes of Jahveh-Elohim. As understood in the twentieth century by Abraham, so it was expressed in the eleventh century by Solomon. On the rock of Moriah, with all the art and mechanism of that age, a sanctuary was erected, a fitting symbol of the national God of Israel and Lord of the world. Therein the ancient Ark of the Covenant was placed, not again to be disturbed or carried about till the flames of Nebuchadnezzar's avenging soldiers changed it into a burnt-sacrifice. Solomon had assembled all the tribes to witness the ceremonies, doubtless with special services for the occasion; and he may have trespassed on the priest's office in parts of the consecration. He, indeed, offered one of the most memorable prayers ever addressed to the throne of Heaven. Dr. Crosby suggests the prayer was prepared for the king by the High Priest. It should cause critics to think twice before saying that then "Jahvism was established as the religion of a local God." The record shows that He was invoked for every emergency, whether in Israel or in captivity, in peace and in war, in famine and in plenty. Moreover, the *stranger* who had come, or should come, from a far country, was prayed for, and that Jehovah would hear him from His dwelling-place, and do according to all that the stranger prayed for; that all the earth might know His name and fear Him, even as did His people Israel (verses 41–43). It is surely difficult to restrict the favor of such a God to any locality. His purview took in the world of mankind. So, two centuries later, He promised to pour out His spirit upon all flesh (Joel 2 : 28).

Pardon of all sin was there to be sought and found; the covenant was to be pleaded and remembered by Jehovah; blessings were to be implored and obtained. The God of Moses would not forget to maintain the cause of His worshippers, as the matter should require, with the refrain that *all the earth* may know that Jehovah is God (1 Kings 8 : 44–60; 2 Chron. 6). Forgery of such records would be as easy as to create a Palestinian sun. They prove how Jacob worshipped the LORD of the world.

And it was by a liturgy, which was a growth in Israel. It hardly began before the service at Sinai. It was enriched for use in the tabernacle and at Shiloh, and again augmented for the service of the Temple. No scholar regards it as the same alike under Moses and Solomon. Nor have we evidence that Samuel introduced any great change in the worship and theology of his country. Two ideas seem to occupy his mind: to bring back, or to bring up, the people to loyalty to their Covenant-religion, and to unify them as a nation for God. He found an established ritual little observed, perhaps, during the sojourn of the Ark at Kirjath-jearim, partly revived under Saul and his priest Ahiah, and fully restored under David when the Ark was placed in the tabernacle at Jerusalem; 1 Samuel 14 : 18, 19 suggest far more than express how it was under Saul, while 2 Samuel 6 and 7 recount the restoration under David. That, together with his preparations for building a splendid temple, which was erected by his son, properly designates him as a religious man and a theocratic prince. Such illustrations of piety would have secured the canonization of any king from Constantine to the Tudors of England. It does not appear to have been the product of a "priestly party" nor of "prophetism," but the outcome of a religious character as developed by the legislation and appointments of Moses. The God who found Jacob at Bethel spoke to Israel through Samuel and David (Hosea 12 : 4).

This era also further proves the antiquity of the laws of the Pentateuch. Recall what has been said in this chapter touching oaths, eating flesh with the blood, where sacrifices of atonement must be offered, against witchcraft, and the provision for a developed kingdom, with the restrictions upon royal prerogative. Consider also Samuel's hesitancy to anoint a king, and the stubborn self-will of Saul; then believe, if you can, that such a monarch would submit to the restrictions found in Deuteronomy 17 : 14–20. Clearly, only if existing at the time of his accession to the throne would a king like Saul, or David, or Solomon submit to such limitations of royal prerogative. They were provided by Moses, or imposed by the prophet, after a night of prayer to God. Compare 1 Samuel 8 : 10–22 with the passage in Deuteronomy 17. If possibly some later editor transferred that of Samuel to the Pentateuch, as some hold, several points remain to be accounted for, notably the writing out a copy of the law respecting himself by the king, which was in care of the priests (verse 18), which he was to read daily, that he might learn the fear of Jehovah, to obey Him (Josh. 1 : 8). It could have little meaning to a *sub-king* like those after the exile. But when the government was consolidated under Saul the worship of Jehovah and sundry detailed laws for prince and people were recognized and established— laws ordained of old.

During the previous centuries the Church had witnessed to the truth, and was the keeper of it as delivered to her. But from Moses to Samuel the sacred deposit was small. It then received a larger increase. Even at the dedication of Solomon's temple, Jacob's Bible comprised the Pentateuch, which was then completed as to substance—the Books of Joshua, Judges, Ruth ; the history, in probably the present form, of 1 and 2 Samuel ; the subject-matter of 1 Chronicles and the first seven chapters of 2 Chronicles ; 1 Kings 1 to 9 ; Job ; probably the first forty-one Psalms ; also 65 to 68, 72, 77, 78, 83, 89, 90, 96, 105 to verse 15, part of 106. The subject-matter and the authority of St. Peter in Acts, second chapter, prove the antiquity of Psalm 16, while Exodus 15, Numbers 10 : 35, 36, Judges 5, 2 Samuel 22, 2 Chronicles 16 : 8–36 prove others as early existing ; but the question is too large and important for treatment here. There were many Psalms doubtless arranged for public use under David and Solomon. The 47th and 48th are adapted to the new temple. But only half the Bible was then written ; many Psalms and prophecies were yet to be added. This illustrates the slow growth of Hebrew literature before David. As a boy he had heard the story of Ruth, but it is said not to have been written out before his coronation. The writing prophets of the eighth century often refer to the Pentateuch, and imply a knowledge of it in those to whom they wrote, otherwise they would be unintelligible. Prophets, in fact, preserved the continuous history of Israel from the Judges to the Exile. Jacob's Bible grew up with him. Never was he unable to write. The history of Israel was not a work of art by Ezra, but a record of the deeds of the leaders and actors in that history. So also its laws were for the most part enactments beforehand for the prospective needs of that people. They were largely anticipatory. Thus the Nazarite vow was early provided for, and we have personal illustrations of it in Samson and in Samuel, who from their birth were dedicated to Jehovah (Judges 13 : 2–25 ; 1 Sam. 1 : 11–28 ; Num. 6 : 1–21 ; Lev. 27 : 2). The removal of the bodies of executed persons was practised by Joshua, according to the law in Deuteronomy 21 : 22, 23 ; Joshua 8 : 29 ; 10 : 26, 27. So the excuse which Saul made for David's absence from table on the feast of New Moon implies the then existence of the laws touching personal uncleanness as well as feast-days (1 Sam. 20 : 18–27 ; Lev. 15 ; Num. 10 : 10 ; 19 : 11–22 ; 28 : 11). In all such cases the ritual prescribed the duty of the priests and how they should perform it. Continuing to judge Israel till the end of his life, Samuel guarded the observances of religion, and the nation lamented his death. The relegation of civil affairs to the king rendered the prophet's conduct more illustrious before the people. Schools of "Sons of the Prophets" lasted with some changes down to Jeremiah. They were occupied in expounding and copying the sacred writings, servants at once of God and man; inciting to patriotism, inculcating and illustrating loyalty and devotion. They blessed Israel for five hundred years, and after the Exile their local work was carried on by the synagogues, whose officers provided for authorized copies of the Law, the Prophets, and the Psalms for reading and exposition. In every place where twelve Jews dwelt, there might a synagogue be formed, which was organized in almost every town and village of Palestine, in Alexandria, in Greece, and in Damascus. Prophets visited Syria in flight from Ahab, or in the discharge of special duty (1 Kings 19 : 15 ; 2 Kings 8 : 7-15). As Elijah erred in thinking that he only was left a servant of Jehovah in Israel, when *seven thousand* other Hebrews were faithful, so now many err in supposing that only one copy of the Law of God existed in Judah under the reign of Josiah. Men of Jerusalem remembered and quoted the prophecy of Micah in defence of Jeremiah's predicting the destruction of their city by Babylon. Very likely they could repeat other early prophecies, and knew the law of the Divine covenant and the teaching under it. The revival which commenced with Samuel continued under David, and new prophets arose who kept alive the religious fervor, even when it implied separation from the rulers. Modern history abounds with examples of the court falling below the moral standard of the people. Witness Charles II. and Louis XIV. Even our Franklin fell below the public demands. It was the function of the prophets to elevate the practice to the covenant requirements. King Mesha knew of Jehovah, and sought to drag captive Hebrew women to Molech's altar, perhaps to offer them as victims. His vindictive feeling found excuse in the oppression he endured, and in the law (Deut. 23 : 3) that no Ammonite or Moabite should enter the congregation of Jahveh to the tenth generation. Verse 7 forbade an Israelite to abhor an Edomite, for they were brothers; to abhor an Egyptian, because Jacob had been a stranger in his land. It is legislation which no late writer would incorporate into a recent Deuteronomy. He would remember that David was a great-grandson of Moabitess Ruth, and that her adoption of the Hebrew religion did not eliminate the taint of corrupt Moab. Dr. Kalisch says the author of the Book of Ruth was in favor at David's court. He certainly could not originate the prohibition of Deuteronomy, nor could any later writer. Ezra would not thus have dishonored a theocratic king. In his resoluteness for marital purity, he could not forget the sin of Lot, neither would he forge an example of license. The passage of ten generations exscinded the blot in the royal pedigree, but proved an ancient legislation, and the anointing oil of Samuel cured all defects in the shepherd king.

Such are some of the facts in the era of Samuel which have withstood all redactors and editors of the sacred books for three thousand years. They leave us in possession of Jacob's Bible, his law, his history, his prophets, and his prayers. They are laws, predictions, and prayers which imply Divine Inspiration. None are mere copies of any other records, nor simply borrowed from other nations. Even when adapted for

Hebrews resident in Palestine, they illustrate how the world-embracing love of Jehovah provided to bless and save mankind. The Book of Ruth evidences the existence of a law respecting gleaners, of a law regulating the sale and redemption of real estate, of the Levirate law and duty of a near kinsman; these were operative in the twelfth century B.C. (chs. 2, 4 : 1–12). The law and vow of the Nazarite were yet earlier (Judges 13); of vows in general, but misunderstood by Jephthah (ch. 11); laws against idolatry (8 : 24–35; 6 : 11–37); cities of refuge recognized by Joshua (20 and 21); the law of the lot (15–19); removal of bodies of executed persons (10 : 15–27); about slavery (9 : 16–27); of circumcision and passover (ch. 5); the priesthood was the inheritance of Levi (Josh. 18 : 7). A word of history is worth a mountain of theory. It is a perversion of truth to represent that the Jewish religion was not completed till 450 B.C., and was then an abridgment of the religions of the world! Even if this were true of *Jewism*, when the prophets had ceased in Israel, it is *not* true when said of the Hebrew religion *before* the Exile. My argument is not with mere *Jewism* after Inspiration became silent. It is concerned with the religion of Abraham, the legislation of Moses, and the voices of the prophets expounding the religion of the Hebrews.

Moreover, important facts of that history, of law, covenant, even recorded judgments, as witness Sodom and Gomorrah, Egypt and Nineveh, Midianites at Oreb and Zeeb, are explicitly mentioned by prophets of the eighth and the ninth century B.C., as being well known among the people to whom they spoke;

also how the lintel of the door was anointed with oil ; how the trumpet told of New Moon and Jubilee ; how Dan was reproved for departing from the Covenant and ritual of Israel, and how Ephraim was entreated to forsake the sin of Samaria. (Cf. Amos 4 : 11 ; 8 : 14 ; 9 : 1 ; Joel ; Nahum ; Micah ; Hosea, 11th and 12th chapters ; Judges 7 : 25 ; Ps. 19 ; 68 ; 78 ; 83 ; 89 ; 99 ; 105 ; 106.) Many of these writers lived a thousand years after Abraham and Jacob, yet they give such details as show that the facts were generally known, forming a part of the national history which was then written. Hosea and Amos certify to the truth of Jacob in Genesis and in Egypt, and to deliverance from it.

VIII.

THE PROPHETS AND THEIR PREDICTIONS.

Ewald on "Revelation" says, "God speaks by His Word and by His Spirit. The Spirit vivifies, energizes; the Word decides and determines; the Spirit endows to right action, the Word directs that action. Original Revelation was given of God with the human spirit in creation. It is *not poetry, nor conscience,*" nor the product of thought, but the inspiration of thought in man. "Human speech, without the antithesis of God and man, and so without a word for God, is not thinkable, and never actually existent. The Bible, the Veda, the Avesta, Egyptian memorials—all have a God, who is the God for their people" (pp. 2–17). This was a grand fact in human life and thought. The records of primitive history are charged with religion and God. Under various names He is everywhere represented as speaking to man. And the most emphatic and most valuable of that speaking was by Hebrew prophets—Abraham, Jacob, Moses, Samuel, and his successors. Even Balaam claimed to voice for Balak only what God put into his mouth (Num. 22 : 38).

Dr. M. M. Kalisch says, Balaam's book was written

in the latter part of David's reign, about 1030 B.C. He compares it with the Book of Ruth, and claims they both belong to the same period, David himself being third in descent from Ruth. Yet he calls Numbers, into which Balaam's account was embodied, a "priestly book." The narrative teaches that the God of Balaam is undoubtedly the God of the Hebrews; that the several altars had a symbolic meaning, referring to the Ruler of nations and of individuals, including all men. Ruth, the Moabitess, accepts the God of Naomi in the most beautiful and touching asseveration ever penned. The book was written while David yet dwelt at Hebron. Deuteronomy was the first heavy blow dealt at the work of the prophets. ("Bible Studies," pp. 11, 37, 60). We have only his guess at dates and origins, because long after the writing of Deuteronomy the prophets were a vast force in Israel; they flourished notwithstanding. Even if it was of the late date claimed by some, the prophetic work had been done; their mission was accomplished. Elijah and Elisha, Jonah and Nahum, Micaiah and Micah, Amos, Hosea, and Isaiah, had each delivered his message, now to the King of Israel, of Judah, of Nineveh, and now calling the peoples of those lands to repentance and right living. It was before the Exile and before restoration to Judah's desolated lands and burnt temple that the prophetic work was performed. From the time of Alexander the Great, the prophets had no mission. The political commotion of the country was best met and managed by men like the Maccabean princes, by exhorters in the newly-risen synagogues, by scribes and expounders of the law, by preachers like John Baptist. I marvel that a scholar such as Kalisch did not see this, and correct his error. Whether Deuteronomy was of early or late origin, it dealt no heavy blow at the work of the prophets. Their era is fixed, and they accomplished their work.

Wellhausen, however, errs in a different way: "The prophets had *long* been preparing for the overwhelming catastrophe which burst upon the house of Omri" (article "Israel," p. 407, in "Encyclopædia Britannica"). What prophets had thus been preparing for that catastrophe? Ahab was only the second king of the house of Omri, Omri himself being the first, and also an usurper, or, as some would say, an avenger! (See the account in 1 Kings 16 : 8–28.) Jehu, the son of Hanani, Elijah, Micaiah, and an unnamed son of the prophetic guild (1 Kings 20 : 35; 16 : 1; 21 : 17–24; 22 : 8–28), are the only prophets of Israel who are reported as prophesying against that reigning house; Jehu, in fact, uttered his word against Baasha. Evidence is wanting of any combination of prophets against Omri-Ahab till after they proved themselves disloyal to the worship of Jehovah. It is, however, true that, from the days of Jeroboam, who made Israel to sin, the voices of the prophets were often raised in remonstrance against the royal, even priestly and popular apostasy of Israel. Samaria's priests were man made, most of them, priests and prophets of Baal and calf shrines.

The chief of those warning prophets was Elijah of Thisbe, who warned Ahab of his danger, and made him tremble on his throne, for the iniquity practised

by himself and queen. It was the only preparation
for the catastrophe which burst upon his house.
" The prophets," says Wellhausen, " first made their
appearance before the beginning of the Philistine
wars. They were a novel phenomena in Israel, lived
in societies, wore a distinctive dress, and had a *recognized place* in religion;" so they could not be very
novel, or they would not have had a recognized place
in the popular religion. " In solitary grandeur Elijah
towered conspicuously over his time. Legend has
preserved the memory of his figure. To him it was
revealed that there exists over all one holy and mighty
God, who reveals Himself in law and in righteousness.
Elijah was no invented figure; he was a prophecy of
the future rather than an actual agent in shaping the
present." Yet he was chief in preparing for the
downfall of Ahab ! " The prophets had foreseen it,
and declared, in the name of Israel's God, that it was
inevitable" (" Encyclopædia Britannica," p. 412).
The cause was the erection of a richly-endowed temple
to the Syrian Baal for Queen Jezebel ; but Ahab " had
no intention of renouncing Jehovah, who still continued to be the national God, after whom Ahab named
his sons Ahaziah and Jehoram. The destruction of
Jehovah's altars or the persecution of His prophets
was not [at first] proposed, nor the introduction of a
foreign cultus, except in Samaria. Solomon had done
so one hundred years before. Nor were the people
offended. But Elijah strenuously opposed. To him
only, not to the nation, did it seem like a halting between two opinions, an irreconcilable inconsistency,
that Jehovah should be worshipped as Israel's God,

and a chapel to Baal be erected at the same time in
Israel. He thought of Jehovah as a great principle,
which cannot co-exist in the same heart with Baal."
Certainly in those who acknowledged and worshipped
Jehovah there could not be another God, His rival!
A Baalite might acknowledge the God of Israel, not
the reverse, for Jahvism was exclusive and absolute,
while Baalism was only local and changeable. Hence
there must be a thorough clearance of it from Samaria
and from the house of Ahab. Hence Jehu, son of
Nimshi, was anointed to be king, and the avenger of
Elijah's God upon Ahab's house. He made quick
work of the clearance; not one survived him. He
extirpated Baal and his worshippers from Samaria.
The king was shot with an arrow right through the
heart; the Queen-mother, Jezebel, was thrown out of a
window; and Ahab's seventy sons were beheaded,
their heads being sent to Jehu. He left none remaining of his great men, his kinsfolks, and his priests (2
Kings 10 : 1–11, 18–28). Nevertheless, Jehu continued the calf worship in Bethel and in Dan. As
Ahab humbled himself before Jehovah, the judgment
was inflicted upon his sons, which does not justify
Renan's saying, "The prophets would destroy, if
they could not reform the world." Before the Exile
idolatry existed in some form; images, stones, trees,
groves were resorted to as accessories of worship, and
witnessed to the patience of the Lord's prophets.
Mesha's inscription lends confirmation to their patient
endurance. 1 Kings 1 : 1–16 ; 3 : 1–27 recount crimes
against humanity and sin against God. No; the majority of the prophets were not revolutionists—reform-

ers often—but often predicting smooth things as the only means of obtaining a hearing. They had no sanctuary nor confessional, while priests of Baal were sure of attention because of their position. At this time we must not forget that Jehovah's priests exercised no functions in the northern kingdom, in the chapels of Baal, and before the calf shrines. The Ten Tribes went not up to Jerusalem. They had no true priest nor true sacrifice. We must also distinguish between the rebukes of priests by Jeremiah and Ezekiel, and of Elijah and Hosea (Jer. 5 : 31 ; 14 : 14 ; Ezek. 13 ; 1 Kings 18 : 17–21 ; Hosea 5 : 1, 2). From Jeroboam to King Hoshea that kingdom was apostate from Jahveh (2 Kings 17 : 5–16), and served Baal. Wellhausen ignores the account in 1 Kings 18 ; how the minister of Ahab protected Jahveh's prophets from Jezebel's wrath, hiding them by fifty in a cave and feeding them on famine fare. The narrative indicates that whatever Ahab might have been, Jezebel was hostile to Jahvehists, and bent the king to her will.

Because the Baal prophets were only augurs and soothsayers, following the popular ways for gain, it would be unjust to charge the prophets of Jahveh, as a class, with timidity, self-seeking, or time-serving. They did *not* attach themselves to the party in power for gain ; not Elijah and Elisha, not one of the so-called greater prophets, nor any of the twelve which galaxy around them in our Bible. Simply as men they honored humanity ; as prophets they honored Jehovah. Only one of them ever shrank from promptly delivering the Divine message, and he was moved by his patriotism to let Nineveh fall, because he foresaw what that people would do to his people in later times. But even he obeyed the second voice of command. Elijah and Jeremiah might have fattened and feasted under royal favor, and have established a house full of the good things of life, if they had been content to follow the party in power ; but instead they preferred to be loyal to Jehovah, though they seem to have suffered the loss of home, of wife and child, which meant very much more in those days than in ours, in order to devote themselves to their mission. It is time to have done with minimizing the early prophets of Israel for the purpose of minimizing *prophetic Inspiration*.

While some of the judges and kings illustrate valor and national heroism, patriotism in the broad sense, the prophets illustrate moral and personal heroism of the grandest sort. They carried their lives in their hands, rebuking wicked kings, exhorting a passionate people to awake from self-indulgence, and to practise the virtues of godliness. They preached the duty of righteousness, heralded the advent of the Messiah, and sought to prepare the people for Him. They were reformers of the ages in which they lived. They warned, rebuked, threatened, or tried to woo the men of their day to be men of God, even those of neighboring and distant nations—Ammon and Moab, Edom and Egypt, Arabia and Assyria, Babylon and Tyre. Joseph in Egypt and Daniel on the Euphrates interpreted dreams sent of God to warn the rulers what Heaven was about to do as affecting their welfare. Now a prophet had a word for Judah, now for Zidon, now for Samaria and Damascus ; now he must

travel to a distant land and cry, " Yet forty days, and
Nineveh shall be overthrown!" and then write out,
and send his message to be read in the streets of Babylon, and afterward sunk into the great river, saying,
" Thus shall Babylon sink, and shall not rise from the
evil brought upon her" (Jer. 51 : 64). No; God's
truth was never barrelled up and restricted to Israel
alone. The hand and voice that provided for Jacob
provided also for Japheth. The God of Jeshurun
was not a local deity, but the God of mankind. Where
no Aaronic priest ever officiated, there prophetic
voices might be heard from the coasts of Phœnicia to
the regions of the two rivers and among the Egyptians.
They denounced idolatry and polytheism, sensuality
and all unrighteousness overreaching between man and
man, and impiety toward God. They declared what
would come to pass according to His will, and how
His judgments might become blessings. They also
had a word of comfort and encouragement for some
lone widow, some fatherless child, some oppressed
laborer, or some praying believer in the saving grace
of Jahveh. And they thundered against the inconsistency of being among the covenanted of the Lord,
while the national conduct belied its profession. Ever
did they proclaim that conduct proved character and
was the index of it, and that punishment would follow
transgression. The Judge of all the earth held a just
balance ; rectitude and righteousness were the habitation of His throne ; adjustments and compensations
were administered by Him. His prophets were pa-
triots and seers, reformers and conservators of the old
ways and truths and teachings of religion. The God

of the Law and the Testimony would deliver His people from all oppressors: now by Deborah and Barak from Midianites; now by Samson and Samuel from the Philistines; now by His angel from the hosts of Sennacherib. Joel would free them from Phœnician corruption and from the Northern Army; Hosea, Isaiah, and Jeremiah from Assyrians, Babylonians, Chaldeans, and Zechariah from foreign captivity to a restored city and temple wherein God dwelt as their everlasting Lord. (Compare Amos, Micah, Zechariah 8th to 14th, Malachi 3d and 4th.) The prophets were thus political as well as religious reformers, heralds of the Messiah and precursors of Him, who should suddenly come to His temple.

If there were indulgent priests like Eli, there were also austere priests like Ezra, who extirpated evils at the root; a scribe of the law who enforced its faithful observance, its fasts as well as feasts, its marital and Sabbatic requirements. From Phinehas to Hilkiah and Mattathias, the father of Maccabæus, there were never wanting priests and prophets who were zealous, loyal, and ready to sacrifice their lives in defence of the law of their fathers and the worship of their God. It needed not a forged Book of Daniel to arouse the patriotism and religious enthusiasm of the Jews to endure the cruelties of Antiochus Epiphanes, and to believe that He who had delivered their fathers from Egypt and from Captivity would also deliver them in the second century B.C. from a monstrous tyranny. Only the God of Daniel, *not his book*, could achieve their civil and religious emancipation. The personal agents in it were the sons of Mattathias.

The sages and seers of Israel ever found the means of having their deliverances reach those for whom they were uttered, whether in Palestine or the regions beyond. Already we have seen the affinity in language among the Semitic families, especially in the vicinity of Canaan. As late as Sennacherib and Hezekiah, Jerusalemites understood the Assyrian dialect. Trade and commerce made those people acquainted with each other's speech. Letters were conveyed to and commercial dealings had with many separated centres of civilization long before the establishment of the Persian posts. Nahum tells us how the merchants of Nineveh were multiplied above the stars of heaven (3 : 16). Ezekiel makes the traffickers a great multitude between Tyre and Bashan, Arvad, Lud and Phut, Tarshish and Meshech, Javan and Tubal, Togarmah and Dedan, Syria and Judah, Kedar and Arabia, Haran and Canneh, Asshur and Chilmad. They comprised every class of artisans, skilled workers, seamen and merchants, traders in precious metals, gems, rich fabrics, spices and gums for sacrifice ; far excelling in quality and variety the trade of our American colonies. Ezekiel's twenty-seventh chapter contains names not written in our modern bills of laden. Herodotus tells of the traffic in " Assyrian wares," which were carried *via* Phœnicia and sold to the Greeks. In his time trade flourished between Armenia and Babylon and Susiana, up and down the Euphrates and Tigris. Diodorus makes the cities on those rivers marts of commerce with Assyria, Media, and Paraetucéne. Thapsacus and Opis, Tadmor, Tyre and Joppa became centres of trade. Solomon built Tadmor as a grand depot and mart for traffic in gold, tin, ivory, lead, precious stones, cedar-wood, pearls, and engraved seals, for export and for tribute. The route from Elath to Jerusalem was *via* Babylon and Thapsacus. The treasures of Arabia and Africa, Egypt and India, were shipped on boats and on camels to Tadmor, Damascus, and the Holy Land, or to Tyre and Zidon. Tin was early brought from Cornwall, Wales, and the Scilly Isles, to be exchanged for the rich fabrics of Babylonia, and the tin was mixed with native copper for the production of "Assyrian bronze." So during the entire era of the writing-prophets ancient carrier-merchants could promptly convey any prophecy to the several points between the most Eastern and Western civilization. Wherever trade went the customs-officer followed, and prophetic voices readily penetrated. From Susa, east of the Tigris, to Sardis in Western Asia Minor, there was a good military and commercial road which occupied ninety days to travel, and was provided with stations some fifteen miles apart; and public hostelries had been established along it before Herodotus wrote. They are described as like the caravanseries of modern Persia, while the road they dotted formed the highway of travel for post and potentate between the Indian Ocean and the Ægean Sea. It was equally available to Phœnician merchants and Hebrew seers. (Layard's "Babylon and Nineveh," p. 429; Rawlinson's "Ancient Monarchy," vol. ii.)

Isaiah could transmit his messages to Babylon and Egypt, to Dumah and Damascus (chs. 17–21). Between Judea and Nineveh the route was better known and more frequented than in our day, so that it was as easy for Jonah to go and preach in the capital of Assyria as for a Bostonian to visit the capital of Texas in 1850. The servant of Jeremiah could as readily read what Jahveh had spoken concerning Babylon and its pending desolation in that famous city, as he could throw the roll on which it was written into the midst of Euphrates (Jer. 51 : 60-64 ; Ezek. 31 : 3-15). Early prophets of themselves could not foresee how corrupt and debased Assyrians would become. They were of the same Semitic family, and in the days of Isaiah were in the acme of their power and influence. He could not tell, except by revelation from God, that the Medes, who were then a rising nation, would overturn the dynasty of Sargon and Sennacherib in about a century after their invasion of Palestine. "In the argument from prophecy we have to do with a forest, not with a single bough or a basket of leaves ; with the whole trend of a coast, not with single headlands or inlets of the sea ; with a zone of constellations, not with a few scattered stars" ("Old Faiths in New Light," p. 248). And the stars of our prophetic zone illumine human history from the promise of Genesis to its perfect fulfilment. All critics admit the work of prophets from Samuel to Ezra ; prophets who wrote and who did not write their predictions. Elijah, with his one known letter to Jehoram, and Elisha of many messages ; Micaiah, who withstood the false prophets of Ahab as well as his sentence to bread of affliction and water of affliction, and whom Mr. H. Spencer misrepresents as advising that Jezebel-ruled king to war against Syria, when his advice was to the contrary, thus: "I saw all Israel scattered upon the mountains, as sheep that have no shepherd.... If thou return at all in peace, the Lord hath not spoken by me" (1 Kings 22 : 17, 28). The whole chapter is a refutation of Mr. Spencer. As well say that the prophetess Huldah predicted the continued prosperity of Jerusalem and its king, when she foretold what would befall it because of prevailing wickedness (2 Kings 22 : 14 ; 2 Chron. 34 : 22–28). We count the non-writing prophets as about twice the number of those who recorded their deliverances. Their order expounded special revelations. Israelites were watchful of new members, and asked with seeming surprise, Is Saul also among the prophets? Will he leave his paternal acres and the vocation of his fathers? Will he be yeoman, seer, or king? (1 Sam. 10 : 1–27.) Of the predictions from Enoch to Anna enough remains for our instruction ; more would doubtless have been preserved if needed for our edification or for preparing for the reign of the Lord. We have all that is necessary to occupy our minds and to interest our affections, and the Bible was not written to gratify our curiosity. We need not lament the loss of historical books which prophets incorporated into theirs.

It is said that *all voicings of seers were not* the revealing of new ideas and events. Jacob, when predicting the future prosperity of his sons, may have spoken from what he knew of their personal character, as well as by the inspiring Spirit of God. Thus his *pre*dictions were also *de*scriptions. He foresaw somewhat of the future by his knowledge of the past. He knew who were stern and self-willed among his boys ; who were strong for labor in the field, and who would bend under the burden of taxes ; who was of a commercial mind and required a harbor on the sea for his ships ; who would become a valiant warrior and chief in Israel ; who swift of foot, fruitful in tillage, producing royal dainties, even those of distant commerce ; who would speak goodly words of comfort and instruction ; who receive the ever-watchful protection of the Almighty Shepherd of Jacob. He foresaw that his beloved Benjamin would raven as a wolf, devouring the prey and dividing the spoil ; and that Judah would sway the sceptre in Israel and give a Saviour to the world. That 49th chapter of Genesis is masterful in prophetic discrimination, in parental and national ratiocination. Jacob was no dervish in dress or speech, but a true shepherd of his family, his final blessing disclosing the digested observations and thought of a father, the wisdom of a sage, and the illumination of an inspired seer. But he was not a legislator like Moses, nor a preacher of a new religion ; rather he accepted as true what he inherited, and to that he added the revelations made to him at Bethel, at Mahanaim, at Peniel. And when he stood before Pharaoh, in his one hundred and thirtieth year, blessing him in the name of the God of his fathers, he evidently made a deep impression on that monarch, who commanded Joseph to give him the best of the lands in the district of Rameses. There was no obsequiousness in his manner, for he was sustained by Him who had sustained his fathers, and had fed him to that day (Gen. 48 : 15 ; 47 : 11, Revised Version).

We can only note the repeated mention of the

"Lord God" of Abraham by Jacob and all later patriarchs to Moses; yet Wellhausen says that Amos is the first writer who thus names Him (4 : 6–11 ; 6 : 8). In Exodus 3 and Genesis 15 the twofold name is also used, Jehovah God ; read also Hosea 12 : 2–6, showing that the expression is as ancient as the thought, and the thought as old as Abraham.

The prophets have been happily styled "the Swiss Guards of the true religion," who stood in no fear of kings or of people. Witness Samuel reproving Saul; Nathan, Gad, and Iddo reproving David and Solomon. Ahijah was a thorn in the side of the Wise King, and Shemaiah restrained the avenging wrath of Rehoboam (1 Kings 11 : 29–40 ; 12 : 22–24). A man of God out of Judah rebuked Jeroboam and proclaimed the destruction of his false altar. The rest of that chapter treats of the same old man of God, who was induced to turn aside from his duty, and for his disobedience was slain by a lion. But his word against the altar was fulfilled. The king presumed to make for his groves and asherahs in high places priests who were *not* of the tribe of Levi, thus completing the apostasy of his reign (1 Kings 13 : 1–34). Jehu, the son of Hanani, reproved King Baasha for walking in the ways of Jeroboam (16 : 2). Again, the Spirit of the Lord moved Azariah, the son of Obed, to a memorable interview with Asa of Judah and Benjamin, because they had long neglected the worship of the true God ; were without a teaching priest, and without observed law. When the king heard Obed, the prophet, he put away the abominations copied from Ephraim, renewed the altar of the Lord, and summoned all the people to Jerusalem to a great sacrifice to Jehovah; which was only a restoration of the old way of worship (1 Kings 15 : 11-15 ; 2 Chron. 15 : 1-16), and clearly indicated that the prophets did not yield to the ruling party when in error.

The non-writing prophets have left enough recorded by others of what they said and did to show how they met the needs of the times ; how their admonitions and remonstrances were suited to the cases before them, the presumption of Saul, the lust of David, the heavy hand of Solomon, the avenging spirit of Rehoboam, the calf-worship of Jeroboam and Baasha, the neglect of Asa, and the persistent Baalism of Ahab-Jezebel. The tragedy at Carmel was the climax of Elijah's zeal and determination to destroy idolatry. The extirpation of it was by a baptism of blood ; it was the slaughter of four hundred and fifty of Baal's prophets and of Ahab's seventy sons. The apostasy called for just such a character as the Tishbite, and just such an avenger as Jehu. Apostasy from Jahveh required heroic treatment and correction. The calves at Dan and Bethel did not exclude the worship of Jahveh, but the new Baalism of Samaria did, and hence the onslaught of Elijah was quite justified. He was prophet, priest, and statesman for the time ; was commissioned to appoint Hazael king over Syria, and Elisha as his own successor ; thus blending the ordinary functions of his prophetic office with priestly and political duty. Thus the vast importance of his work made his memory ever dear to Israelites, and he was thought to have reappeared in John Baptist.

Why Elijah and other prophets of the ninth and

tenth century B.C. did not write their predictions, Wellhausen explains by saying, "They were *not* literary; that a large part of Israel's early history has been preserved to us in the Books of Judges, Samuel, and Kings; in collections of the laws and decisions of contemporary priests, as Exodus 21, 22, which were committed to writing. Somewhat later, perhaps, the legends of the patriarchs and primitive times; that between the early prophets and Amos a non-literary developed into a literary age!" This is given in the "Encyclopædia Britannica," and reprinted with a "Prolegomena" several times its length, retailed at four dollars a copy! But the author asks the reader to compare the progress made by Isaiah in chapters 15, 16, and his orations. Doing this we find those two chapters contain an unvarnished prophecy against *Moab*, the long-time enemy of Isaiah's country, which are as explicit as language could make them. A rhetorical setting would have been out of character, whatever the ability of the prophet. If Jahveh had a word against Moab by a Jew, He would not spoil it by fine writing. This is the explanation of the style? That learned men put forth such criticisms is a marvel. Confessedly, when Samuel, Nathan, Micaiah, or Elijah had anything to say to the kings and men of their generation they said it in clear, terse, and forceful language, and so suitable as not to be improved. Nor is Elijah wanting in rhetorical power and literary skill. As reported in 1 Kings 17, 18, 19, Elijah indeed is unsurpassed by Amos. The reader may easily compare the two. We must not forget that the earlier prophet lived near the age of Solomon, when literature did flourish, when the temple ritual was largely enriched, and that comparative peace favored literary art; that in the first half of the ninth century B.C. Jehu revolutionized the government and Baalism of Samaria; that the armies now of Syria and now of Assyria kept the country in commotion, and a century later Shalmaneser and Sargon carried tens of thousands of Israelites beyond the Euphrates. So the era of Amos was no more favorable to literary growth than that of Elijah. Indeed, less so, if we may judge those times by other countries. Ordinarily, an era of revolutions is preceded by discussions, as in the Greece of Demosthenes, in the England of Cromwell, in France before the Revolution. So it was in Israel. Jacob was warned, exhorted, threatened; Elijah and his compeers were now here, now there with their prophetic thunders, which they voiced in tones of alarm, accompanied with impressive gestures. One letter was written to the King of Jerusalem, but the direct mission of the prophet of fire was with Israel, and his message oral and repeatedly spoken, not written as history, but spoken to those whom it concerned.

This is the reason why those prophets did not write their messages: they were for the men of their day then in Israel, not for posterity, not for distant nations, but for living men and rulers; thus: " Go, show thyself unto Ahab;" and " As Jehovah liveth, before whom I stand, I will surely show myself unto Ahab to-day!" It is masterful in its setting, this eighteenth of 1 Kings, and strong against the charge of a new literary age as against a new evolution of the Hebrew religion. Jahveh's apostates must renounce their apostasy and return to Jahveh; His altars must be repaired; His worship re-established; His enemies be put down and extirpated. Jehu of Nimshi, Hazael of Syria, Elisha, son of Shaphat, even Mesha of Moab, and Assyrian kings, are agents in the clearance. Work of that sort is never done by letter, but by terrible words, and sword in hand. Thus Baalism was extirpated from Israel, and to that extent the reformation was effectual; but for " state reasons" Jehu failed to abolish the calves of Dan and Bethel. They were reserved for the Assyrians to carry away. (See Chapter X. of this work for other corrections of critical writers of this period.)

Again, Wellhausen says, " that the Torah was at first small, but grew by additions, counsels of priests, ethical maxims, etc., of which there was a common stock—there were moral intuitions and convictions" (" Encyclopædia Britannica," Art. " Israel," p. 409*b*). That is, in Israel there existed what we call an *unwritten law*, some of which was gradually incorporated into the written code. Elijah complained that he was left alone of Jehovah's followers, and Jeremiah lamented the mourning of Zion, because none came to her solemn feasts (Lam. 1 : 4). Jehovah's altars were broken down and His written Laws despised.

After all the analysis of Kuenen, the history of Renan and of Wellhausen, I can see no sufficient reason for not insisting upon a well-known code of law and of ritual *before* Elijah the prophet, for Israel and for Judah. Moses and Samuel were legislators and organizers, and their successors in the tenth, the ninth, and the eighth century B.C., were reformers who sought to restore the old ways and bring their people back from the calf-worship into which they had fallen to the worship of Jahveh. Hosea would remove even the name of Baal, the moon-feasts and desecrated Sabbaths from Israel. He exhorts to *return* unto Jahveh and His Law; else the calf of Samaria shall be broken in pieces; for the great things of the Law had been written for him. Ten thousand precepts were counted a strange thing. Only in the Lord was there help for Jacob, therefore should he return from his backslidings to the covenant which he had transgressed (Hosea 2 : 11, 17 ; 6 : 1, 7 ; 8 : 1, 6, 12, 14 ; 13 : 9 ; 14 : 1, 4). Isaiah also speaks of the ways and paths of Zion, of the law and the word of Jahveh, to which the people were to be willing and obedient. To the law and to the testimony they were to appeal for judgment of the true as against the false (1 : 2–19 ; 2 : 3 ; 6 : 9–11 ; 8 : 20). It is teaching based upon previously existing and acknowledged law, and otherwise has little force or meaning. Obedience to a standard was enjoined and required by prophets of Israel and prophets of Judah.

A prophet is authority for saying, that Jahveh gave laws which were not the best possible but the best practicable at the time (Ezek. 20 : 25). Some precepts of life, rules of procedure, details of ritual in the temple worship, and maxims of conduct between the nations are of later date than the legislation of Moses and the reorganization under Samuel; and are adapted to the period of the temple and the disruption of the kingdoms. But it is impossible that a prophet like Samuel for Saul and Elijah for Ahab could have done as they did without the existence of a recognized law for king and for people. A standard of law and of duty must have been known in Israel and some ritual for worship, or they could not have been expounded and enforced. Kings are not wont to listen to a preacher who has no authority to preach, and no text to explain. The recognition of duty to God or man arose from some existing law of God or man. This is as evident in the utterances of the earliest prophets as in the latest, in the rebukes of Nathan as of Elijah, in Jehu the son of Hanani and in Huldah the prophetess. They all reproved for the violation of some known law, or enjoined some acknowledged duty, or sought to reform and correct abuses which had grown up in Judah or in Ephraim.

Moreover, it should be remembered that *a rule* of right living and of worship was recognized in Assyria and Babylonia, in Egypt and Phœnicia, in Edom and Moab. They were not, indeed, expected to worship the God of Israel, but to worship the God whom they acknowledged and in the approved forms. This is what Jonah and Nahum, Isaiah and Jeremiah taught. The Gentiles should live righteously and worship in sincerity. But a Hebrew dare not bow down to any other than Jahveh God of Israel. (Compare Jonah, chs. 3, 4; Nahum 1-3; Isa. 12 to 23; Jer. 47-52.) Jehovah would take of the nations priests and Levites to minister unto Him (Isa. 66: 21), and all flesh shall worship before Him (verse 23). It is part of Isaiah's prophecies which Kuenen claims to have been written before 500 B.C. It speaks of the Jerusalem temple as burned and desolate, but whose restoration should be a joy and a rejoicing (65 : 19). In chapter 30 : 9, 10, the prophet rebukes Jerusalem for her rebellion in not hearing the law or teaching of Jehovah; "Which say to the seers, See not; and to the prophets, Prophesy not unto us right things, speak unto us smooth things, prophesy deceits." It is very evident that they knew the right way and what the right teaching should be. Amos 3 : 1, 2 is quoted as showing that God delivered Israel from Egypt, and *covenanted* with him, not because he was better than others, but because He loved him; therefore should Jacob fear Him (6 : 2-8; 1 : 3-15; 2 : 4-16; 9 : 7-15). (Compare Isaiah 7 : 5-17; 4 : 2-6.) These imply a *law* of Jahveh and loyalty to it and Him. It matters little how that law and ritual compared with the liturgy of Egypt and Babylon, nor even how much of them was copied from others. The fact of supreme importance is that to Abraham and to Moses God gave a law of life and a law of worship—*i.e.*, a theology and a liturgy, brief and explicit. Every instructed Hebrew knew what to believe about God and how to worship Him acceptably; that He was not only God of Israel, but also God of all nations. In this especially is seen the Divine element of the Pentateuch. It has a God for all mankind, not a local Deity for Jacob alone, but also for Japheth and the enemies of Israel (Deut. 23 : 3-8). We have this illustrated in the prophetic messages for distant nations and to the isles of the sea; in the kings who acknowledged Daniel's God to be God of gods, Lord of kings, a Revealer of secrets (Dan. 2 : 47), to whom Nebuchadnezzar gave praise and honor (4 : 37). The decree of Darius was "that in every dominion of his kingdom men tremble and fear before the God of Daniel ; for He is the living God, and His kingdom shall not be destroyed (ch. 6 : 26). By Cyrus also He is recognized as the LORD God of heaven (Ezra 1 : 2) ; by Darius as the God of heaven (ch. 6 : 2-12) ; by Artaxerxes Ezra is designated the priest and scribe of the law of the God of heaven (7 : 21-26). Even Alexander the Great acknowledged Him in Jerusalem. From Melchizedek and Abraham in the twentieth century B.C. to the Ptolemy who erected a temple to Jehovah in Egypt in the second century B.C., He was acknowledged as God of all nations of men ; by Assyrians in the time of Jonah, by later Babylonians and Persians, by the men of Hamath and of Egypt, by Jews in Palestine and in the centres of trade and commerce from the Persian Gulf to Damascus and Joppa. Pythagoras visited Babylon, and probably became acquainted with some leading men of the captivity, and held conversation with Daniel the prophet. However that may be, some of the reported teachings of Pythagoras bear a striking likeness to Hebrew theology—viz., the unity and purity of God, as taught in that era, and the importance of music and of silence in the religious life (Ps. 4 : 4 ; 32 : 3 ; Isa. 41 : 1 ; 46 : 10 ; Zech. 2 : 13 ; Hab. 2 : 20 ; Zeph. 1 : 7). That Jewish bank in Babylon looks like a fulfilment of Deuteronomy 28 : 12 and 15 : 6, where it is said that Jacob " should lend unto many nations, and should not borrow, as he borrowed," from necessity upon leaving the house of bondage (Ex. 12 : 35). It is difficult to show that those verses are of later origin than the Babylonian house. Or

would we necessitate two miracles in history rather than
accept one inspired prophecy ? Exodus 12 says how
they borrowed ; Deuteronomy in two places says that
Jacob should become a " lender to others ;" George
Smith in 1874 bought certain terra-cotta jars at Bagdad
full of tablets, and now translators say they describe
the business of a firm of exchange while Hebrews
were captives in Babylon ! Those verses of Exodus
and Deuteronomy were not late additions suggested
for the glorification of a banking firm ; but they seem
to perforate the " later origin" theory, till it cannot
hold together. A Divine element runs all through
the Old Testament. Inspiration, like an endless or
continuous chain, connects and guards all the several
links and books of Scripture, and whichever one you
strike, it is sure to return a celestial sound, even
though we occasionally must wait for the echo.

Some recent criticism claims that there were two
authors of the Book of Isaiah, one who wrote the first
forty chapters, and another, who, however, died before 500 B.C., and wrote the last *twenty-seven* chapters. This affects the inspiration of certain matters,
which, being accomplished facts, needed not to be revealed, yet in those chapters are many things which
imply inspiration. But passing this, it is important to
inquire about the relation of the " Great Unknown,"
as the later Isaiah is styled, to the Pentateuch. Turn,
then, to Isaiah 49 : 2 ; 51 : 16 ; Exodus 33 : 22,
where the sentiment of each passage is very similar :
Exodus, " I will cover thee with my hand ;" Isaiah,
" In the shadow of His hand hath He hid me ;" and
" I have covered thee in the shadow of mine hand."

Any modern writer following another in using such striking expressions would be said to have imitated or borrowed from the older author. This is precisely what the Isaiah writer did. He copied from a well-known work, as familiar to his Hebrew brethren as to us to-day; but, says Kuenen, he was in his grave before 500 B.C., which is doubtless true; how, then, if Ezra largely re-wrote and revised the Pentateuch fifty years later, did he get this expression from the Great Unknown, who was a captive somewhere in the northern empire? The expression was as ancient as Exodus, well known to the second Isaiah who, however, was not, as the ancient Exodus was well known to Ezra. Works must have been well authenticated to be acknowledged by those who returned from captivity. Add this to the points already stated, and the reasons for an ancient Exodus and Deuteronomy—*i.e.*, *ancient* for readers of the sixth century B.C., cannot be evaded. Compare the creation account in Genesis with Isaiah 40 : 28, "The Lord is an everlasting God, the Creator of the ends of the earth;" and the calling of Abraham with 41 : 8, "Jacob whom I have chosen, the seed of Abraham my friend." Then "Jahveh magnifies the law, or makes the teaching great and glorious (42 : 21). I am the Lord, your Holy One, the Creator of Israel, your King" (43 : 15), and to chapter 45, showing how the author was permeated with the spirit and matter of Deuteronomy. In the later Isaiah and in Jeremiah there is so much that clearly echoes the Pentateuch, that it is impossible for one who has no theory to sustain not to see the relation and dependence of these prophets upon that

teaching. It is also a significant fact that the life of
Jeremiah was saved because of the agreement of some
of his utterances with those of previous prophets,
probably Micah a century before Jeremiah. But the
exhortations and predictions they delivered were in
complete accord with the existence of an ancient Pentateuch (Jer. 26 : 4–24) : " Walk in my law. Hear ye
the words of this covenant ; Obey my voice" (Jer. 11 :
2, 6). The people were rebellious, had wandered from
God, and were exhorted to return to Him in loyal
obedience. All this implies covenant, law, duty,
which had long been recognized. Jehovah never
punished for violation of laws which did not exist, and
which were not understood as obligatory. Neither
Israel nor Judah could plead the baby act—viz., ignorance of the law and covenant they had transgressed,
and of which prophets had so often warned them.
Upon their return from exile, Nehemiah (8 : 2–9) read
to the assembly and translated into the vernacular from
the Book of the Law of God. The word " translated
or interpreted " implies that during their captivity
their language had become changed. Compare Ezra
3 : 1–7, and remember that there were those present
who could compare what they then heard and saw with
what they had heard and seen long years before.
Isaiah had predicted that kings should be their nursing
fathers, and the isles should wait upon Jahveh, their
Deliverer (49 : 1 ; 60 : 9, 10 ; Jer. 33 : 7–26) ; and
in Ezra 6th, 7th, Nehemiah 8th, 9th ; 10 : 28 to
11 : 2, are the proofs how Cyrus, Darius, and Artaxerxes, became nursing fathers and supporters of the
Jews in rebuilding their temple, and in re-establishing
the worship of Jehovah in it.

To suppose that Ezra originated the detailed legislation of Jacob is as unhistoric as to suppose that Sargon II. created the legislation and ritual of Assyria, or that Sargon I. created the legislation and ritual of Babylonia and Accad, or that Rameses created that of Egypt, or that Solon created that of Greece, or that Edward III. created that of England. These all enlarged and improved what already existed. So the non-writing prophets of Israel did *not prepare for a law*, but enforced and applied acknowledged principles of conduct both toward God and man; principles which had long been acted upon in Israel before they arose to enforce them.

In no civilized country do we find a code of laws embodied and detailed in its literature before its existence as a legislation. Rather, laws are tabulated and enacted before they are expounded and enforced upon the nation's observance. Israel is no exception to this fact of universal history. Rules of life and conduct gave tone to a literature in which they were early incorporated.

We see no contradiction between the "mercy and not sacrifice" of Hosea 6:6 and the teaching of Ezra, for Hosea addressed an apostate people, who sacrificed to idols, at the shrines of Dan and Bethel and in chapels of Baal, which were offensive to Jahveh, and therefore rebuked. Moses and Samuel could not restore Jehovah's favor to them. Ezra, on the contrary, sought to guard his people from such sin, and to tone them up to the loyal service of God and His worship. As in Deuteronomy 10:12; 13:3; 30:16, he taught a principle which reached to the depth of all love and sacrifice. Kuenen overlooked this in his criticism, and also the teaching of Malachi, than whose writing nothing in Hosea is more spiritual, nothing in Ezra more exacting. The margin of the Revised Version reads "kindness" for mercy. In either case Ezra is right and Kuenen wrong. But he rightly says that "the pressure of Herod's rule no less than that of the Romans revived and strengthened Messianic expectations in post-exilian Israel. There was a dominant conviction that the subjection of God's people to the heathen was an anomaly that could not long last. Hence the spirit of *Proselytism* earnestly manifested itself, which induced many Greeks to submit to Jewish laws" ("Hibbert Lectures," English edition, p. 222; St. Matt. 23 : 15). After so much suffering and exile, it is no wonder that later Jews became narrow, strict in attention to details, and limited in their national sympathies. Their law, their literature, their worship, all spoke to them of *Jacob's* God as for them. They knew that the vital matters in Exodus 34—viz., the preparing of a second set of law tables which replaced the first that Moses had broken, the grand theophany described in verses 5-9, the appointment of annual assemblies and festivals, the consecration of the first-born, the long fast of their leader, and the transfiguration of his countenance—were all for them, and were not the fabrications of a later age.

IX.

JACOB'S PROPHETS SERVE JAPHETH'S KINGS: A LIGHT TO LIGHTEN THE GENTILES.

"The letters of the Hebrew books," says Renan, "are not many, but they are letters of fire. Its language does not say much, but what it says is beaten out upon an anvil. It pours out floods of anger, and utters cries of rage against the abuses of the world, calling the four winds of heaven to assault the citadels of evil. Like the jubilee horn of the sanctuary, it will be put to no profane use, but it will sound the note of holy war against injustice, and the call to great assemblies; it will have accents of rejoicing and accents of terror; it will become the clarion of the new law in Christianity and the trumpet of judgment" ("Hist. People of Israel," vol. i., p. 86). Her reforming prophets were the forces which swept the world before them, now by ministry in Samaria and Jerusalem, now in Nineveh, in Babylon, in Egypt, and in Moab.

1. Jonah, the dove, was son of Amittai of Gath-hepher, and was probably one of Elisha's guild, the young man sent to anoint Jehu, the son of Nimshi, to "smite the house of Ahab, and avenge the blood of Jehovah's servants at the hand of Jezebel" (2 Kings

9 : 1–10). He also uttered a prophecy which was accomplished by Jeroboam II. (2 Kings 14 : 25). I place him in the reign of Assur-natsir-pal, 883–858 B.C., who made the name of Assyria terrible to the nations, and whom Professor Sayce calls "the most brutal of her kings." It was probably while Assur-natsir-pal ruled Assyria that Jonah visited Nineveh and delivered his message. How it astonished that people to hear the prophet, as he walked their streets and high walls compassing the city, crying: "Yet forty days, and Nineveh shall be overthrown!" From king to child the people humbled themselves, fasted, prayed, put on sackcloth, and besought God to turn away His fierce anger, that they should not perish. And God saw that they turned from their evil way, and deferred the threatened punishment. The walls of Nineveh were nine miles around it, enclosing a population of half a million persons, one fifth of whom were young and ignorant. No wonder that God sent His prophet to lighten those Gentiles (St. Matt. 12 : 40 ; Acts 13 : 46, 47). Our Lord's reference to Jonah certifies his historic character, for He would not compare Himself and His resurrection to a fabulous person. Kalisch treats the prophet as actually historical, whose personality and work need not be misunderstood. His book is composed of three acts of one Divine drama, each complete in itself, and all illustrating the goodness of God to the Gentiles.

If the reigning monarch was Assur-natsir-pal, one of the most cruel kings, his repentance is the more remarkable. We like to think of such a tyrant being humbled and reformed. That text and sermon all in one sentence struck the conscience and bore fruit. It caused the doom of sin to be postponed, but only postponed, for a new generation which adorned the prophet's tomb, forgot his preaching. Yet the city flourished till 606 B.C., when it fell by the conquering Medes. Its ruins are as famous as its former renown. They were seen by Xenophon and his retreating Greeks two hundred years later. Jonah's tomb is still shown near them, and in its dilapidation is said to cover forty acres. The ruins are estimated to contain six and a half millions of tons of débris. Many are the historic marks of this historic prophet and his mission to Nineveh. Mere difference in dates does not change the facts, and these clearly disprove Renan's statement, that "Jahveh showed Himself simply as *Unser Gott*, local, national, and tribal, partial and ferocious, a political slaughterer, *per fas et nefas!*" In such criticism Renan lets his zeal for a theory become fanatical and grotesque. It overrides his judgment and the truth of history. God ever discloses Himself as ready to bless mankind, *not* as partial and jealous in a bad sense, hating the rest of the world, except the chosen in Abraham, but seeking to save men from sin and Satan, and by the laws of eternal righteousness. In illustration of this endeavor, we pass on to consider,

2. The author of the latter portion of Isaiah. I have no theory or preference for *two* writers of the book. Some words in the present tense speak of Jerusalem and the temple as being a wilderness and burned up with fire (64 : 10, 11); that the sanctuary is profaned, and Jacob given to the curse (43 : 28); that the sons of strangers shall build thy walls, and

their kings shall minister unto thee (60 : 10); and the call to arise, shake off the dust and loose the bands of captivity (52 : 2, 3), all which may have been written between 586 B.C., and the reign of Cyrus in Babylon, 538 B.C. But to make the predictions touching Cyrus *history* and *not* prophecy is to force a meaning upon them quite foreign to the letter: "Thus saith the LORD to His anointed, to Cyrus, whose right hand I have holden, to subdue nations before him, and I will loose the loins of kings; to open the doors before him, and the gates shall not be shut; I will go before thee, and make the rugged places plain; I will break in pieces the doors of brass, and cut in sunder the bars of iron: and I will give thee the treasures of darkness, and hidden riches of secret places, that thou mayest know that I am the LORD, which call thee by thy name, even the God of Israel" (Isa. 45 : 1–3). For the same reasons that we accept the then present desolations of the holy city do we insist that these verses were written before the capture of Babylon in 538. Truth demands consistency. The prophet at once encourages Cyrus and exhorts Israel. She was yet to be delivered from captivity; Cyrus was yet to take Babylon. Neither was then done. Hence, we must add *thirty-eight* years to Kuenen's date, and say, those prophecies were probably uttered before 540 B.C., and whether the writer ever saw Cyrus or not, he served him as a noble king of Japheth, for whom Jahveh had a special work; and who became a nursing father of Jacob's children.

Moreover, this prophet not only serves Cyrus, he also calls upon the islands and the peoples to renew their strength, and to consider the wonders which Jehovah was about to perform; the LORD, the first and the last, was He (Is. 41 : 1–5). A Saviour and a righteous worker or Judge shall be given as a light for the Gentiles and a covenant of the people (42 : 1, 6). Saith Jahveh : Egypt, Ethiopia, Sabeans, men of stature, shall come and confess that God is in thee, and there is no other. But the God of Israel, the Saviour, who had hidden Himself, should now be known and acknowledged by all the ends of the earth, who were invited to look to Him (45 : 14–22). Mark verse 23 : "By myself have I sworn, the word is gone forth from my mouth in righteousness, and shall not return, that unto Me *every knee shall bow, every tongue shall swear.*" It evidently includes the people of Japheth as well as of Jacob.

Then Babylon is exhorted to humiliation and repentance. "Hear now this—two things shall come upon thee in one day, the loss of children and widowhood." From the context we may infer that "widowhood" included the loss of sovereignty or kingship and the loss or purification of their religion, of their astrologers, sorcerers, and prognosticators (Is. 47 : 1, 8–13). As history certifies, the Persian conquest of Babylon led to the reformation of its religion, and the successor of Cyrus was an iconoclast. The images were broken to pieces. Jacob was avenged in Babylon, and delivered from it, with the restoration of his sacred things (Ezra 1 : 1–11 ; Isa. 48 : 20). In chapter 49 : 1, 22, 23, 26, "the people of the isles, the Gentiles from far are to bring Israel's sons in their arms, and his daughters upon their shoulders ; kings are to be nursing fathers, and their queens nursing mothers to them; they shall bow down to the earth, and all flesh shall know that I the LORD, am thy Saviour and thy Redeemer." (Compare Is. 60 : 3–16.) Again, "Behold, the LORD hath proclaimed unto the end of the earth, Say ye to the daughter of Zion, Behold, thy salvation cometh; behold, his reward is with him, and his recompense before him" (62 : 11). Even "the isles afar off shall declare my glory among the nations. And of them also will I take for priests and for Levites, saith the Lord" (66 : 19–21).

"The author," says Dr. Briggs, "stands on the loftiest peak of prophecy. He masses more Messianic predictions in his book than any who preceded him; carries the Messianic idea to a much higher stage of development, and becomes the evangelical prophet, the nearest to the Messiah and the theology of the New Covenant" (p. 337). But the striking fact which emphasizes God's providence for mankind, is that a prophet of the captivity should be enabled to rise above his surroundings, and by inspiration utter such strong, comforting words to his brethren, and such sacred truths to the Gentiles, at once making known the power and grace of the LORD in the restoration of His people to Judea, and also in setting Him forth as the God and Saviour of the nations. The isles shall wait upon Him; all flesh shall worship Him. We have nothing preserved to us of prophets of the ninth century, which is superior to this of all who uttered Messianic predictions. They were Reformers of their age, as Amos, Hosea, Micah were reforming prophets for the eighth century, and their voice went out in preparation for the Redeemer of Jacob and of Japheth.

3. Micah, the Morasthite, flourished in the days of king Hezekiah and others, between 750 and 700 B.C. His earliest utterance was not before 757, nor his latest after 697; and he was probably thirty years old when he began to prophecy. His work is undoubted by critics, and his era fixed. Yet he prophesied that the Assyrian should come into Israel, and tread in her palaces, but the land of Assyria should be wasted with the sword, and the land of Nimrod (5 : 5, 6). It is a prophecy of the most demonstrable kind, a making known of what was to come to pass. But we are concerned with this prophet as Messianic, and as the one whose deliverances saved the life of Jeremiah a century later. Both uttered their oracles against Jerusalem, and when the enemies of Jeremiah said that he ought to die for his unpatriotic prediction, his friends replied that Micah in the days of Hezekiah had also declared that Zion should be ploughed as a field, Jerusalem become heaps, and the mountain of the house the high places of a forest (Micah 3 : 12; Jer. 26 : 4–19). This precedent of bold truth-telling saved Jeremiah's life at that time. It connects together those two prophets, who thus authenticate each other. Jeremiah predicted that " seventy years should be accomplished at Babylon" (ch. 29 : 10; 25 : 12-14); he repeats the threatening and deportation in chapters 21 and 22, and declares the destruction of those who carried them captive and the deliverance of Israel in chapters 51 and 52. Those prophecies were studied by Daniel, who is also authenticated and com-

mended by Ezekiel (14 : 14, 20) ; he asks the prince of Tyre, whose pride had inflated him as though he were a god, " Art thou wiser than Daniel ?" (28 : 3). These references are enough to show that oracles spoken in Judea were known at Nineveh and Babylon, that Micah and Jeremiah, Ezekiel and Daniel, testified of each other and foretold future events.

Moreover, if there were two Isaiahs, the second of them wrote while captive in Assyria, and, like other Exile prophets, was acquainted with the cuneiform writing. Hence it is not too much to expect that a cuneiform second Isaiah, if there ever was one, a cuneiform Ezekiel, and a cuneiform Daniel, in sets of tablets preserved in terra-cotta jars, may be found, and satisfy all inquirers. Already such a "find" has silenced forever those who doubted Isaiah's correctness touching Sargon of Assyria. His inscriptions have illustrated the prophet who for two thousand years preserved his name in human memory. A similar "find" is probable, which shall illustrate the prophets of the Exile.

4. Even from his birth Jeremiah was called to be a prophet, and began his work in the thirteenth year of King Josiah, who had already commenced his reformation of religion in Judah. This prophet and this king were contemporaries during eighteen years. What the continued life of Josiah for twenty or thirty years longer, with such an adviser, would have effected we cannot say. But his premature death in his thirty-ninth year left the sinners in Zion and the enemies of Jeremiah free to plot against and persecute him. He suffered much from well-to-do Jews, because he re-

buked them for their wickedness and predicted the destruction of their temple and city by the Chaldeans. But he also prophesied against Babylon, and when a captive in the Nile land raised his voice against Egypt. By keeping the names distinctly before us, we shall find this gentle and lone man of God as true as steel in denouncing all unrighteousness; now prophesying against Jerusalemites and their wicked rulers, now against Babylonians, Egyptians, and Ethiopians, now against Philistia, Moab, and Ammon, now against Edom and Damascus, Kedar and Hazor and Elam; even as God overthrew Sodom and Gomorrah, they shall be overthrown by the Medes and northern nations. The last dated utterance of Jeremiah is in chapter 44, about 570 B.C., and while yet a captive at Tahpanhes. If born in 629, he was only about sixty years old when he ceased his prophetic mission. He had for sixteen years survived the destruction of Jerusalem, when he died in the land wherein Jacob was a stranger. Yet he was as confident of his country's restoration as of her punishment, and sent his servant to purchase the field at Anathoth, a town of Benjamin, of his nephew Hanameel; and the purchase was duly certified to, and the money paid before witnesses, according to the law and custom of the place (Jer. 32 : 1–25). This chapter of Jeremiah is at once a judgment and a promise, a threat and an encouragement: "Men shall buy fields for money, and subscribe deeds, and seal them, and call witnesses, in Benjamin, in Jerusalem, and in the cities of Judah, in the hill country, in the lowlands, and in the south; for *I will cause their captivity to return*, saith the LORD" (verse 44). This assurance prompted Daniel in Babylon, in the first year of Darius the Mede, to look for the end of the captivity of Judah—viz., the seventy years which had been appointed (Dan. 9 : 1, 2). In Ezra's first chapter we read how Cyrus issued an imperial decree for all the Jews of his dominions to return to their native land; for, saith he, "The LORD God of heaven hath charged me to build Him a house at Jerusalem in Judah" (verse 2). All the sacred vessels which Nebuchadnezzar had taken away were to be restored to the new temple, with the captives from Babylon (verses 7, 11). Such is the evidence of the genuineness and credibility of Jeremiah's book that it has been universally received as authentic. Some confusion exists in the present arrangement of the different predictions. Emphatic is his word against false prophets in Jerusalem and in Babylon (chs. 23, 28, 29).

5. Next in order of the exilo-prophets is Ezekiel, who was early carried captive into the region of Chebar, or Nahr Malcha, the royal canal upon which Nebuchadnezzar employed vast numbers of those whom he had forced away from their homes. It ran from the Euphrates at Sippara to a lake near Borsippa, and irrigated the adjacent lands—so Rawlinson; but, according to others, from Sippara *to Cuthah*, which is mentioned among the places from which the king of Assyria carried those whom he located in Samaria (2 Kings 17 : 6, 24), which means an exchange of the inhabitants of those cities, Cuthah being among them. The Chebar of Ezekiel can hardly be the Chaboras which enters the Euphrates two hundred miles north of Babylon. Cuthah seems to have been an old town

with fixed traditions, and so a safe place for Hebrew captives. To such a place Ezekiel, with many others, was taken, the king, nobles, priests, and well-to-do persons being of the number. Hence it appears that he was of high respectability; he married, lived in his own house, in a colony of fellow-exiles. Suddenly, however, his wife died (Eze. 1 : 1 ; 3 : 15, 24 ; 8 : 1 ; 24 : 18). He began his prophecy in the thirtieth year of his age, or of the reigning dynasty, B.C. 597, and eleven years before Jerusalem was destroyed. His last deliverance is dated in the twenty-seventh year of his exile, or 570 B.C. (Eze. 29 : 17–20). He predicts that Egypt shall be given to Nebuchadnezzar, a reward for his services against Tyre, and that soon after the house of Israel should bud forth in the midst of them. Sometimes his fellow-exiles were offended at his plain speaking against them, and for his reproving words while in banishment; but the LORD said: "Speak my words unto them, whether they will hear, or forbear" (2 : 1–8). Later they held him in high esteem, and the rulers visited him in his house (14 : 1–14 ; 20 : 1–4). From chapter 4 : 1 it is evident that Ezekiel understood cuneiform writing, and that he may have written some of his oracles in cuneiform character for the use of Babylonian Jews and natives. Indeed, he was commanded to portray upon one of the writing bricks the city Jerusalem as besieged, with embankments and battering rams placed around it. Even if this was in any one of the first eleven years he was a captive and before the ruin of his city, it was a revelation to his fellows of what was about to happen at Jerusalem (24 : 1–21). There were no newspapers in those days, and so, though living near the capital of the empire, he and they might be as ignorant of transpiring events in Judea as we are of occurrences in Alaska. And if it was Sippara or Sepharvaim which gave name to his district, that was noted as an old literary centre. Many are the reasons why prophets of the Exile should write the cuneiform style, even as the disciples of our Lord wrote in Greek. Hence the reasonableness of discoveries of tablets in Babylonia of prophets of the captivity. By comparing chapter 8 : 18 with Micah 3 : 4 and Zechariah 7 : 13 one observes the close agreement in the thought and expression of each writer. So also in Ezekiel 8 : 2-4 ; Daniel 7 : 9, 10 ; Habakkuk 3 : 3-6, we have similar descriptions of the God of heaven, of the Ancient of days, of the glory and brightness of Him before whom the mountains were scattered and the hills did bow. Clearly they are not accidental coincidences, but designed, and evidencing an inspired authorship. The denunciations of Ezekiel against Judah are all the more striking when we reflect that they were made in exile and to exiles, and sent from them to Jerusalem. Compare those beginning at chapter 16 and continued to chapter 25. He has a word against Ammon and Moab, Edom and Philistia ; in chapters 26–28 against Tyre and Zidon. In chapter 29 he prophesies against Egypt, and continues his description of her desolations by Babylon in chapter 30 ; while in chapters 31 and 32 he proclaims against Babylon herself, which shall fall by the sword of the mighty. Then he returns to lament Israel, Egypt, and Edom. But as dry bones may be reclothed and made to live by the breath of

God, so shall Jacob, His chosen, be restored by the Spirit and power of Jehovah (37 : 1–12); in verses 13–28 the everlasting covenant shall be renewed and the sanctuary forever established, and the nations shall know that He is the Lord. Chapter 38 foretells the war of Gog and Magog, in which many Gentile nations shall be involved, and they shall know that God is the Lord. Thus Ezekiel discloses many things for Jacob and for Japheth. God will set His glory among the nations (39 : 21). The prophet of doom becomes a prophet of hope and deliverance and salvation. But he, like the later Isaiah and Jeremiah, died in captivity, and saw not the good days of which he spoke. Of the manner of his taking off we know nothing at present, nor is there any good reason for believing that he gave Pythagoras an audience, nor that his pretended tomb, shown near Bagdad, ever contained an autograph copy of his prophecies. It is, however, assuring to know that his book is recognized as genuine by all critics, even by those who cavil at his fellow-exile and contemporary. If he was thirty years of age when he began to prophesy in 597, and he died soon after his last, in 570, he scarcely lived and rounded sixty years.

6. We pass now to him whom he left in Babylon, whom he authenticates and resembles in the passages already noticed: *Daniel* was a prophet of royal descent, royal associations and royal favors, whose prerogative it was to proclaim the King of kings in the palaces of Babylon, and to foretell the progress of earthly kingdoms and of the kingdom of righteousness. He was born in about 618 B.C., was carried a

captive to Babylon at the first appearance of Nebuchadnezzar against Jerusalem in 605. Then he was put in the training school of the Chaldeans and educated for the service of the king, whose wonderful dream, which he had forgotten, greatly troubled him, but which, after a night of prayer with his companions that God would reveal it, Daniel interpreted to Nebuchadnezzar, and so saved the lives of the whole college of learned men of Babylon, because they could not make known the dream nor, of course, its interpretation. This was in the second year of the king's reign, and when Daniel was not more than seventeen years old. Yet as a reward he was highly promoted in office, rank, and dignity, being made chief of the college and a counsellor of the royal court. It was fifteen years before the fall of the holy city. Thus early did this prophet preach the truth that *the God of heaven* had revealed such and such things to Nebuchadnezzar. Whereupon the king said to Daniel, "Of a truth your God is the God of gods, and the LORD of kings, and a revealer of secrets, seeing thou hast been able to reveal this secret." Then the king promoted Daniel and his three young friends (ch. 2 : 1–49). Captain Arioch was the instrument of communication with the king. The event was a marvellous and impressive one, and the whole court, the learned and religious orders, with their families and the chief men of Babylon, were deeply concerned both at the possible and the actual issue of affairs. A young Hebrew captive had become chief counsellor, and his three youthful friends, who were also captives, were set over the district of Babylon ! It is as if some Hindoo hostages were suddenly advanced to the highest trusts in the gift of the British sovereign! Yet we are expected by certain critics to believe that such an affair as the king's dream, the wonderful interpretation by Daniel, and the consequent promotion of those young men by the king, were the invented forgeries of some patriotic Jew three centuries later! Let those who can swallow such a camel do it; we prefer to accept the record as a true account of the events and persons concerned.

It was an age of commercial and literary activity. Prompt despatch of the news of the fall of Nineveh had been carried to Egypt, had been known at Babylon and in Jerusalem. Pharaoh-Necho had prepared to contend with any who opposed him for the government of the East. He routed the army of Josiah, and slew him at Megiddo. But this battle only delayed the final struggle of Egypt against Babylon for the empire of the world. If Josiah had remained neutral, or if he had united with Pharaoh-Necho against Nebuchadnezzar, a very different issue might have followed the contest at Carchemish, and Egypt, not Babylon, might have succeeded in the mastery of Assyria and her provinces. But that was not to be, and the foolishness of Josiah caused his own death and sealed the doom of Egypt, while it also sealed the doom of Judah. The first part of Nebuchadnezzar's dream was fulfilled when he conquered Egypt, dominated the countries about the Tigris and in Syria, subdued Phœnicia, and destroyed the city of David, with the temple of Solomon. The old Semites, mixed as they had now become, were better fitted for the world's empire than the unprogressive Hamites of the

Nile land, who also had had their day of glory and of power. Moreover, beyond the Tigris, north and south, were the rising Medes and Persians, whom Providence had appointed to the sovereignty of earth for a time, to break in pieces the images of Babylon and of Egypt, to cure his people of their tendency to idolatry, and restore them to their own land. Among Judea's mountains should arise a Power not of human hands, which should become an everlasting kingdom; this was the last part of the royal dream and its interpretation. It had no sort of relevancy to the times of Antiochus Epiphanes and the Maccabeans, but to the Everlasting Light for the salvation of the Gentiles. Thus, Hebrew captives in Babylonia would be tenfold more a blessing to the world than if in Egypt, and it would repay the Chaldean fostering care of Abraham fifteen centuries previously. It also illustrates how Providence attends upon the birth and destiny of nations, yet leaves all free to work out their own natural tendencies. Evidence is wanting that Jeremiah advised or approved Josiah's attack on Pharaoh-Necho, though he lamented his untimely death (2 Chron. 35 : 20-25). The prophet proved himself to be a loyal Hebrew. At Babylon there was another equally noble and loyal, of wonderful knowledge, piety, and devotion, and of marvellous faith that God heard and answered prayers to Him (Dan. 2 : 14-23). Thus we see how sacred history is the manifestation of God to the world in preparation for His Son. It was in Exile that Hebrew prophets became in a new sense prophets of Japheth. It led to the enlargement of the kingdom of God among men. Inspiration went forth from the city and temple where Jehovah was enthroned and His people dwelt, among all nations. Thenceforth the Jew as such retires to the background of the prophetic scene, and a new kingdom, also rising out of the mountains of Judea, is to be established for the healing of mankind, and take precedence in human history. This is a grand fact, which has been only partly understood, that the Exile of Israel prepared for the reign of Jesus Christ among men. And in the accomplishment of this Daniel was an active agent. With all the learning of the Chaldeans added to that of the Hebrews, he served Nebuchadnezzar through his long reign of forty-three years, and survived him and his successors down to the fall of Babylon and the capture of the city in 538 B.C. Darius the Mede then began to reign, and Daniel became one of his chief governors. What Joseph had been to Pharaoh in the interpretation of his dreams and the management of affairs, that and more, perhaps, was Daniel to Nebuchadnezzar. Both kings acknowledged Jehovah as the One Supreme, King of kings and Lord of lords.

It is no part of my plan to write a commentary on the Book of Daniel, which is well done in the "Speakers' Commentary;" in Dr. Pusey's "Lectures;" by M. Stuart; in Keil and Delitzsch; on chapters 1–6 by the present Dean of Canterbury, etc. Yet it is fitting, now that the book is assailed by Renan and Elsmere, and those for whom they stand, to consider some points which tend to authenticate the text and an inspired authorship. In the memorable incident of those three young men recorded in chapter 3, we have the grand spectacle of an image set up in the plain of Dura. Not caring for its size and composition, we note the defiance of the king's mandate by three of his officers. They would not bow to the image, symbol of nothing living to them. Nay, they even told the monarch they would not serve his gods, nor worship the image he had set up (verse 18). In punishment for such disobedience and rebellion, they were cast into a heated furnace of flame, which instantly killed the officers who were about to throw them into the fire. The king passionately observed the details of procedure, and to his amazement beheld a fourth form, like a son of God, walking with them in the burning furnace, but not a particle of harm had come to the young men! Impulsive as he was, he knew that was not natural, and he would test what it was, and why the scene was as it appeared. He called the saved ones from the fire, carefully examined them, and confessed that none but their God could have preserved them alive. Then he made a decree that no one in his dominions should speak a word against the God of those young men, and he promoted them in office in the province of Babylon (verses 19–30). As we all know, the account is that of an Eastern despot, who was religious in his way, and who tried to force the observance of his way upon all his subjects. He was the most famous of the last Babylonian dynasty. He was surrounded by courtiers and learned men—Daniel himself being among them—but was not implicated at this time. Records of such occurrences, of the new god, of the disobedience and the penalty inflicted, were usually made in the bricks. Perhaps the priestly influence was such as to prevent such record then, and perhaps such a record may yet be found in the ruins of the city not yet examined. But, however that may be, it is not the sort of events which writers fabricate, nor a rôle which impostors care to play. All the chances of discovery are against them, and the punishment of failure is greater than the reward for success. Just as sure as we detect the true and the poetical in Shakespeare might the men of the second century B.C. detect what was true or false in the prophecies and visions of Daniel. Whatever the additions in the Greek version, the old text affords no ground for doubting the account as we have it. Of course it contains the miraculous; so does the history of Joseph and his brethren, of Samuel and Eli, of Elijah and Ahab, of Micah and Jeremiah, of Isaiah and Ezekiel; why not, then, the visions and events of Daniel?

Pagan Porphyry would palm off upon his readers things more strange, and without sufficient reason. Every reader of his "Pythagoras" knows how he tries to represent the followers of that philosopher as more enduring than Christians, more spiritual and charitable than those baptized disciples who distributed to every member of the Church according to his need. From his time till now there have been those who urge objections against Daniel *as they read him*, which, however, arise *not* from want of authentication of the contents of the Book, but because portions of it are palpably supernatural, and Christians claim inspiration for the writer! Precisely. But no Christian is bound to accept a line of the contents till competent men have sifted the evidence upon which its truthfulness depends. Clearly there is no *a priori* reason against the miraculous and the inspiration of Daniel, which may not be urged against his contemporaries, Jeremiah and Ezekiel. Yet they are undoubted and accepted by all critics whom any Christian would recognize as authority in the matter. The fact that some fabrications of second-century Jews got added to the Alexandrine version—whether now accepted by the Roman Church matters not—does not bind any reader to acknowledge more than is duly authenticated in the Hebrew and Aramaic text. All know that it is only the genuine, not the spurious, which is counterfeited. Of the miraculous, the one question for us is, *Is it properly authenticated?*

And this brings us to chapter 4, the very crux of the book. The school of Kuenen and Renan admit that there was an increasing tendency to Jewish exclusiveness after the return from Exile, and that this spirit was active and dominant in the second century B.C. We accept this admission as entirely true. But consider: no patriotic Jew of that era could therefore forge or fabricate a story like the account in Daniel 4; for it represents a heathen and idolatrous king as privileged with visions from Jehovah touching his *personal* concerns. And the account is found in the most reliable text, not doubted by many who doubt about the last half of the book. It is genuine and historic. An enthusiastic Jew would as soon think of committing suicide as of fabricating a Divine vision like that for a pagan. Surely, if he dared thus to symbolize the fall of Antiochus Epiphanes, he would not permit him to sprout and live and reign again, re-established in his kingdom (verse 36). That would be acting as insane as the king. Moreover, he would not afflict him with such an *uncommon disease*, occurring indeed but very seldom, and making belief in it as difficult and less credible than belief in the whole vision. Nor would he set a captive in Babylon as the chief minister of affairs during Nebuchadnezzar's incapacity. Such critics have considered only half the case and its belongings. The supernatural of Daniel cannot be explained away by still more supernatural traits in Jews of the second century B.C.

Reading the story of the Maccabean princes in Josephus inspired me with enthusiastic admiration for them many years ago. This prompts me to say that not one of them, not one of their heroic companions and followers, would possibly allow to a conquering king, who trampled down their rights and their religion, to be privileged with such visions from heaven, as warned him of his *personal* duty to God, and promised him a glorious restoration after a seven years' penance! This is unparalleled in the history of the Jews, who would not invent such things of Antiochus Epiphanes. As I am writing for intelligent readers, I will not weary them by further remarks. With the chapter open before them, they will see how absurd it is to attribute the writing of it to a Jew in the second century B.C. As every one knows who knows anything about this question, there is no pretence that it is the work of any one after the year 150 B.C.; for then Daniel was done into Greek, with some additions by the translators and editors, which, however, all Protestant Christians reject, and reject for similar reasons which compel them to receive the contents of our version. It was not till *seven hundred* years after Daniel was sleeping on the banks of Euphrates that any one is known to have doubted the authorship of his prophecies, and then it was a pagan who wanted to enthrone Pythagoras in his place! A cuneiform copy may yet be found which shall confound all his detractors. It is quite evident that Daniel was a cuneiform writer as well as a Hebrew prophet, and well read in the literature of the Euphrates and the Jordan. For years the chief minister of Nebuchadnezzar, he survived his death in 561; that of his successor, Evil Merodach, in 558; of Nergilissar in 555, and of Belshazzar in 538, becoming a prince councillor of the new government under Darius the Mede the same year, when, if born in 618, he was about eighty. Such a character was not to be fabricated in *three hundred* years, nor his work forgotten in Babylonia, Syria, or Judea. As well try to invent, in our day, a Lord Bacon or a Sir Edward Coke for the reign of Elizabeth; but Daniel's life and work were even more closely identified with the government, while his voice and visions were for the instruction of the court and a light for the Gentiles. His captivity in 605 to the decree of restoration by Cyrus covered the seventy years' Exile.

It is proper to add the testimony of Josephus the Jew to Daniel the prophet, for he lived and died a Jew. Even if he exaggerated or embellished his account of Alexander's visit to Jerusalem, the fact that he mentions the prophecy of Daniel as being shown to Alexander is conclusive of Daniel's prophecy. And he may have used the fact of that prophecy to give greater credit to what he said of Alexander. Josephus was too intent upon glorifying his country to seek support for his picture about Alexander's visit in a weak or worthless frame. Rather he endeavors to sustain what he says of the king—even upon the supposition that it is pictorial—by citing Daniel, who was well known and believed. That this item is not mentioned by Greeks only suggests that the incident, occurring in Jerusalem and of local importance, in their judgment had no interest *for Greeks*. I care not a straw whether Parmenio questioned the king, or whether the king saw a vision at Dium, or in what robes the priestly procession met him; the facts remain that Alexander visited Jerusalem, pardoned the Jews for their disobedience, and conferred upon them the privileges allowed them by the Persians; also that Josephus, writing of this in the first century A.D., says that the Book of Daniel was shown to Alexander as containing predictions respecting the King of Greece! This certifies that *Josephus and those for whom he wrote knew of and recognized the ancient authority of Daniel.* It is the inevitable conclusion from the narrative—viz., the *existence of Daniel's prophecies in the year* 332 B.C. Josephus's "Antiquities," Book 10, 10 and 11; P. Smith's "Ancient History of the World," vol. ii., pp. 60, 61; Justin Martyr and Origen also confirm the belief in the early existence of Daniel's book.

7. Consider what modern discoveries have done for Isaiah 20:1: "*Sargon*, the King of Assyria, sent Tartan to Ashdod, and fought against it, and took it"—a time-mark of the prediction in that chapter. Yet

the world was troubled and puzzled at it for two thousand years, for want of the brick-knowledge which the discoveries at Nineveh have supplied in our generation. Sargon was one of the most famous of Assyrian kings from 722 to 705 B.C.—about seventen years. Yet the mention of his name by Isaiah was objected to by doubting critics as an error of the prophet! He was the shuttlecock of historians and expositors; now confounded with Shalmaneser IV., whom he slew; now, with Sennacherib, who was his son; and then doubted whether *read out of or into* the inscriptions! Even as late as 1845, Dr. Kitto thought there was such a king who had reigned *two or three years;* altogether presenting a striking illustration of current objections to our Daniel, and a similar exhibition of learned guesses touching Isaiah and Sargon. Wherefore that old usurper and warrior king had to wait *two millenniums* before he was recognized as the most powerful monarch of the world during seventeen of the last years of the eighth century B.C. It was he who captured Samaria, finishing the siege which Shalmaneser IV. had begun, and carried the Ten Tribes into Assyria and Babylonia, which he subjugated. His "Annals," written under his direction, occupy forty pages in the translation made in 1876. They tell how he plundered the country and house of Omri—Omri being the Assyrian designation for the King of Israel, which was continued in use two centuries after the extirpation of that dynasty, and is incorrect; how he routed the king of the Moschians, overpowered Egypt, treated the King of Gaza like a slave; the great Phœnicia, Syria in its totality, cities of remote Media, he made tributary, and forced under his authority. From Samaria he took 27,280 captives, 50 chariots, and much other booty. He expelled Merodach-Baladan from Babylon, and immediately immolated the expiating victims to the great gods, leaving that city in the thirteenth year of his reign, and capturing the ensigns of royalty, the throne of his royalty, the golden sceptre ; . . . oxen, camels, sheep, and lambs were taken. He carried off 80,570 men, 2070 horses, 700 donkeys, 6054 camels, 30,000 instruments of gold, etc. Sippara, Nipur, Babylon, Borsippa, he did not destroy, but of some places he made a desolation. And he closed the record of his deeds with a prayer for blessings upon himself and his successors, but a curse upon whomsoever should alter his writings or change his name—" May Assur, the great god, exterminate his name and his offspring, and never pardon his sin !" The details are translated in " Records of the Past," vols. vii. and ix. But they were unknown to Europeans for two thousand years ; not indeed changed, but buried amid the ruins of his palace. His name only was found in Isaiah the prophet, who lived before and after him. Emerging again into light after that long eclipse, Sargon now elucidates the writer who made him a time-mark of a prophecy. It was Sargon who fulfilled the prediction in 21 : 16, that " within a year, according to the years of a hireling, and all the glory of Kedar shall fail ; . . . the children of Kedar shall be few ; for Jehovah, the God of Israel, hath spoken it." Now, within that time, Sargon invaded Northern Arabia, punished Kedar and its Ishmaelite inhabitants, B.C. 716. It was the enthronement of prophetic truth. So of the prophecy against Tyre (Isa. 23), and against Egypt in chapter 30. The Egyptian party in Jerusalem would find no aid from the Nile land against Assyria; "for the tramp of her soldiers and the roll of her chariot wheels were soon heard in the defiles of Lebanon and in the valley of Orontes. The nations which spake treason Sargon chastised and rendered obedient. None could save the calf of Dan and the Baal of Samaria." For his many victories the king offered costly sacrifices to his god in acknowledgment of the greatness conferred upon him, and for his successes. He erected a magnificent palace near Nineveh, formed a large library, and placed in it the narrative of his royal deeds. At length he was slain in his court, as he had probably slain his predecessor, and was succeeded by his son Sennacherib, the foe of Hezekiah, who was obliged to retire from Jerusalem, according to the word of Isaiah. Thus time and Providence will solve all the difficulties of prophecy for the nations, illustrating how its light enlightened the Gentiles, and was a progressive preparation for the Son of God. If there is any fact demonstrable from the history of mankind, it is that Jehovah, the Elohim of Israel, has ever manifested Himself as the God of Japheth. In Egypt, in Palestine, in Syria and Hamath, in Babylonia and Assyria, and to the isles of the sea, He who was worshipped in Hebrew tents, in the Tabernacle and in the Temple, has all through the ages sought to draw all men unto Him. For them He gave the Son of His Love.

X.

GENERAL REVIEW OF MATTERS CONSIDERED IN THIS BOOK.

We have learned the story of how the Bible grew and was written. We have seen that the legislation contained in the Pentateuch existed for the most part before the regal history; that Hebrew judges and priests administered a law and urged obedience to a ritual which were of recognized obligation in the two centuries which preceded Saul; that many precepts of the code were early incorporated into the national literature, and continued to be so used during six hundred years; that Hebrew kings did at the outset submit to certain restrictions and limitations of royal prerogative, and with some exceptions continued such submission to the last days of their history; and that none of them ever repudiated the *authority* of Mosaic institutions, even when they added to them, or apostatized from the covenant religion. Critics admit that neither Ahab nor Manasseh, Jezebel nor Athaliah denied the authority of Moses and the prophets, even when they set up Baal instead of their teaching, or as supplementary to it. Jacob's Bible grew with his history—psalms, parables, proverbs enriched his book. The facts related in Genesis 37 and 42 are of such a personal character, that each one concerned must have contributed his own share in the matchless story of Joseph, which, like the blessing of Jacob, no late writer could have composed.

We learn the religion of Abraham by a careful study of the religion of Ur, where he long lived and whence he came to Haran and to Palestine, and that Joshua was quite right in saying their "fathers served other gods beyond the river." Days of Passover and Atonement now observed by the Jews are derived from similar observances in the time of Moses. Even when the ritual varied the substance remained the same. Micah's exhortation to remember "the righteous acts of Jehovah from Shittim unto Gilgal," includes the memorable passage of the Jordan, and proves that Hebrews of the first half of the eighth century B.C. knew of and believed them. Yet some critics who acknowledge eighth and ninth-century prophets fail to see the folly of putting the writings of those prophets *before* the law on whose existence they depend, and without which lose all their force. Thus the life-work of Samuel proves Moses; so does the conduct of King Saul; so does the mission of Elijah to apostate Israel. But some forget the apostasy after Jeroboam, and that she never recovered from that fatal lapse. Prophets threatened and remonstrated in vain.

To relegate the origin of the Law to 444 B.C. is to ignore the veritable history of Israel, and to treat its literature as a forgery. But the great names of some who hold this view gain disciples to their error, not seeing that Church and nation were alike disrupted at the same time, from Jeroboam to Ahab. Some difficulties in chronology and some errors of copyists exist, but there is nothing which disproves Hebrew law in the early ages—the law of the Nazarite, the law of Jehovah, and a ritual of worship, which we trace back from Hilkiah to Samson. Though we have no manuscripts of that era, neither have we MSS. of the era 444 B.C. Nor have we the original MSS. of Homer and Plato, of Cicero and Cæsar. But the uniform testimony of men who knew the writings, if not the writers, renders it impossible for us to reject their works as genuine productions of the age which claimed them. Moses, indeed, was before Homer, and he was read by priests, prophets, and kings many centuries before he was heard in the synagogues of post-exilian Jews. Tracing backward we find that Roman writers prove Hebrew history after the second century B.C.; that Greek writers prove it for the two previous centuries; that Persian and Babylonian history proves it for the fifth and sixth century B.C.; while Assyrian, Hittite, Moabite, or Egyptian records prove it from the sixth to the fifteenth century B.C.

Moreover, we also learn that Jehovah was the God they worshipped by a ritual observance and sacrifices, by Sabbaths and holy days, and that ever and anon during this long period they carefully obeyed certain laws, observed certain rites, practised circumcision, kept the passover, regarded the mandates of prophets who uttered predictions now for Jacob, now for Japheth, in Palestine and in Exile. Even the first eight verses of Zechariah ninth chapter would be remarkable, if not preceded by some still more striking passages in Daniel and Ezekiel, in Jeremiah, Isaiah, and other prophets. So Hosea (12 : 3, 4, 9, 12, 13) proves the patriarchal history in Genesis and Exodus by the facts which the prophet mentions in detail. Before his birth Jacob took his brother by the heel ; in his manhood he had power with the angel of God ; at Bethel he found the Lord God of hosts in His memorial or covenant name ; therefore his sons should wait on God continually. Ephraim should remember the deliverance from Egypt, and that his riches were from the Divine bounty. Prophets and visions had been multiplied to secure the people's obedience to the covenant of Sinai ; but Ephraim had provoked the Lord most bitterly, therefore his blood should be upon him, and the reproach of Jehovah, because he had transgressed at Gilgal, offended in Baal, and made idol-gods ; his men had kissed the calves in sacrifice. We count a dozen historic facts in half as many verses. Early prophets epitomize both history and law for Israel.

Modern history relates how English kings and Parliaments often resisted the imposition of Papal laws upon the English people ; how French and German sovereigns often disobeyed Papal mandates ; how Hildebrand failed in his struggles against imperial power ; how Boniface VIII. failed to humble Philip IV. in a contest of which the world took notice. But none of those monarchs ever suggested that the Church of these haughty popes was only a new establishment of recent authority. Rather they were content with disputing Papal claims to dominate *civil* affairs. The peoples ruled by Jeroboam and Ahab, Ahaz and Manasseh were as numerous and as religious as those of the European kings we have named ; but while they tried to introduce new ways of worship, or new gods to be honored, neither the son of Nebat nor the son of Omri ever excused his apostasy from the worship of Jahveh *because* His worship was a new thing in Israel. They admitted its antiquity. Even the most reforming of Hebrew prophets only demanded obedience to the old covenant law of that people. Ezekiel reminds them of Noah, Job, and Daniel, while Elijah and his successors exhorted them to loyalty to Jahveh. The Jew was assured by his national teachers of the ancient character of his law.

Without a page of new documentary evidence, and with many probabilities against them, some now assume that because Ezra or some other authority in Jerusalem may have made some additions or adaptations to the old law of Moses or to the ritual of the second temple, *therefore* the code itself and the ritual are of the date 444 B.C., when, in fact, there was then only a *re*publication of it. Just as wisely could those European kings have based their resistance to Papal claims upon the assumption that the Church of which there were popes was a new thing, rather than that their claims to dominate over princes in civil affairs was recent. But neither Hebrew kings nor European monarchs made such objection ; rather they acknowledged the priority of the Church in each country to themselves. There is surely no objection to conceding that after the return from Exile some supposed safeguards were added to the Hebrew law and ritual, and that returned Jews became narrower and stricter than their fathers : but there is every objection to saying that those laws and that ritual had not been long observed in Israel, and, in fact, are found interwoven with its history during *fifteen hundred* years, and are certified to by the prophets. That "Jewism began from that moment" means nothing. The teaching of Ezra depends on that of Moses and Abraham. The Hebrew religion began with the patriarch some two thousand years B.C.

Wherever we find the observance of any law in Israel; of the Sabbath, of sacrifice, of sin and penalty, of the Nazarite and other vows, of witches and necromancy, of the removal of dead bodies, of ceremonial uncleanness, eating flesh with the blood, of the place where atonement was to be made, laws about feasts and fasts, new moons and first days, circumcision and Passover, of priests, prophets, judges, kings—there we have proof that such laws then existed, existed in the era from Joshua to Saul. It is interwoven with the history of that period, and cannot be exscinded without fraud and violence, unless it can be shown that the records were forged, which is impossible. Not a King of Israel can be shown to be mythical; not a recognized priest was without a duty or an altar; not a prophet of Jahveh failed to deliver his message to whom he was sent--Jonah only hesitated. In Samaria, in Jerusalem, among other nations, the Divine voice was heard; for there was great occasion for remonstrance, contrition, reformation; nobles and people wandered from God. Yet the preparation for a new evangel went on in Palestine and in Exile. Perfection was not yet.

Some writers ignore the consequences of the Disruption of the nation under Rehoboam upon the religion of Israel. Thereafter Israel and Judah were as distinct governments as Syria and Edom, or Moab and Phœnicia. They tell us how " priest and prophet reeled through the influence of strong drink in the very ministration of their sacred offices !" So might the priests of India ; so in Babylon, Egypt, Phœnicia, " prostitution was throned upon the altars !" But that had little to do with the development of Hebrew religion in *Judea*. In the century after Amos, when Hezekiah invited the remaining tribes after the capture of Samaria to keep the Passover with his people, they laughed at his proposal to go up to Jerusalem to worship. They followed the cultus of Bethel and Dan. It was all they recognized. From Jeroboam I. to Sargon II. there was no development of Jahvism in Israel. At Bethel, at Gilgal, transgression had not ceased. Some idol worship continued after the capture of the shrines of Dan, and longer yet was the influence felt by the covenant people. Kuenen, Renan, and others seem to forget that the Disruption of Israel applied alike to the government and to the Church of Jacob. Her drunken priests and prophets were those of Baal, not of Jahveh, and though denounced by Amos, he sought to bring them back to covenant loyalty. " The nation, as a whole, was recreant." They did not go up to the temple at Jerusalem, and unless they repented as a nation and returned to Jahveh, He would avenge His cause by the Assyrians carrying them captive. But Judah had not wandered so far and so long from her covenant God. If " Amos was the first to preach the principles of pure *ethical monotheism*" to the *Ten*

Tribes after their separation, it does not follow that a similar ethical monotheism did not prevail in Judah nor under David and the early years of Solomon, nor when Samuel administered affairs in his annual circuits from Ramah to Gilgal and Mizpeh. The prophets must not be severed from the local history of their times. During *two hundred and fifty* years those of the northern kingdom had to struggle against the sin of Jeroboam, to which was added the sin of Ahab and Jezebel; but in the southern kingdom Jahvism more generally prevailed, and the people went up to Jerusalem at the great feasts to sacrifice and worship. Neither so far nor so long did they wander from the temple-service. But we are told that Ahab did not mean to apostatize from Jehovah worship! It is difficult to see that he ever was a Jahvist. He was in succession from Jeroboam in Israel, who had made as radical a revolution in the religion as in the government of the country. He apostatized from the temple worship; would not allow his people to attend the feasts at Jerusalem; set up calf shrines at Bethel and at Dan, which were served by priests from the lowest of the people. The priests of the Law and the Temple would not serve him, for he had become a separatist and an apostate. So were his successors, from Nadab, his son, to Hoshea, who was carried captive in 721 B.C. Prophets of the ninth century had failed with Ahab; prophets of the eighth century failed with the successors of Jehu. Prince and people were incorrigible. It is a perversion of history to give a different setting to these facts. From Rehoboam to Sargon II. there was no true development of theology in Israel. Ahab was but one of a series of apostate kings, whom neither the warnings of prophets nor the preaching of the Law of the Lord could long restrain from following the rival cult set up by Jeroboam, chiefly in order to keep his new subjects from worship at the Jerusalem temple. The priests of Baal were slain by the hundred, and the prophets of the Asherah, but soon others took their places; for the king would not risk his people attending the sanctuary of his rival in Judah. It is this, and not the development of a new theology, which is the key to the prophecies of Amos and others of his era. Theirs was a last effort to bring back apostate Israel to the God of Jacob. Only in Judah was there any true temple or altar of sacrifice. But to that, after the Disruption, the Ten Tribes did not return. The sword of Jehu did not exscind the calf worship of Samaria. Hence that baptism of blood was followed by deportation of Israel to Assyria, and of Judah to Babylonia.

The Hebrews were not chosen to be the most illustrious and powerful nation under heaven, but to be conservators and disseminators of true religion among men, now here, now there, a light to lighten the Gentiles in preparation for that Light who should illumine the darkened hearts of mankind. But the prophetic mission closed with the return from Exile. Thenceforth it was waiting time. From Malachi to John Baptist no new truth of God was given to men, leaving the old to leaven and permeate the world. And as there was no new prophet to authenticate Scripture, so no new book was admitted to the Sacred Canon. It is in evidence that Daniel was already enrolled into Jacob's

Bible. He could not have been accepted for translation into Greek, unless he had been authorized by a prophet before the order ceased. The necessity of prophetic endorsement of a sacred book ruled out Sirach and 1 Maccabees, and it would have excluded Daniel if he had not already been admitted to the Sacred Canon. Hence it is really more difficult to accept a second-century writer of Daniel than the received Daniel of the sixth century B.C. Ezra presents the same objection of being written in two languages, and there is a similarity with Ezekiel, yet the personal independence of these three writers remains intact.

It is an honor to American scholarship that M. Stuart, in 1850, thoroughly refuted the criticisms of Lengerke and Knobel. Daniel's Hebrew in 2 : 4 to the end of chapter 7 resembles that of the golden age; he is always himself, now writing like an adept in Hebrew upon Hebrew matters, and now like a Babylonian in the Chaldean parts. In each the style is equally perfect. Grounded in his native tongue in his boyhood, his education as a youth in Babylon enabled him thoroughly to master its language, so that he could pass from one to the other with the ease of modern Germans and French resident upon the borderlands of those nations in speaking those tongues. "The Greek historians," says Stuart, "do not mention Nebuchadnezzar as King of Babylon!" Was he therefore not a king there? Josephus on such points is a better authority; and he says that Daniel 8 : 3–7 and 11 : 2, 3 were shown to Alexander the Great, and produced a favorable impression upon him. His anger for the Jews not sending him the aid he asked and for not submitting to his authority was appeased. He forgave them, renewed their privileges granted by the Persians, and kindly treated them. This was in 332 B.C. It establishes the date of the prophet as before that time. Justin Martyr corroborates Josephus. (Stuart's "Daniel," pp. 380–408 ; 1 *Macc.* 2 : 59, 60.)

In his "Address to the Greeks" Justin shows the antiquity of Moses's writings ; his divine and prophetic gift ; that the heathen oracles testify of him, and that his works were early translated into Greek and written in the Greek character (chs. 9–13). In his "Dialogue with Trypho" he testifies of Isaiah and Jeremiah as quoting from Moses. In chapter 70 he shows that priests of Mithras *imitated* some of the *text of Daniel* as well as Isaiah 33 : 13–19. His critical acumen is seen in his charging the Jews with recently "cutting out some passages in Jeremiah and Esdras " (ch. 72). And in his " Apology" (ch. 54) he says, "The prophet Moses was before all other writers. Even Plato borrowed from the Hebrews." As Justin was a converted Greek, a man of vast learning, who addressed a long epistle to the emperor in defence of Christianity, and suffered martyrdom for the faith in 165 A.D., his testimony is of great weight. He flourished a century and a half before Porphyry, and knew the authority of Daniel's prophecies. Only a little later Origen collated them in his famous " Hexapla." " The merits of Daniel," says Josephus, "must excite the wonder of all who hear of them." And Josephus was a thoroughly educated Hebrew, who had no Christian bias to prejudice him. Antiochus Epiphanes sought to destroy every copy of the Jewish Scriptures, and punished with death those who concealed them.

No one well read in history would compare Nebuchadnezzar with that mad persecutor of the Jews. Except in the matter of conquest and pillage, there are no analogies between them. To mistake one king for the other, or to identify them as equally hostile against the Jews, betrays an ignorance very uncomplimentary to the writer. No Hebrew would lack the skill, even if he lacked the courage, to detect and explode such a misconception of history in the second century B.C. Moreover, the Jews then were zealous and very strict, even fanatical in their ideas of religion. The Maccabean fought for his Church and his home against oppression. Nebuchadnezzar did not persecute in efforts to foist his creed upon others. The order touching the golden image was but a local and temporary injunction. No penalty came to Daniel; his three friends were officers, punished for disobedience. Alexander the Great worshipped in the same temple which Antiochus desecrated in ways the most revolting to a Jew. No wonder at the resistance and storms of war which followed; stubborn rebellions and cruel usurpations; till down went Pan and his pipers; up went pæans and chants to Jehovah. Then came peace, and the temple of Janus was shut.

The stone of the old altar at Bethel was said to have been removed to Jerusalem, where it became the pedestal of the Ark, fit emblem of the conservation and perpetuity of truth. However that may be, it is certain that the God of Bethel revealed Himself at Zion, and fulfilled His promise in the birth of One who crushed the serpent, broke in pieces the images of false deities, and became the Saviour of men, "wherever the earth bears a plant or the ocean rolls a wave." *He* has verified the Revelation in Genesis, accomplished the Exodus, fulfilled Numbers, superseded the priests of Leviticus, perfected and amended Deuteronomy by the new law of Christianity, and proved Himself the Joshua of all believers by opening the way to a heavenly inheritance. From Eden to Sinai, to Calvary, to Olivet, one voice was ever speaking to man; one God watched over him from heaven. Abraham circumcised *all* who would receive the rite; it was renewed at Gilgal; looking upon the brazen serpent gave healing to wounded Israelites; even so shall all who look to JESUS and believe in Him be saved, whether of the seed of Jacob or of Japheth. (See "God Enthroned in Redemption," chapters 4 and 5.)

But Panism and Pyrrhonism now ignore the foundations of true religion, and would decide biblical texts and interpretation by a majority vote of persons ignorant of monumental discoveries. Because some critics in Germany, in France, and their "captives" in England, adopt erroneous views of the dates and purposes of Scripture, why would you have us fall in their line and surrender our judgments? We dare not do so. It is hardly a century since the French National Assembly (September, 1792) abolished the Sunday or Sabbath of six thousand years' observance, and in its place enacted a Tenth-day as the "Rest-day" of the people; with five other holidays in the year, or a total of seventeen days for rest from ordinary labor; poor substitute of man for God's gift of fifty-two Sabbaths

11*

a year! By so much less is human generosity when compared with the Divine bounty. And a woman of loose morals was enthroned as a goddess, to be worshipped by those new Reformers! As might be expected, that change of calendar was tolerated but a short time, and in twelve years plus three months the government returned to the old-time Sabbath order, January 1st, 1806. (See Carlyle's "French Revolution.") The votes of a majority cannot change the nature and needs of mankind, nor abolish the facts of ancient history.

True, Charles I. lost his head by a majority vote, and Cromwell vaulted into his place; but other votes and voices within a dozen years called another Charles to the throne of England. The Prayer book, rejected by one set of voters, was re-established by another set, and the old Church returned to her old place. Missals and liturgies may be enacted by votes; but no votes ever provided an atonement for sin, or gave the world a revelation, or opened the door to everlasting blessedness.

Moreover, some modern voters forget that they cannot expunge the records of human thought which lie buried in the ruins of Assyria and Babylonia, or are inscribed in the tombs and on the monuments of Egypt. Even now those treasures are being deciphered, and flash new light upon some dark questions. They corroborate Genesis and Moses, the history and prophets of Israel; they bid us not interpret his writings by modern notions, but by contemporary records where such exist, and to wait for other unfoldings of buried scrolls which may supply all the aids we require to read and understand the heritage of the ages and the disclosures of God to man. No; the pillars of monumental knowledge cannot be shaken by guesses of to-day. Inscriptions are older than mss., and may outlast them. Moses and Mesha speak louder than modern assemblies.

Fantastic is the dogmatism which would fix absolutely 165 B.C. as the date of Daniel—so Mrs. Ward in the *Nineteenth Century* for March, 1889—even while a party of explorers in the region of his exile may find jars of tablets containing an original copy of the book! Neither our preferences nor our prejudices should attempt to settle by a majority vote questions of fact, especially the facts of ancient history. Its records cannot be disposed of or dispensed with in that way. The method was tried upon Homer, but the excavations of the spade have been turned upon, and buried those who denied him an early place in Grecian song and civilization. Nor is it long since German critics flouted his personality. So with Hebrew and Christian writings. Few linguists are good historians; specialists are usually as narrow as they are positive. Critics may try to eliminate and explain away an author, but they neither make him nor destroy him. The Creator reserves that to Himself, for Jacob and for Japheth. Wonderful as was the origin of the Bible, its history and preservation are equally remarkable. Everywhere hunted, proscribed, burned, it is everywhere found and read of all nations. We cannot be more sure of the contents of Homer's Iliad than of the contents and books of the Old Testament. The authority of Herodotus touching Egypt and the

East is now past; but the absolute credibility of the Old Testament is daily illustrated and confirmed. The Jews could truly say, We have a very sure word of prophecy. Prophets and priests authenticated and guarded the Sacred Books, and were expounders of them. If seers of the ninth century B.C. did not record their utterances, others took pains to write them out. Hence were preserved the doings and sayings of Elijah, Micaiah, Elisha, and others of that era in the nation's history, constituting a large part of it. The prophetic and Messianic matters form the greater part of the later Bible. In 444 B.C. the whole then known seems to have been authenticated and republished by authority, and could be tested by the memories of intelligent men. The history discloses that it was easier for books to be lost than for supposititious writings to be received as genuine.

When the order of prophets ceased, men of the great synagogue guarded and certified to the Law, the Prophets, and the Psalms, which were read to the people every Sabbath; and Scribes performed the duty of writing out copies for use and preservation. Moreover, the Samaritan Pentateuch, the jealousies of the different sects—Pharisees, Sadducees, Essenes—served for four hundred years like so many watchmen as custodians of the MSS. and their interpretation. Then the translation of the Hebrew books into Greek, completed by 160 B.C., is further guarantee against errors, and rendered them more difficult. Of course, some verbal variations would occur in the passage of generations, but there was too much jealous care for serious errors. No other ancient books are more pure and true to the original.

The connection and relation of events in the later records emphasize the prophetic writings, their accuracy and value. For six hundred years Hebrew kings reigned, but the prophets ever illumined the foreground of the historic scene, exhorting the sinners in Israel and Judah to truth and righteousness. Thus Elijah became more famous than apostate Ahab; Isaiah sheds more lustre upon his king than Hezekiah does upon his prophet and prime-minister. A hundred readers remember the character and predictions of Jeremiah to one who can recall the death of Josiah at Megiddo. Illustrious as was Nebuchadnezzar as conqueror and builder, Daniel of the captivity has increased his renown. And our Lord authenticated that prophet for us and, in a sense, all the prophets. Even the fanaticism of second-century Jews proved their scrupulosity about the Scriptures, and illustrated their discrimination touching Hebrew literature. They could not be imposed upon by a Greek writer. They admitted no Greek book into their Sacred Canon. That the sceptre should not depart from Judah till Messiah came led to careful inquiry among those who cherished expectations of Him, and to earnest longings for His appearance. Many mothers fondly hoped to become the honored and favored one, the blessed among women, for giving the Redeemer to Israel. Jews in Palestine and in colonies among the Gentiles could not forget the predictions of Micah nor the last verses of Malachi. Their misunderstanding of Messianic prophecies may have narrowed their ideas of religion in Jerusalem, but they also intensified their convictions. They indeed thought, "Salvation is of the Jews," and often limited it to them; but they looked for it with confident assurance. Yet their later intolerance, if such it were, could not hide the Light of Him and of His Gospel, who came to save both Jew and Gentile.

Remarkable is the fulfilment of Isaiah's prophecy (19 : 19), "There shall be an altar to Jehovah in the midst of the land of Egypt." Josephus, in his "Antiquities" (Book 13, chs. 3 and 4), narrates the building of a temple at Bubastis, in the nome Heliopolis, like that at Jerusalem, with an altar to Jehovah, but smaller and poorer than that, and tells how a Jerusalem priest celebrated the worship of the Hebrews' God in that Egyptian temple. It furnishes a memorable fulfilment of the prophecy. In the "Wars," Book 6, chapter 3, section 3-5, he says, "The people ate what the dogs would not touch, even girdles and shoe-leather, which is testified to by innumerable witnesses. Nay, a woman of wealth and family was so terribly reduced by famine that she slew her nursing son, roasted him in an oven, and ate one half herself, and concealed the other half. The brutal robbers who had plundered her of all she possessed were attracted by the smell of food, and returned to get what they could find. The lady then produced the remainder of her hidden son, saying "she had eaten the other part, and they might eat this!" They were too horrified to touch it, and departed. Thus literally was fulfilled Leviticus 26 : 29; Deuteronomy 28 : 49-57, in the terrible famine during the siege of the Romans under Titus. No Jew *after* the Exile would have written such prophetic cannibalism into the Pentateuch, and no Jew like Josephus would have *invented its fulfilment.* Both alike prove its truthfulness. Thus Jacob's Bible is authenticated by Jacob's history, as written by his sons and by the sons of Japheth.

Very touching is the prayer of Esdras, "Wherefore, O Lord, is Israel given as a reproach to the heathen, and for what cause is the people whom Thou hast loved given over unto ungodly nations, and why the Law of our forefathers is brought to naught, and the written covenants come to none effect, . . . and our life is astonishment and fear, and we are not worthy to obtain mercy?" St. Paul answers him: That Israel had fallen for a time, for the saving of the Gentiles; that all, both Jews and Gentiles, Semites and Aryans, may be saved (Romans, ch. 11). It was the Divine purpose in the calling of Abraham, in the legislation of Moses, and in the voicings of later prophets.

I have endeavored in this book upon "Bible Growth and Religion" to illustrate and establish the truth of Revelation, answering those current objections which strike at its origin and authority, especially those of the naturalistic school; and I have purposely emphasized the grand fact of inspiration rather than the mode of communication.

Those who want a brief "Introduction to the Books of the Old Testament" will find it in Dr. Stearns's recent work, in any good Bible Dictionary, or in the Manuals published by Mr. Whittaker, New York.

May the HOLY SPIRIT give life to the words and conviction to the readers, that we all may rejoice together with HIM!

NEW NOTICES BY THE PRESS OF "GOD IN CREATION" AND "GOD ENTHRONED IN REDEMPTION."

The New York Evangelist said: "Some months ago we had the pleasure of noticing 'God Enthroned in Redemption,' which was the second part of a work of which the first part had appeared under the title, 'God in Creation and in Worship.' Between the two editions a book appeared containing statements which, without proof, tend to weaken the foundations of the author's argument. A new introduction was written, showing the baselessness of some of 'Squire Wendover's' statements, and the inadequacy of the results reached by him. It goes carefully over the question of the testimony of history to revelation, which forms the basis of the book, showing triumphantly that no fair-minded seeker after truth can be indifferent to 'the historical impressions of an eternal tendency in men.' This was also printed in pamphlet form, serving a good purpose, both in setting the book to which it belongs upon a firm basis, and counteracting the harmful tendencies in others."

The Standard of the Cross and the Church said: "'God in Creation' and 'God Enthroned in Redemption' deserves careful reading. The author gives no clew to his identity, but he need not conceal it, or be ashamed of his work. He argues for the original belief in monotheism, and strongly combats the assumptions of Herbert Spencer on this point. The neglect of historic evidence by sceptical theorists is dwelt upon, the latest discoveries of archæology are summarized, and the general purport of the work may be gleaned from the preface; that God originally taught men how to live, and how to prepare for a future life, was the belief of the first ages. It is attested by Hebrew Scripture, by the monuments of Egypt, by the inscriptions and religion of Assyria and Babylonia."

The Living Church said: "In compact form, with every evidence of the erudition needful to the task, and with keenness and good spirit, the author disproves prevalent naturalistic theories. He shows where Mr. Spencer is at fault historically, and where he has ventured upon false inferences, even from correct historic statements. We lay the book down with the conviction that it was well worth the author's while to write out his views upon the subjects treated and to give them to the Christian world. Part first contains Christianity not Evolved from Ghosts and Hero-worship, God in Creation and in Worship, Legends about God and Creation, Legends about Satan and Evil Spirits, Deluge Legends and Pagan Deification, with an examination of the testimony of Tacitus, of Tertullian's Apology, asserting the proposition of Tiberius to the Roman Senate that Jesus of Nazareth should be enrolled among the gods of the empire."

Of the First Part, *The Christian at Work* said: "It is a well-written, interesting, and forcible argument. The inscriptions of Babylon and Nineveh and the records of old Egypt are found to corroborate the accounts of Moses."

The Old Testament Student calls it "a vigorous book against the theory of worship and religious belief being an evolution from burial rites. These customs give no account of themselves in the most ancient times. Records inform us that temples were erected long before tombs. Nimrod was the first recognized hero. The oldest piece of literature in the world is a hymn to the Maker of Heaven and Earth. Herbert Spencer has even perverted the text of Scripture. Along a line of cumulative reasoning our author has marshalled an abundance of interesting citation and historic illustrations, the book being a good source of information."

The Home Journal said: "The author maintains that the doctrine of One God is older than belief in many gods; polytheism is a degeneration of the idea taught to our first parents. He marshals history, tradition, and legend, making a very interesting show of learning and research."

The Open Court said: "The author's view concerning the fate of 'creators of discord' is anthropomorphic, and almost as picturesque as Breughel's famous paintings. The facts are as vivid as any romancer could present them."

The Lowell Times said: "We readily recognize the conspicuous merits of this remarkable little treatise—the abounding research, the curious scholarship, the graphic and business style, and, above all, the scientific spirit which pervades and governs the whole. The central idea is easily grasped: that the conception of the Jewish and Christian God was not evolved at all in the historical sense, but was in the nature of a direct revelation."

THOMAS WHITTAKER, 2 & 3 BIBLE HOUSE, N. Y.

GOD ENTHRONED IN REDEMPTION.

BEING THE SECOND PART OF "GOD IN CREATION." IN ANSWER TO MODERN THEORIES OF THE EVOLUTION OF CHRISTIANITY.

OF this book *The Christian at Work* said: "This is a small volume, but it is compact with research, vigorous thought and profound truths. Its five chief divisions are: I. Legends and Expectations of a Coming Saviour. II. The first Sabbath and Primitive Worship. III. Immortality in Legends and Longings. IV. The Lamb Slain for Man's Redemption. V. The Spiritual Kingdom a Realm of Ransomed Souls. There are an hundred embryo volumes in this grand little book, which historically demonstrates the grand facts of Scripture upon which to-day is shining new light and attestation from the monuments of Egypt and from the inscriptions of Assyria and Babylonia. The reader will find it a remarkable volume."

The New York Evangelist said: "The *central* point of the argument is that the solidarity of mankind, being perfectly exemplified only in Adam, the salvation of the world was provided while mankind was in solidaric unity, the sacrifice of Christ having been truly made at the time of Adam's fall. All men, therefore, having sinned in him were also saved in him. The substitution was a righteous substitution—viz., of a perfect Man for a sinful man; and being accepted while man was a unit, all his children were thereby put in the same redeemed position. The author brings a good acquaintance with the most recent discoveries to support his position."

The New York Mail and Express said: "Among new publications, 'God in Creation' and 'God Enthroned in Redemption' rightly command attention for condensed, vigorous statement and sustained power. It sweeps the whole field of historical research, especially recent discoveries in the East, presenting them in very readable form, and is buttressed by highest authorities. It is compact, clear, and strong, giving the substance of many volumes not readily accessible. Thus it truly enthrones God in creation, in primitive worship and sacrifice, giving the legends about Satan and evil spirits in early ages, with a valuable chapter on deluge legends and pagan deification. The second part enthrones God in redemption, as illustrated in legends and expectations of a Saviour, in the Sabbath of primitive times universally observed ; immortality in legends and longings among ancient peoples, and so prepares for a new treatment of the Lamb slain for man's redemption."

The Independent said : " The author asserts, and cites history to prove that Christianity is not an evolution in history, but a force divine from the beginning which has shaped history. This volume is the supplement of an earlier one on ' God in Creation,' which followed a line of reasoning similar to that pursued in the volume before us, the author's aim being to show that the idea of God was not evolved either from ghosts or from hero-worship, but can be traced back through the history of the race. This volume applies the same reasoning to the hope of a Redeemer, traces of such hope being widely diffused in the oldest legends of the race ; those of the Sabbath, primitive worship, and the doctrine of sacrifice. The two parts taken in connection form an interesting argument based on a patient and earnest study of the history of the race, for the truth of the Christian doctrine that God has never left himself without a witness in the world, and that religion was divinely taught to men from the beginning."

The Christian Advocate said : "The book sweeps the whole field of historical demonstration, and quotes from the recognized authorities. While compact and scientific it yet has the elements of interest to the general reader, and is an able argument against Spencer's ' Ecclesiastical Institutions.' It is an earnest defence of the foundations of Revealed Religion."

Upon announcing that the second part was ready, *The Church Chronicle* said : " The author in a scholarly way sets the reader to thinking in fresh lines of old thought. The first part was warmly received in many quarters."

The Church Record said : " This is a marvellously strong book, suggestive of thought sufficient for many volumes, and meets the crude speculative heresies of modern materialism with unanswerable power."

The Board of Missions of the Protestant Episcopal Church, at its May meeting, 1889, voted to place the completed work, two parts in one volume, among the approved books for the use of its Missionaries and Teachers.

THOMAS WHITTAKER, 2 & 3 BIBLE HOUSE, N. Y.

www.ingramcontent.com/pod-product-compliance
Lightning Source LLC
Chambersburg PA
CBHW021344230426
43666CB00006B/403